Charting the Plantation Landscape from Natchez to New Orleans

READING THE AMERICAN LANDSCAPE

Lake Douglas, *Series Editor*

Cane for the Mill, by George François Mugnier, Courtesy of the Collections of the Louisiana State Museum, 09813.0807.1.

CHARTING THE PLANTATION LANDSCAPE *from* Natchez *to* New Orleans

Edited by Laura Kilcer VanHuss

Louisiana State University Press
Baton Rouge

Published by Louisiana State University Press
www.lsupress.org

Manufactured in the United States of America
First printing

Designer: Barbara Neely Bourgoyne
Typeface: Garamond Premier Pro
Printer and binder: Sheridan Books

Jacket illustration: Portion of *Norman's Chart of the Lower Mississippi River,* 1858, by Marie Adrien Persac, steel engraving with watercolor on paper. Courtesy of The Historic New Orleans Collection.

Library of Congress Cataloging-in-Publication Data
Names: VanHuss, Laura Kilcer, editor.
Title: Charting the plantation landscape from Natchez to New Orleans / edited by Laura Kilcer VanHuss.
Other titles: Reading the American landscape.
Description: Baton Rouge : Louisiana State University Press, [2021] | Series: Reading the American landscape | Includes bibliographical references and index.
Identifiers: LCCN 2020050831 (print) | LCCN 2020050832 (ebook) | ISBN 978-0-8071-7479-1 (cloth) | ISBN 978-0-8071-7571-2 (pdf) | ISBN 978-0-8071-7572-9 (epub)
Subjects: LCSH: Persac, Marie Adrien, 1823–1873. Norman's chart of the Lower Mississippi River. | Plantations—Louisiana—History. | Slaves—Louisiana—Social conditions. | African Americans—Louisiana—Social conditions. | Louisiana—Social life and customs—19th century. | Louisiana—Social life and customs—20th century.
Classification: LCC F375 .C45 2021 (print) | LCC F375 (ebook) | DDC 976.3/05—dc23
LC record available at https://lccn.loc.gov/2020050831
LC ebook record available at https://lccn.loc.gov/2020050832

CONTENTS

Charting the Plantation Landscape from Natchez to New Orleans

INTRODUCTION

PERSAC'S PRECISION

Almost a full year prior to the publication of *Norman's Chart of the Lower Mississippi River,* an ad was placed in the *New Orleans Times-Picayune* on February 16, 1857, announcing the map serial. Promising to have "great value to . . . all who have anything to do with the Great Father of Waters," the blurb asserted that the map would be a "complete view of all the points on the river—plantations, with their titles, proprietors' names, and products raised; landings and roads to interior plantations; islands, bars, hills, creeks, post-offices, churches—everything, in short, that it can be desirable to know."[1] When the map was published the following year, a subsequent announcement was made with the claim that the map "defines the great River, and describes the rich and beautiful country through which it passes, with the greatest possible accuracy."[2]

These advertisements had some share of truth. The artist commissioned for the chart, Marie Adrien Persac, was a surveyor, painter, and photographer whose strength lay in his execution and not-inconsiderable precision as a draftsman. Illustrating a landscape positively exploding with agricultural and economic success was the ideal assignment for an artist for whom precision was a forte and details his means of expression.

As faithful as Persac was in the particulars of his renderings, however, the assemblage of those details, the resulting narrative, was not necessarily accurate. In the case of *Norman's Chart,* a series of decorative vignettes framing the map belie their creator's willingness to bend the truth in search of perfection. The sketch of Baton Rouge shows a completed St. Joseph's Cathedral that while begun in 1853, was not completed, and the "Sugar Plantation" tableau, clearly

Belle Grove in Iberville Parish, reduces the presence of the plantation's 150 slaves to a handful of tidy cabins, rearranged from their actual configuration for a more picturesque presentation. Indeed, Persac's minimizing of slavery—the foundation of this agroindustrial corridor's success—becomes a standard for much of his work. The result is a landscape of perfection more than truth, the kind of elegant presentation a planter would want to own.

Persac seems to have been quite cognizant of potential buyers' interest. *Norman's Chart* is useful in the navigational sense, but its attraction lies in the fact that it is stuffed with every indicator of success. It is a map of celebration. His choice of Belle Grove as his "sugar plantation" suggests a deliberate move to reference the newest and grandest estate the area had to offer. He includes examples of activity and industry with paddle wheels and busy wharves, activity showcasing the lower Mississippi River's bustling economy. In the context of the Persac map, the swath of land lining the Mississippi River from Natchez to New Orleans is a land of plenty and a landscape of triumph—a depiction of accomplishment, prosperity, and wealth.

Less than ten years later, the landscape Persac meticulously created with such certainty was unrecognizable, its message of success inapplicable. With the Confederacy's loss in the Civil War, many of the same estates Persac had illustrated were burned, abandoned, sold, leased, or became bank property. Sharecroppers, tenant farmers, contract freedmen, and investors replaced the names previously touted on *Norman's Chart.* Agriculture had little economic support. Most important, emancipation overturned the idealized success Persac depicted in his work. Many of the estates listed were sugarcane enterprises, and sugarcane requires consistency and an immense number of workers at every stage of its cultivation and processing. Previously both were guaranteed by slavery, no longer an option in a postemancipation world. In addition—and perhaps more importantly—emancipation changed the plantation landscape by reshaping the plantation's social and political topography. Persac had cataloged a terrain of planters who stood as the unchallenged masters of the lower Mississippi, and that supremacy was no longer assured. With emancipation, planters found themselves challenged by people who were once their property, even to the point of disputing their ownership of the physical plantation: "Here [on the plantation] is where secession was born and nurtured," a committee of former slaves protested. "Here is where we have toiled nearly all our lives as slaves and treated like dumb driven cattle. This is our home, we have made these lands what they were, we are the only true and loyal people that were found in possession of these lands."[3] Indeed, the celebration of the antebellum planter depicted in Persac's map was challenged by the most rudimentary of American societal beliefs: that those who labor own the fruits of that labor. Subsequently, those who work the land have a claim to its ownership.[4]

THE RISE OF THE PLANTATION MYTH

While the plantation landscape offered in Persac's map was certainly altered—and in some cases is now nonexistent—that ideal of perfection held more value than accuracy as it informed his interpretation, one that was soon embraced by a new generation. As the Civil War moved from current conflict to past trauma there was a growing interest, particularly in the former Confederacy, in how its participants and their culture would be remembered. Beginning with the Southern Historical Society (1869, New Orleans), a series of associations dedicated themselves to shaping public memory of the Confederacy specifically and the antebellum South in general. Riding the wave of patriotic enthusiasm demonstrated nationally with the Daughters of the American Revolution (1890), the United Daughters of the Confederacy was founded in 1894. Monuments appeared in public spaces in New Orleans, Baton Rouge, Natchez, and many smaller towns in between. The concept of an antebellum "Golden Age" began to take shape in the public consciousness as memoirs of private citizens made their way to publication.[5] While writers certainly were not overtly referencing Persac's artistic approach of perfection over reality, it nonetheless became an embraced perspective.[6]

Eliza Ripley was one such writer. She could have been describing a Persac-painted scene when she wrote:

> Those grand autumnal days, when smoke rolled from the tall chimney of the sugar-house, and the air was redolent with the aroma of boiling cane-juice; when the fields were dotted with groups of busy and contented slaves, and their cabins resounded with the merry voices of playing children; when magnolia and oak trees were musical with the mocking-birds, whose throats poured forth melodies unknown to any other of the feathered tribe, and nimble squirrels gathered their winter stores in the pecan-groves—oh, those grand autumnal days![7]

So vivid and precise is Ripley's description of her plantation that the reader can easily ignore the realities of the same described landscape: an agroindustrial enterprise supported and sustained by human bondage. She mentions activity in the sugar mill and slavery, but like Persac's depiction of Belle Grove, such are described in sanitized terms. Where Persac showed us Belle Grove's quaint quarters and busy smokestack, Ripley gives us "the smoke rolled from the tall chimney" and "contented slaves." The nostalgic, incomplete nature of Ripley's writing is particularly apparent in that what she describes is sugarcane harvest season, also known as "the grinding." Frantic and rigidly systematic, the grinding amplified the uniqueness of sugar plantations as environments that were just as industrial as they were agrarian. The "groups of busy and contented slaves" Ripley describes were in reality overworked gangs working shifts of more than sixteen hours a day for what could be months, urged alternatively over the course of the season by promises of harvest pay or a driver's whip. The season's compulsory intensity reached fever pitch in the mill, where steam engines and progressive mechanization established a factory work pace—with factory hazards.[8]

None of this, of course, is detailed in Ripley's account. For her and writers like her, the plantation was a peaceful, ordered, and noble institution deserving of reflection. It was the same act of memorialization and value representation being exercised by the newly formed Daughters of the Confederacy but applied to a place, rather than a person, and articulated through literature, rather than statuary. The "plantation myth" was born. A fictional cultural landscape, the myth found definition in plantation aesthetics, meaning in their agricultural achievements and significance in their economic successes. The associated subtext to this myth read that the plantation as an institution was the epitome of noble agrarian life and previous generations had been quite right to fight for its preservation.

PLANTATION: FROM AGRICULTURAL ENTERPRISE TO DAY-TRIP DESTINATION

Plantations in the early twentieth century began to engage in an activity somewhat foreign to their original purpose: tourism. Armed with nostalgic language like that of Eliza Ripley, young people flocked to the estates as part of the latest craze of "automobile outings." Particularly in the New Orleans area, plantations became a destination for automobile enthusiasts for a number of reasons. They were easily accessible by car and offered a bucolic setting for related activities and free admission. One announcement in New Orleans read: "An 'Automobile Outing' to Diamond Plantation, where participants will enjoy an 'old time picnic' in the sylvan precincts of the old Diamond Plantation, one of the finest estates in the South."[9] Further upriver in St. James Parish, young people from nearby Donaldsonville catered a luncheon and hired a local orchestra to entertain them while they relaxed at the Valcour Aimé plantation for the day.[10] In both instances, and in similar advertisements, the emphasis is placed on the house and grounds. While the plantation varied, such ads and reports peppered New Orleans newspapers in the early twentieth century, invariably advertising a quaint activity and a superlative environment, the plantation almost always being described as "the finest in the South."

The surge of interest in activities such as picnicking at plantations—or more accurately, on the immediate mansion grounds—underscores two important points. First was an emerging tourism-dependent definition of a "plantation" as the house and immediate grounds. No one is picnicking in a sugar mill or mule barn. Second, the outing was never advertised as an invitation by the property owner, which would have been required if there was a homeowner present. Rather it was simply an announcement. It was a demonstrable shift from plantation mansions as private homes to being de facto attractions.[11]

Tracing Persac's map north, homeowners in Natchez, Mississippi, felt the pinch of meeting the needs of their sizable townhomes without the revenue from their now-defunct plantations.[12] Leveraging the national popularity of "pilgrimages" to places like Mount Vernon, the Garden Club of Natchez sought to bring attention to their city's own antebellum architecture by presenting the first Natchez Pilgrimage in 1931, hosted by a Mrs. Balfour Miller.[13] The following year, the pilgrimage was officially announced. Historian Jack Davis observed that later depictions of the first pilgrimage made the event seem epochal, "a cataclysm in the course of Natchez's future that occurred with the redemption of its history."[14] Certainly, more was at stake than old structures. In a postemancipation world, the Natchez elite were frantically trying to find cultural and racial redemption.

And it was a redemption driven entirely by women.[15] It is debated whether Mrs. Miller alone deserves credit for establishing "The Pilgrimage," but she was undeniably proactive in its promotion and larger recognition. She lectured at various women's clubs on topics that were generally antebellum in content but Natchez specific. Her strategy was unabashedly ambitious and impressively thorough. As Jack Davis writes, "Pilgrimage folks showed an almost messianic fervor in their resolve to share Natchez with the rest of the world."[16] When giving a lecture, "Natchez, Where the Old South Still Lives," at the Greenwood Women's Club, Mrs. Miller accompanied her presentation with "[60] exquisite tinted slides" and appeared in full costume: "picturesque and becoming dress of the 19th century. She carried a corsage of pink rosebuds."[17] It was a stroke of promotional genius. In a single lecture Mrs. Miller not only defined antebellum life through personification but underscored Natchez as *the* place for anyone interested in the Old South. The attendees that day at the Confederate Memorial Building in Greenwood were thrilled.

The club and Mrs. Miller's hard work proved successful. As early as 1938 the Natchez Garden Club was producing professional marketing material, complete with poems contributed by former attendees:

I had not thought these things were so:
Unreal they'd peered from out the page
Of romance of another age.
I had not dreamed that I might see
A lady fair with stately grace
Descend broad stair or slowly pace
Through vaulted hall to welcome me.
But now at Natchez—now I know

I had not thought how sweet 'twould be
To look with reverent eyes upon
The treasures of a people gone;
To catch the gleam of candle light
On priceless china, and the glow
Of fire-shine spreading rich and slow
On ancient brass made newly bright.
But Natchez vouchsafes these to me.

And who am I that I should see
So much of beauty: spiral stair,

Coin-silver service, rosewood chair,
Tall mirror set in leaf-gold frame,
Wrought-iron lace against the sky?
All these I've seen and rich am I—
Ah, richer far than when I came.
So much as Natchez done for me.

Lucy Louise Hatcher
Dean, Gulf Park College[18]

In 1939 the club received an unexpected boon as *Gone with the Wind* took movie theaters by storm. Interest in the Old South soared, and the Natchez Pilgrimage was firmly entrenched in the social season. "Negroes sang spirituals, citizens wore dress of before the war and young men donned Confederate uniforms," a writer enthused, noting that there was even a Confederate ball with an honorary king and queen.[19] For those who had seen the movie, such pageantry was *Gone with the Wind* come to life. What had begun as an interest in the designed landscape transformed into a celebration of all things antebellum, contextualized by the plantation myth tradition. The fact that these were townhomes, rather than plantation mansions, merely made it easier to focus on nostalgic narratives, divorcing the success of plantation operation from its source and any associated ugliness.[20]

That is not to say that the identity so carefully being crafted by the Daughters of the Confederacy, the Natchez Garden Club, and others was completely without counterpoint or challenge. As early as 1941, Allison Davis, Burleigh Gardner, and Mary Gardner's groundbreaking book, *Deep South,* detailed the race-based caste system that ordered the interactions between Black and white in the Jim Crow South. The plantation was not the focus of their study—they were contemporary social anthropologists—but their work nonetheless challenged the perfection of the plantation landscape by deftly outlining its legacy, specifically how that legacy was articulated in existing social constructs. Among others, historian John Wesley Blassingame addressed the plantation myth directly with *The Slave Community: Plantation Life in the Antebellum South* (1971) and *Slave Testimony: Two Centuries of Letters, Speeches, Interviews and Autobiographies* (1977). Yet despite their significance, such works remained largely in academia. Plantations themselves—both historic sites and private enterprises—remained committed to the landscape of Persac's idealized plantation, a place of happy slaves, agricultural abundance, elegant women, and a lifestyle fit for nobility.[21] Throughout the 1980s and 1990s, and some continuing currently, the Southern Belle tradition, with its dramatic décolletage, expansive hoopskirts, and hats fitting the Kentucky Derby persisted. Enslaved men, women, and children were mentioned as "servants"—if at all. Those who sought to bring scholarship to their interpretation found the process daunting, often resulting in representations of slavery that lacked character dimension and frequently had little bearing on the material culture around them. As Christy Coleman, CEO of the American Civil War Museum at Historic Tredegar, commented ruefully as late as 2013, "We think if we give them [the enslaved] a name, we give them a function, and our job is done."[22]

PLANTATION COUNTRY

Visitors today climb off buses and out of rental cars to experience the plantations of the lower Mississippi River valley, but they are not visiting plantations. As John B. Rehder observed, tourists visit plantation mansions—not plantations.[23] Not unlike their automobile-outing predecessors, the plantation in the eyes of the contemporary tourist is limited in both physical and narrative scope. Visitors, often ignorant of nineteenth-century history, are guided through the house and immediate grounds where, until recently, much of what they heard was a verbal articulation of Persac's narrative of perfection with its associated Lost Cause ideology. Slavery? What slavery? Have you seen our columns? And any inclusion of slavery positions the institution, and the plantation's involvement in it, as incidental. Even as recently as 2018, a group of visitors on a plantation tour in Louisiana was encouraged to reenact presumptively happy enslaved laborers on their way to the fields by singing a spiritual and clapping their way through the slave quarter area.[24]

There are sites that are intentionally and successfully moving away from the *Gone with the Wind* narrative, but changing the visitor's perception of "plantation" as being just the mansion is a difficult task. The physical landscape is not what it was when Persac first illustrated this agricultural corridor. Barns were demolished when mules were exchanged for tractors; mills were disassembled and sold as cane farmers moved to centralized refineries; and so on. In many cases, the mansion is all that remains, and its permanence, coupled with the absence of any previously existing buildings used for agricultural production tasks, makes it difficult to argue plantations as the agroindustrial enterprises they were.

Tourism promotion underscores both aesthetically driven narratives and the divorce of mansion from plantation. From the bucolic-sounding "plantation country" used to promote sites outside New Orleans to the continuance of the Natchez Pilgrimage, the message is clear. Plantations (in this usage, plantation *mansions*) are the celebrated palaces of the American South, the remnants of a lost agrarian aristocracy. And when visitors stop by the gift shop for a souvenir, neatly packaged posters of *Norman's Chart of the Lower Mississippi River by M. A. Persac* are available for purchase, along with *Gone with the Wind.*

ABOUT THIS COLLECTION

The aim of this volume is to bring perspective to Persac's perfection in a manner and with an approach that makes the material normally reserved for academic discussions accessible to the general reader. Taking Dell Upton's affirmation that "an apparently unvaried landscape may actually be composed of several fragmentary ones, some sharing common elements of the larger assemblage," each contributor to this volume was challenged to consider landscape broadly defined as the aggregate of identifiable markers specific to individual areas of interest, enabling the reader to look at the same geographic area—in some cases the same plantation—through a variety of lenses.[25] This differs from the current trend of examining plantations (and more largely, slavery) primarily through the lens of economics, for instance, and allows the reader a more contextually informed understanding of the plantation landscape. Subjects were identified as those whose combined presentation would best achieve this goal. Subsequently the essays are organized to balance the familiar with the foreign, covering the built landscape and the designed landscape before moving into the territory of medicine, emancipation, and the visual tradition, before closing with a plantation monograph. The focus throughout is on the nineteenth century and primarily on the eras immediately preceding and following the Civil War. There are some aspects that are outlying, but tightening the collection's focus allows the reader to have a detailed and nuanced understanding of a landscape during its most significant—and often confusing—iterations.

Architectural historian Laura Ewen Blokker's contribution, "Construction and Construct: Architecture of the Louisiana Plantation," establishes a clear counternarrative to the mansion fetish of twentieth-century tourism and culture. Placing planters' houses in their proper environment and discussing the built landscape in its entirety, Blokker not only demonstrates the complex and even contradictory nature of plantations but also the degree to which spaces and structures were heavily influenced by the occupant's status as an enslaved or free person.

In "The Plantation Landscape: Spectres of an Unseen Imprint," landscape historian Suzanne Turner considers the plantation as a cultural landscape. Using traditional foci of plantation landscape studies—purpose, ornament, organization—Turner examines how they are the results of human action and interaction. By emphasizing process, situation, and the subsequent cultural patterning that takes place in plantation landscape creation, Turner brings the paradoxical qualities of the plantation environment to the forefront of her work and outlines how they define the plantation landscape even today.

Historian Charles D. Chamberlain III looks at the extent to which Louisiana politicians' activity as slaveholders and sugar planters shaped their political policies as well as their rise—or fall—from power. In "Severed Heads to Statehouse: The Political Landscape of the Sugar Coast," he focuses on the activity between two cities depicted on Persac's map, Baton Rouge and New Orleans, and outlines the early French Creole's assertion of political supremacy, the arrival of the American planter challenge, and the post–Civil War landscape.

Medical historian Christopher D. E. Willoughby's "Plantations as Landscapes of Medicine" offers the most unfamiliar perspective yet exemplifies the complexity of plantations as a social and political construction engaged in large-scale enslavement. The US medical profession of the early and middle nineteenth century earnestly promulgated ideologically shaped best-practices intended to inform plantation health care and support its use of enslaved African labor. Willoughby details both the framework of race-based enslavement and the realities of health care in an environment defined by its agroindustrial nature.

Author William Horne applies the construct of plantation landscape to illuminate an often-murky period: postemancipation. In "Landscapes of Emancipation: Plantations and African American Liberation," he illustrates how the once clearly delineated plantation landscape of power and powerless became both the backdrop and inspiration for political activism on the part of freedmen. His plantation landscape is a contested one, with former slaves seeking to form a body politic even as their former owners look to regain the supremacy they lost in the Civil War.

In contrast to Horne's contribution, art historian Jochen Wierich offers "After Persac: Imagining the Plantation Landscape from the Civil War to the Great Depression." Beginning with the man himself, Marie Adrien Persac, Wierich explores how plantations have been memorialized in art, from planters seeking to bring permanence to their own success, through the postemancipation years as the same planters sought to reaffirm their status as a distinct class, the rise of Lost Cause ideology, to Walker Evans' photographs. Wierich's essay is particularly important because of the role the visual arts have played in defining—or redefining—the plantation landscape.

Christopher Morris's closing essay, "The Rise and Fall of Uncle Sam Plantation," gives the reader an opportunity to see how far disconnected plantations and their associated myths can be. Uncle Sam, marked the Fagot Plantation on Persac's map, was an extensive sugar plantation in St. James Parish. Its mansion was indicative of much of area architecture at that time, and it retained quite a few of its outbuildings into the early twentieth century. Its loss at the hands of the Army Corps of Engineers—a sacrifice in service of a new levee—spurred growing interest in plantation house preservation and propelled Uncle Sam into the realm of myth. Morris carefully outlines what this plantation was, and what it was not, placing the mythical Uncle Sam in its proper, historical context.

The contributors to this collection trace the cultural mythology of plantation life in the South and examine how it does and does not represent the historical reality. From Persac's cartographic delineations to the thunderous pace with which *Gone with the Wind* captured America's imagination, plantations have fascinated the public, and their "big houses" have become towering icons of the American South. They were landscapes filled with meaning: they were important because they were substantial; they were significant because they were beautiful; they were, according to this worldview, representative of a lost time and life we should mourn. In short, plantations were metaphorically raised as monuments to an imagined past.

By separating these places from their fictionalized identity and examining them through varying disciplinary lenses, this volume strives to offer the general reader a nuanced understanding of what actually constituted the plantation landscape. Our hope is that though this is by no means an exhaustive examination, the essays here will demonstrate the true significance of the area so beautifully detailed by M. A. Persac in 1858. Far from presenting monuments to an imagined past, the aim is to demonstrate the true significance of plantations as landscapes of complexity, paradox, and contradiction.

NOTES

The volume editor wishes to extend her appreciation to the contributors for their insight and commitment to scholarly research. She would also like to thank Lake Douglas and Jenny Keegan for their guidance from concept to publication and Kathryn for her talented editorial pen.

1. New Orleans *Times-Picayune,* February 16, 1857, p. 1.

2. New Orleans *Times-Picayune,* April 2, 1858, p. 4.

3. Letter to President Andrew Johnson, October 28, 1865. National Archives Records Administration: B-53 1865 and P-27 1865, Letters Received (series 15), Washington Headquarters, RG 105.

4. This ethos is first seen in the establishment of the United States as a society of colonists, then later in Free Soil advocates of the 1840s and 1850s, as well as the basis for the US Homesteading Acts of 1850, 1862, 1866, 1873, 1904, 1909, 1916, and 1930, all of which were based on the premise of proving legal ownership to land by habitation and cultivation.

5. Examples include *Memoirs of a Southerner, 1840–1923,* by Edward J. Thomas, published in 1923, Savannah, Georgia; *From Flag to Flag: A Woman's Adventures and Experiences in the South During the War, in Mexico, and in Cuba,* by Eliza Ripley, published in 1888 by D. Appleton & Co, New York; and *Social Life in Old New Orleans: Being Recollections from My Girlhood,* also by Ripley, published in 1912 by D. Appleton & Co., New York.

6. There are traces of plantation mythology writing before the war, most notably John Pendleton Kennedy's *The Swallow Barn* (Philadelphia: Carey & Lea, 1832). However it became an identifiable genre with significant contributions as part of antebellum nostalgia in the latter part of the nineteenth century.

7. Ripley, *From Flag to Flag.*

8. Planter Maunsell White of Plaquemines Parish wrote to Messrs. Stillman, Allen, & Co. that one of his female slaves died from injuries suffered in the mill after her hand and arm were caught in the mechanics. *December 1, 1845, Letter Book Vo1.1* in the Maunsell White Papers #2234, Southern Historical Collection, The Wilson Library, University of North Carolina at Chapel Hill.

9. Advertisement for the Diamond Plantation, St. Charles Parish, in New Orleans *Times-Picayune,* May 12, 1905.

10. *Donaldsonville Chief,* August 14, 1915, p. 2.

11. With the shift of plantation management from resident planter to a variety of operational structures, "Big Houses" were often left empty. Groups only had to obtain permission from the operation's management, if at all.

12. See also Steven Hoelscher's "The White-Pillared Past: Landscapes of Memory and Race in the American South," in *Landscape and Race in the United States,* ed. Richard Schein (New York: Routledge, 2006), chap. 3, https://doi.org/10.4324/9780203621622.

13. *Greenwood Commonwealth,* May 9, 1934, 3, http://america.aljazeera.com/articles/2014/4/5/natchez-antebellumplantation.html.

14. Jack Davis, *Race Against Time: Culture and Separation in Natchez Since 1930* (Baton Rouge: Louisiana State University Press, 2001), 69.

15. Karen L. Cox details the role that women in general, and the United Daughters of the Confederacy (UDC) in particular, played in the practice of postwar public history. See *Destination Dixie: Tourism & Southern History* (Gainesville: University Press of Florida, 2012) as well as *Dixie's Daughters: The United Daughters of the Confederacy and the Preservation of Confederate Culture.* (Gainesville: University Press of Florida, 2003.

16. Davis, *Race Against Time,* 59.

17. *Greenwood Commonwealth,* May 9, 1934, 3.

18. Gulf Park College for Women was opened in 1921 in Gulfport, Mississippi.

19. *Shreveport Times,* March 3, 1940, 24.

20. Natchez's landscape is unique in that many planters retained a house on their plantation but lived in and emphasized their city houses.

21. While not a plantation but the one-time stewards of Carters Grove Plantation, Colonial Williamsburg is generally acknowledged to be the first to integrate more complex narratives in its Living History presentations. Yet a decade after their African American Interpretation department was created, Williamsburg had fifteen African American interpreters to represent the historic African American population, which constituted at 52 percent of the total population (A. Greenspan, *Creating Colonial Williamsburg: The Restoration of Virginia's Eighteenth-Century Capital* [Chapel Hill: University of North Carolina Press, 2002, 163]).

22. Christy Coleman, "From Scholarship to Public Interpretation." Day 2, Session 3 presentation at Telling the History of Slavery: Scholarship, Museum Interpretation, and the Public conference held at Thomas Jefferson's Monticello, February 23, 2013.

23. John B. Rehder, *Delta Sugar: Louisiana's Vanishing Landscape* (Baltimore, MD: Johns Hopkins University Press, 1999), p. 3.

24. Author's experience, 2018.

25. Dell Upton, "White and Black Landscapes in Eighteenth-Century Virginia," *Places Journal* 2, no. 2 (1984): 5.

CONSTRUCTION AND CONSTRUCT

Architecture of the Louisiana Plantation

LAURA EWEN BLOKKER

Beginning in the first quarter of the eighteenth century, a built plantation environment emerged along the Mississippi River between New Orleans and Natchez.[1] Over the next century, it came to be populated by a myriad of buildings of varying purposes, styles, and construction materials. Creole and, later, in the nineteenth century, Greek Revival big houses with regiments of columns and colonettes dominated much of this landscape physically and psychologically. These buildings remain foremost in our mind's eye of the imagined plantation and inspire titles like that of the classic 1941 text by J. Frazer Smith, *White Pillars: The Architecture of the South.* Today, images of grand columned homes are prominent in Louisiana's cultural tourism industry. Yet, these buildings are a mere fraction of the constructed plantation environment. The architecture of plantations was composed of a wide variety of planters' and overseers' homes of many sizes as well as countless slave dwellings. These residences were accompanied by many ancillary structures, from kitchens to hospitals, and every possible type of shelter for agricultural pursuits, from basic sheds to elaborate sugarhouses. This architecture—which could impress the visitor with refinement and cleanliness or crudity and lack of upkeep—was as contradictory and dynamic as the personal relationships and experiences in the system of enslavement it supported. While much has been written on the subject of Louisiana plantations, it is difficult to glean an understanding of them as complete architectural complexes through time from any one source. This essay aims to provide an overview of this architecture and to shed new light on this iconic, yet murky built environment.

While the subsequent essay by Suzanne Turner delves into the manipulation of the land itself, this essay examines plantation buildings between New Orleans and Natchez through time and different ownership situations. It begins with the lower river parishes outside of New Orleans, where some of the region's first plantations were developed and where the big houses are the most familiar due to their participation in the tourism industry. It also visits West Feliciana Parish and the distinctly Anglo architectural influence of settlers who came from the Upper South. Finally, it explores Concordia Parish, where the choice of planters to erect their residences in Natchez, Mississippi—across the Mississippi River—left a plantation landscape where overseers' houses were the dominant buildings. In this way, this essay will give the reader a complete picture of this built plantation environment, thereby providing critical context in which to understand the fragments of it that remain. This context elucidates the present juxtaposition between the few surviving slave dwellings and the big houses by filling in the missing pieces.

Plantations between New Orleans and Natchez possessed great variety in styles, scale, and typologies of their buildings. These were shaped by cultural traditions, agricultural processes, and trends of the time. In design, materials, and spatial organization, they were grand and crude; high style and vernacular; ordered and chaotic. Just as every person, enslaved or free, operating within the plantation system was an individual and not a stereotypical actor with prescribed characteristics, the same was true of the buildings. While forms and construction methods might be a common thread, personal choices and the capacity to employ free will were manifest in the construction process. Much more than just examples of architectural styles, form and function, the various buildings forming the plantations reveal their inhabitants' labor practices and their concepts of home, privacy, autonomy, privilege, and power.

BEGINNING A BUILT PLANTATION ENVIRONMENT ALONG THE MISSISSIPPI RIVER

Essential to understanding the architecture of Louisiana plantations is the early French Colonial and Creole building idiom. The French Colonial period is a relatively short span of time in Louisiana's history—lasting from initial explorations in 1699 only until transfer to Spain in 1762—but it had an indelible impact in laying the seeds of a Francophone culture that inhabitants fiercely preserved for generations to come. Creole is a term that has had many meanings through the years in relation to people, cuisine, language, and other elements of Louisiana's cultural heritage. Here the term will be used in the sense true to its meaning in the early colonial days: to describe someone or something born in the New World—in this case, Louisiana—and thus shaped by its particular ways.

Louisiana's Creole plantation houses are both associated with Louisiana's Creole culture—though many were built for French-born people by African-born people—and Creole in and of themselves. The design traces its ancestry to places abroad but is native to Louisiana.[2] Creole plantation homes are characterized by several easily recognizable features. They are raised substantially above the grade level on brick foundations that enclose a ground level known as a *rez de chaussée,* with rooms often used for storage. The main level or *premier étage* is constructed of heavy timber frame filled between with bricks (*briquette-êntre-poteaux*) or daubing (*bousillage*). Wrapping the building on all sides is a deep gallery that provides a sheltered open-air space around the ground level and the main floor. Over it all is a tremendous roof that is either double-pitched or a single-pitched umbrella. These were the first of Louisiana's "big houses." The features of this form emerged on the French Gulf Coast by the early eighteenth century, with many similarities to architecture found in the Caribbean and also manifest in French settlements further north on the Mississippi River, such as Cahokia, Illinois, and Ste. Genevieve and St. Louis, Missouri. Though barely any of the eighteenth-century Louisiana plantation houses survive in their original size and form, a substantial number of extant buildings are heirs of this Creole idiom.

An early and particularly well-documented example of the Louisiana plantation is Destrehan in St. Charles Parish on the east bank of the Mississippi River (fig. 1). A contract for construction of the house signed January 3, 1787, between property owner Robert Antoine Robin de Logny and Charles, a carpenter, woodworker, mason and free man of color, provides telling details about both the design and the labor system employed for its erection.[3] In translation from the original French, the specifications for the house called for a building sixty by thirty-five feet. Importantly, some of the defining Creole design elements are called out in the contract, such as it being raised ten feet on brick

Figure 1. Destrehan Plantation main house, Destrehan, St. Charles Parish. The Historic New Orleans Collection, Acc. No. 2010.0145.2, Gift of Nancy La Fonta de Saintegeme in memory of her mother and her family in New Orleans.

piers and surrounded by a twelve-foot *galerie.* Details such as paneled doors and casing at "doors of communication" were called for and it was noted that all should be done according to the plan the builder "has in hand."[4]

The contract continues with the terms for payment and labor provisions:

> The said Sieur Robin de Logny has given to the said Charles on account on the said enterprise, one untrained Negro from his plantation named l'Eveiller (Rouser) with a cow and her calf . . . obligates himself besides, to furnish to the said Charles, two Negro wood squarers, three other Negroes from his plantation who are those named François, Louis and Jean Louis, and one other Negro to help him with the masonry and to furnish him all the materials necessary for the construction of the said house . . . and the said Negroes listed at his disposal until the finishing of said work.[5]

This agreement reveals the use of enslaved people both as payment for building construction and as temporary construction laborers and specialized craftsmen.

It makes clear some of the divisions of labor in building and the fact that enslaved people of specific skill sets were enlisted.

Meanwhile other enslaved people at Destrehan, of which twelve were included in Robin de Logny's 1782 purchase of the plantation, focused on other primary tasks.[6] The cash crop of Destrehan at this time was indigo. Charles received final payment for his work on April 22, 1790. Two years later Robin de Logny passed away and the inventory of the estate at that time provides a snapshot of both the remnants of the previous plantation ensemble and new accommodations. The description of the house reiterates the contract specifications exactly and adds that there are six rooms on the ground floor and six on the main level. Additionally, other buildings on the twenty-eight arpents (approximately twenty-four acres) were described as:

> a kitchen built in *colombage* [heavy timber frame] on sills, 34 by 20 feet, with front and rear galleries, double chimney and shingle roof . . . ; a storehouse 48 by 24, two old hospitals 17 by 11, 'a pigeon house, twelve feet square in *colombage* above and below, surrounded with planks and roofs with shingles,' . . . a cabin of posts in ground, 30 by 18, serving as a coach house, three cabins, 18 × 12, 'a Negro camp composed of nineteen cabins, good as well as bad, of posts in the ground, roofed and surrounded with stakes' . . . a mounted bell; nine pairs of vats (for indigo processing); 'a shop of posts in ground surrounded and roofed with stakes, 30 × 16 feet'; a drying house, 30 × 15; a shed for repairs, 48 × 20; a shed covering the works of the pump . . . two old sheds covering the grinding machines; . . and 'all the fences of the said plantation, amounting to around 15,000 stakes . . . the enclosure of the yard containing 2,400 stakes and 480 stakes surrounding the garden.[7]

From all of this detail, we get a sense of a rather compact and dense complex with two main fenced areas and thirty-six buildings of many sizes and conditions where fifty-nine enslaved people plus members of the de Logny/Destrehan family (and possibly others) lived and worked. Several clues about the early forms and transformations of plantations are embodied in the descriptions. The very large kitchen with front and rear galleries and double chimney could potentially represent the adaptive reuse of an earlier domicile. First-generation residences remained on many plantations after being superseded by more substantial big houses and were repurposed as needed.

The very brief description of the "Negro camp" offers a key detail of housing of the enslaved in this period: post-in-ground (*poteaux-en-terre*) construction. Placing the upright framing members of buildings directly into holes or a trench in the ground was among the very first construction methods employed by French colonists in Louisiana, but as its ephemeral nature was heightened by the high water table and termites, the introduction of sills and elevation of buildings was soon utilized for more durable construction. In slave cabin construction, however, post-in-ground construction and its dirt floors persisted. The economic advantages of this are obvious and suggest that plantation owners were investing as little as possible in the materials and comfort of slave housing; however, another dynamic also can be seen in such designs. The housing of the enslaved in the eighteenth century was closer in materials, construction methods, and organic spatial relationships with other buildings to African traditions than the later antebellum regiments of identical double cabins.[8] Enslaved people at Destrehan were a mix of Creoles born in Louisiana and those from African nations identified as Congo, Fond, Maquoi, Mina, Bambara, Dina, Mananga, Nago, Guiné.[9] The number of enslaved people to cabins breaks down to three, plus or minus, per domicile.

While Creole influences continued to shape the big houses of the greater New Orleans area through Baton Rouge on to Pointe Coupée Parish, across from the latter, on the east bank of the Mississippi River, a very different influence took hold. In West Feliciana Parish, settlers from the Upper South—particularly the Carolinas—erected their own concepts of appropriate plantation architecture. West Feliciana was part of West Florida, an area controlled by England and then Spain. When families like the Barrows moved there from Halifax County, North Carolina, in 1799, it was Nuevo Feliciana. The 1804 contract for the construction of Highland Plantation (originally Locust Ridge) illuminates what was considered essential for a fine plantation home here. William Barrow specified in his agreement with John Arick:

> . . . a Framed House said frame to be set on blocks. The House to be Fifty eight feet long and twenty one feet wide and two story high, the lower story to be twelve feet from the floor to the ceiling and the upper story to be ten feet from the second floor to the ceiling. The lower story to contain a Hall twenty four feet long by twenty feet wide, one Entry or Passage fourteen feet long by twenty feet wide, one chamber room eighteen feet long by

> twenty feet wide with stairs running up from the lower story into the upper story with a closet underneath the stairs. The upper story to be laid of in Rooms the same size of the lower story, all the floors to be tongued and grooved with chair boards and wash boards . . . [10]

The result was a slightly asymmetrical, center-hall I-house with Georgian and Federal detailing that is unusual in Louisiana but would fit comfortably in the owner's northeastern North Carolina place of origin (fig. 2).[11]

Figure 2. Highland Plantation, vicinity of St. Francisville, West Feliciana Parish. The Historic New Orleans Collection, Acc. No. 2010.0232, Gift of Mr. Thomas S. Allen.

A second story was added to the back shed rooms soon after the house was built, and the front porch was raised to two stories after the Civil War.[12] For completing the original construction in the "best workmanlike manner," John Arick was promised a sum of $800. No exchange of livestock, plantation product, or enslaved person was part of the deal as had been in the case of Destrehan Plantation. Also, there was no mention of building plans as there were in the former's contract. The ample fourteen-foot-wide center passage contrasts sharply with the spatial organization of the Creole house. While human circulation through a Creole house involved the exterior galleries and doors from one room to the next—providing multiple ways to move into and out of rooms—the Georgian house, with its prominent central hall, controlled movement and access, thus further emphasizing the social constructs of privacy and the hierarchy of individual rooms. The Creole house was a realm of more organic spatial possibilities, while the Georgian house supported social construct with its physical construction.

For all of the detail put into the specifications of Highland's main house, there is no mention of accessory buildings, even those closely associated with the big house, such as a kitchen. What those buildings and the houses of the enslaved at this time were like can only be imagined. Four years later in 1808, Barrow's property was described by a traveler, Fortesque Cuming, as including, "a very handsome house, a noble plantation of about four hundred acres of cotton all in one field, and a hundred and fifty Negroes."[13] Both sugar and cotton could be grown successfully in this region and this factor—along with the heritage of the owners—impacted the development of plantation buildings. The house was enlarged in the 1830s, at which time a live oak grove, race track, large sugarhouse, dance hall, and hospital for the slaves were also added.[14]

THE RISE OF THE LARGE SUGAR AND COTTON PLANTATIONS

The patent of the cotton gin in 1794 and development of a process for granulating sugar in Louisiana in 1795 set the stage for a major change in the cash crop focus. Thanks to the climate and rich delta soils being suitable for growing sugarcane and cotton, the improved acreage and number of enslaved persons on individual Louisiana plantations increased steadily over the first half of the nineteenth century. An analysis of St. James Parish based on census records found that in 1810, 39 percent of enslaved persons belonged to holdings with 1–10 slaves; slightly less (23 percent) belonged to holdings 11–20; and even fewer belonged to those with 21–40, and so forth. There were *no* holdings with more than eighty slaves. By 1860, the situation was inverted with 31 percent of enslaved persons living on holdings with 100–200 slaves; 9 percent on holdings with more than 200 slaves; and just 16 percent on holdings with ten or fewer slaves.[15] Louisiana was, by 1860, the state with the most slaveholders owning seventy or more slaves.[16] Some 160,500 or roughly 48.4 percent of Louisiana's enslaved persons, are estimated to have lived on plantations with fifty or more slaves in 1860. Improved acreage on such plantations ranged from 612 to 1, 174 acres and unimproved acreage ranged from 1, 112 to 3,017.[17]

The area addressed by the essays in this book—that along the Mississippi River depicted by *Norman's Chart*—had a high concentration of plantations with holdings of fifty or more enslaved persons: ninety-five in Concordia, seventy-six in Iberville, sixty-two in West Feliciana, sixty-three in Pointe Coupée, and between ten and fifty in each of the other parishes.[18] Thus the large plantations unquestionably constituted a major portion of this built plantation landscape.

Speaking to the size of the plantation near Baton Rouge where she had lived, former slave Catherine Cornelius recalled encountering General Butler on the levee and his asking the name of the town, to which she answered, "Dis ain't no town: dis a plantation."[19] Louisiana plantation scholar J. Carlyle Sitterson observed that the "scores of buildings required on a large sugar plantation made carpentering second in importance only to actual production of a crop."[20] By the time of the Civil War, many of the large plantations that had emerged along the Mississippi River between Natchez and New Orleans were so vast and had so many buildings that they might indeed be mistaken for a town.

At the beginning of the nineteenth century, Destrehan became a sugar plantation. In the second quarter of the nineteenth century, the Creole architecture and organic spatial relationships of Destrehan and much of Louisiana's lower Mississippi River plantation landscape transformed as national trends and the wealth produced by sugar brought new grandeur, rigid geometries, and modular repetitions. Amid a culture not prone to discard tradition lightly, the raised Creole house continued to be a mainstay of plantations in Louisiana's French triangle of influence, but it received an updated appearance.[21] Its galleries were beautifully adaptable to the wrapping colonnades of the Greek Revival style. Slender colonial colonettes gave way to two-story Tuscan, or even Ionic and Corinthian columns. Plantations like Destrehan received stylish updates while, later in the nineteenth century, new residences embraced the full grandeur of complete Greek Revival design. Only a handful of Louisiana plantations adopted other nationally popular styles such as Gothic revival or Italianate revival.[22]

Some scholars have analyzed the dichotomy between the institution of slavery and the democratic ideals associated with the Greek Revival, but it seems likely that the ease with which the columns of the style could be applied to existing plantation house forms and the imposing presence they created influenced design choices more so than philosophical linkages. In any case, both enslaved and free observers of the new Greek Revival edifices certainly took away an impression not of democracy but of undeniable wealth and power. In 1860, J. W. Dorr, an editorial correspondent for the *New Orleans Crescent,* described houses along the road on which Destrehan was located as "costly, elaborate, and expensive."[23] From the Mississippi River, voyagers witnessed a parade of one lavish property after another from Natchez to New Orleans. Not only were the big houses individually impressive, they were increasingly complimented by a carefully composed array of buildings that accentuated the size of the big house and the control of the landscape. No longer would organic mélanges of utilitarian structures and slave housing cluster around the big house or the edge of fields. Slave quarters were situated closer to the fields and toward the back swamp, away from the vistas of the riverfront. For large sugar plantations, the era of calculated design and arrangement of the plantation complex had arrived.

Evergreen Plantation on the west bank of the Mississippi River in St. John the Baptist Parish exemplifies both the Greek Revival influence and the orderly expansion of the plantation complex. It is another Creole plantation that received a Greek Revival update. Its 1832 remodeling for owner Pierre Clidament Becnel by builder/carpenter John Carver addressed the main house but also created an ensemble of Greek Revival buildings framing the garden at the rear of the big house. This white, columned grouping imposes symmetry, order, and grace to the yard of the house.

The *pigeonniers,* dovecotes in English, were a symbol of wealth providing dining delicacy for the tables of the owners. Flanking *garçonnières* were luxuries of extra space accommodating the unmarried young men from the family of the house or visitors. Even the two-room privy, which was included in the 1832 building contract, was refined with its elaborate treatment of scored stucco over brick with pilasters and a parapeted gable. Removed a distance from this scene is the row of twenty-two cabins where the enslaved field-workers lived. This manipulation of spaces with a cultivated buffer around the big house and a straight row of nearly identical houses set apart was to become the standard for Louisiana's big sugarcane plantations. Yet, today Evergreen is one of the few places where such a complete arrangement can be experienced. As noted in its National Register of Historic Places nomination, it is one of the "most intact plantation complexes in the South."[24]

A now-demolished plantation that compared favorably to Evergreen and other peers and was well-documented through the Historic American Buildings Survey (HABS) is Uncle Sam, which is the focus of the last essay in this book. The bird's-eye view of the complex done in 1940 portrays the perfectly symmetrical main house ensemble with outlying ancillary buildings associated with crop production and enslaved labor separated into other areas delineated by fences. By the time the HABS documentation was submitted, the slave hospital, sugar mill, sugarhouse, and an unidentified house had already been reduced to their foundations, but still standing were the big house, *garçonnières, pigeonniers,* "offices," one stable, a carriage house, a barn and stable, blacksmith shop, "foreman's house," twenty-one slave houses, and three houses of unidentified use that the surveyors supposed to have been occupied by white workmen.

Both Evergreen and Uncle Sam have a primary building grouping composed of a big house, two *garçonnières,* two *pigeonniers,* and two matching buildings that have been variously identified as offices or kitchen and servants' quarters, but they utilize slightly dissimilar positioning that impacts the prominence and interface of the components. Both big houses are flanked by their *garçonnières,* but Evergreen's present their side gables to the front river side and face inward toward the front lawn of the big house. Likewise, its offices/kitchen/quarters set behind the house face inward while both offices and *garçonnières* at Uncle Sam present their front facades to the riverfront. This makes a very different impression on the visitor first seeing each from the river approach. In the view of Evergreen, the main house is the focus and the accessory buildings barely register in the background, while Uncle Sam's arrangement frames the main house with two smaller, but still substantial, colonnaded buildings. These supporting actors add to the visual impact of the complex as one of means and power. The visitor who made it to the back of Evergreen's main, however, would be greeted by a carefully composed architectural ensemble that defines a formal outdoor space. This area provided an additional opportunity to stage and direct the visual input a visitor received as well as to control their progress into actual buildings according to their business or social purpose and their status and relationship to the owners.[25]

The two plantations also exhibit variations in site layouts that relate to spacing between work and slave spaces and the main house environs. At Evergreen, the surviving row of slave cabins begins a little over one-sixth of a mile from the main house yard while at Uncle Sam it was shown to be over a quarter of a mile away, with the sugarhouse, sugar mill, and scale house between. If we are to try to imagine what it was like to live in and among these buildings as both free and enslaved people, it is important to consider the impacts of the arrangements of and distances between buildings. For an overseer or slave-owner on horseback, negotiating the whole of this built landscape could be done with some ease. To the enslaved on foot, the physiological implications of distances between plantation areas created greater psychological distances as well. Likewise, for those of the master's household without need to go to the crop-associated places, the quarters likely felt far removed. Thus for both enslaved and free people, there were whole areas of spatial "otherness" on the plantation as distinct as neighborhoods in a city.

Of course, the separation by distance and fencing was just one element of hierarchical dynamics in plantation architecture. As described above, from the 1830s onward, prosperous plantations featured very elegant big houses and immediately ancillary buildings. Slave housing stood in stark contrast to this. This is so much so that from our twenty-first century perspective, it could seem to be obvious evidence of the cruelty of slavery, yet what slave housing demonstrates is much more complicated than that. The surviving slave cabins at Evergreen Plantation are excellent examples of what had come to be the standard dwelling form for the enslaved across the South by 1860 (fig. 3). Most are the symmetrical two-room type with center chimneys, center partition walls, and side gable roofs that encompass full-width engaged porches. Though extremely small when juxtaposed with the big house, they are not nearly so dissimilar from very traditional house forms like the Creole and Acadian cottages of Louisiana or the Anglo-American hall and parlor house. When comparing with such *petite maisons,* size is not so much a distinguishing factor, but the craftsmanship and finish details are.

Unlike finer small houses of the early nineteenth century, Louisiana's slave cabins commonly lacked interior wall sheathing. Studs were left bare without the thermal or aesthetic benefit of plaster or paneling. Often whitewash was employed on the inside and out. This was thought to provide certain antiseptic qualities that would contribute to healthier living conditions as well as provide a bright look. Former slave Catherine Cornelius noted that all the cabins of Smithfield Plantation in West Baton Rouge Parish were white.[26] In 1850, a *Southern Cultivator* column advised, "A coat of whitewash inside and out, every summer, adds very much to the neat and comfortable appearance

Figure 3. Evergreen Plantation slave cabin, St. John the Baptist Parish. Photo taken in 2012 by Laura Ewen Blokker.

of the buildings, and is also, by its cleansing and purifying effect, conducive to health. The cost is almost nothing as one good barrel of lime will whitewash a dozen common sized negro houses, and any negro can put it on."[27] A common whitewash recipe that appeared in an 1857–58 and 1862 memo books from plantations in Iberville Parish included lime, molasses, salt, alum, and warm water.[28] One of the same books listed marble mantels to be ordered for the big house, emphasizing the contrast between big house extravagances and the parsimony regarding slave housing.

Elevation of houses off the ground on piers was also considered conducive to cleanliness as rubbish could be seen and swept out from beneath. Windows typically had no glass, but only board-and-batten shutters. Doors were also typically board-and-batten. While these details clearly make slave housing cruder than the few examples of finer small houses that have survived, there is so little evidence of the housing of poorer free people of the time that we cannot derive any concrete conclusions about their comparisons. For example, window glass was an expensive item not always included in home construction even among free persons. It is very likely that the houses of poor yeomen were little better than the standard slave cabins on large plantations. As discussed shortly, sometimes they could have been of worse construction.

The average size of the double houses was between twelve by twenty-four feet and sixteen by thirty-two feet. Four-room variations of this plan also survive at Evergreen and a four-room brick building at Evan Hall Plantation in Ascension Parish is believed to be a slave cabin. Far less common in rural settings were two-story quarters like those at El Dorado Plantation in Pointe Coupée Parish.[29] Driven by our modern perceptions of reasonable ratios of persons to square footage, much emphasis has been placed on how many people occupied slave cabins. However, in the eighteenth and nineteenth centuries, most households had more individuals living in less space than we are accustomed to today. Perhaps more telling of the conditions of slavery is the relationships of persons living together because there was far less choice at play in this regard for the enslaved than for free people.

The occupants of a cabin were not necessarily family units as might be imagined. The 1817 quarters bill for Oakland Plantation in West Feliciana Parish provides a rare detailed look at actual cabin occupant composition.[30] In relatively low-density examples, one cabin was occupied by four unrelated single men; two cabins were home to married couples with no children; one family of two parents and two children had a cabin to themselves; and two married couples shared another cabin. Other cabins were more crowded with one occupied by two parents and their daughter along with a single mother and her two children; another by two parents and their son plus a single mom and her four children; and in another, two women who had two children each, one of whom who had a husband who might have also shared the cabin. Other cabins were shared by families and single adults without children. Ann Patton Malone, who analyzed this and other Louisiana plantation lists, concluded that "Very rarely did a standard nuclear family have the privilege of a cabin for its exclusive use—and even then only if that family was larger than average or was very favored."[31]

In many cases, enslaved house servants are known to have had different accommodations from those who worked in the fields, but the overall picture of such in Louisiana is unclear. Even though house servants are more often mentioned in correspondence by plantation-owning families because of the close relationship that often existed among family members and house servants, details of their housing are elusive. Appraisals of Evergreen Plantation note two small buildings serving as kitchen and four servants' rooms apart from the listing of twelve slave cabins. These are presumably the two brick, Greek

Revival buildings that stand just to the back of the big house today. Kitchens were traditionally kept apart from the main house to remove the excessive heat of all-day cooking. Even though they were closely affiliated with the big house, most have not survived and were barely documented.

Toward the end of the antebellum period, the very elaborate big houses brought the kitchen and cooks' and servants' quarters into the house. Belle Grove in Iberville Parish, designed by New Orleans architect Henry Howard and constructed between 1852 and 1857, was such a house (fig. 4). The two-room kitchen was located on the ground floor with a servants' stair leading to the dining room on the first floor. On the first floor, across the stair hall from the dining room were the servant's rooms: one 15′ 5″ × 16′ 8″, one 15′ 5″ × 11′ 11″, and two about 15′ 5″ × 10′ 6″. These rooms and kitchen were roughly contained within their own wing with outside doors and a stairway for ingress/egress and connection to the main house for service.

An image of the ruins of the hearth and oven at Belle Grove plantation was captured by HABS and is a rare indicator of such configurations. Former slave Rebecca Fletcher recalled that on her plantation the children too young to work

Figure 4. Belle Grove Plantation house showing service wing, 1938. Photo by Richard Koch. Library of Congress, Prints & Photographs Division, HABS, LA 24.

were looked after by an old woman in a big kitchen where she cooked and fed them.[32] Some plantations had houses for the care of the children. In the 1920s, Elizabeth Ross Hite recalled there being one where she was a child in slavery.[33] Such a house was described as existing on Houmas Plantation in Ascension Parish where children as old as eleven were looked after by an elderly woman.[34]

VISITING THE QUARTERS

Since so few slave cabins survive today, looking to period descriptions gives us some augmented sense of what the quarters were like. In 1861, Briton Sir William Howard Russell traveled through Louisiana and recorded his impressions in a diary he subsequently published. As with any personal account, we must take his descriptions at face value and anticipate biases and errors. However, Russell's observations as a traveler trying to understand a foreign culture, are helpful to our own quest to interpret plantation architecture. In the sense that, "The past is a foreign country, people do things differently there," we are like travelers ourselves.[35] As he visited plantation after plantation, Russell's expressed emotions transitioned from pity for slaves, to belief that they were well provided for, to uneasiness over the highly controlled management of slavery.

Russell's first visit was to the St. James Parish Cabahanoce (also spelled Cabanocey) Plantation of André Bienvenu Roman, a very wealthy Creole and two-term governor.[36] He described his accommodations as a detached building close to the big house, with four bedrooms, a library, and a sitting room.[37] Roman led Russell out from the back of the house and past a "high paling" to see the quarters on the "part of the estate" where Russell estimated seventy to eighty people lived.[38] It was a Sunday and the quarters were filled with their residents. In 1860, Roman owned a total of 142 slaves and sixty-five slave dwellings.[39] Russell's description aligns with the typical organization of quarters and the standard two-room house form. He wrote, "We entered by a wicket-gate, a square enclosure, lined with negro huts, built of wood, something like those which came from Malta to the Crimea in the early part of the campaign. They are not furnished with windows—a wooden slide or grating admits all the air a negro desires. There is a partition dividing the hut into two departments."[40] His phrasing regarding the minimal fenestration oddly suggests the enslaved persons as the clients in the house design, as if it all was executed to their taste. Russell continues by describing spare furnishings within the cabins.

Next he was led to the quarters of the house slaves, which, he explains, are separated from the quarters of the field-workers by a paling. Beyond this, he offers no particulars on the designs of their houses, but notes of the interiors "not a sign of ornament or decoration was visible; not the most tawdry print image of Virgin or Saviour." Russell explains that he felt reluctance at examining the interiors at all, although he was urged to by Roman, because he could not "divest [himself] of some regard for the feelings" of the enslaved "who stood by, shy, curtseying, and silent as I broke in upon their family circle, felt their beds, and turned over their clothing." He even asks and leaves unanswered the question, "What right had I to do so?" It is clear he felt torn between acknowledging the right of ownership asserted by his host and respecting of the right to privacy of fellow humans. Despite this, he seems to leave favorably impressed by the provided housing, just as Roman surely would have wanted him to be. After riding down the road, he commented on neighboring properties saying, "Men making eighty or ninety hogsheads of sugar a year lived in the most wretched tumble-down wooden houses not much larger than ox sheds." (Roman produced 342 hogsheads in 1860.) Perhaps it was in contrast with these personal abodes of poorer planters that Russell found the slave housing provided by his host to be so good.

From the Roman property, Russell crossed the Mississippi River to stay with an even wealthier planter, John Burnside, who was not only one of the wealthiest planters in Louisiana but also one of the wealthiest in the South. His multiple plantations in Ascension Parish, consisting of 23,600 acres, were valued at $1,400,000 in 1860.[41] His personal property, which would have included slaves, was estimated at $800,000.[42] With additional property he owned in St. James Parish, his real and personal property was valued at a staggering $2,600,000.[43] In St. James Parish, he owned 187 people and 60 slave dwellings; in Ascension Parish, he owned 753 people and 192 slave dwellings.[44] Russell stayed in a *garçonnière* at Burnside's home plantation, Houmas. There he found the quarters to be "a row of single-storied wooden cottages, divided into two or four rooms. An avenue of trees runs down the center of the negro street and behind each hut are rude poultry hutches."[45]

Although Russell said nothing more of the quarters here, the overseer's proclamations of the benefits, good provisions, and management caused him to reflect, "I declare that to me the more orderly, methodical, and perfect the arrangements for economizing slave labor—regulating slaves—are, the more odious and hateful slavery becomes."[46] Russell had perceived one of the ironies of slavery: better conditions such as in housing did not necessarily indicate care on the part of the planter for the humanity of the enslaved. Often, the pure aim of good housing, clothes, or food was for the enslaved to be in good condition—like well-oiled machines—to provide labor and thus profit for the owner. It was also a means of control. In setting out the rules of Highland Plantation, West Feliciana Parish, in 1838, Bennet Barrow reasoned that "... such a settled arrangement should exist on the plantation to make it unnecessary for a negro to leave it—or to have a good plea for doing so. You must therefore make him as comfortable at home as possible, affording him what is essentially necessary for his happiness—you must provide for him yourself and by that means create in him a habit of perfect dependence on you."[47] Good housing was also utilized by slaveowners as exhibits in their defense of slavery to outsiders such as Russell in 1861. Nearly a century later, segregationists also used architecture to support their position when they built new school buildings for Africans Americans to assert there was equality in separation.[48]

Russell continued to visit other Louisiana plantations and observed that at Burnside's neighboring Orange Grove plantation, managed by another overseer, "the negroes unquestionably seemed less comfortable than those in the quarters of Houmas, separated from them by a mere nominal division." Conversely, of the nearby plantation of John Lawrence Manning, Russell remarked, "one plantation is as like another as two peas ... but the slave quarters on Governor Manning's were larger, better built, and more comfortable-looking than any I had ever seen."[49] Manning was governor of South Carolina from 1852 to 1854, a signer of the Ordinance of Secession, and one of the largest slaveowners in the United States. In addition to his holdings in South Carolina, in Ascension Parish he owned 616 people and 150 slave cabins.[50]

In sum, over 14,000 slave cabins existed in the parishes along the Mississippi River coast of Louisiana between Natchez and New Orleans.[51] They varied in their exact form and quality, but by the Civil War, most often they were wooden, two-room dwellings brightened by whitewash on the inside and out, with a center chimney, a full-width porch, minimal window openings with no glass, and no interior sheathing. During the colonial period, enslaved people may have had greater control over their habitations and even built their own homes to their own designs, but in the first decades of the nineteenth century, slaveowners increasingly standardized their slave housing. Although design was taken out of the hands of the enslaved, some scholars have argued that enslaved people did have agency in their domestic environments. For instance, in his study of Louisianan and Jamaican sugar plantations, Roderick A. McDonald concluded that "slaves assumed extensive command over what happened in and to their houses. Despite amorphous questions concerning property rights, for most practical purposes the slaves largely determined life and living patterns in the quarters and behaved as property owners."[52] It is also very important to remember that while Americans in the twentieth-first century spend a great deal of time indoors, people in the nineteenth century spent more of their time outdoors. Scholars such as Garrett Fesler, Dell Upton, and John Michael Vlach have asserted the importance of outdoor space as extensions of domestic space and places of agency for enslaved African Americans.[53]

With knowledge that, in some cases, slave housing would have been better than that of free, but poor, yeoman farmers and imagining the enslaved assuming some control over their spaces, we might see slave cabins as slaveholders would have wanted: proof of the good conditions of enslavement. However, accepting slave housing as a mark of good treatment is as flawed as seeing it as evidence of mistreatment. Both conclusions miss the deeper nuances of enslavement which cannot be traced through architecture alone, yet are interwoven with it. Enslaved households fluctuated not just with births, marriages, deaths, and family circumstances, but also with unpredicted arrivals (purchases) and departures (sales). Ultimately, enslaved people could not control with whom they lived today or where they might live tomorrow. Uncertainty was an overlying theme for the life of the enslaved and so the home, of whatever construction, was infused with it. Regarding very different circumstances of time and place, James Baldwin wrote in *Giovanni's Room,* "Perhaps home is not a place, but simply an irrevocable condition."[54] Within the irrevocable condition of enslavement, perhaps home was not just a place and not just a building, but yet deeply tied to it under the ever-present threat of displacement.

CAPITALS, HOSPITALS, AND CHURCHES

Every town has its institutional buildings, even small towns. This was also true of expansive plantations that might be mistaken for towns, as the previously quoted Catherine Cornelius, who was once enslaved on a plantation outside of Baton Rouge, recounted. Plantations had buildings or structures for every purpose, including such things as carriage houses and well shelters, but a few of the buildings provided significant communal spaces in the enslaved plantation experience. At large sugar plantations, the sugarhouse was often in close proximity to the slave cabins. Russell aptly described the situation by saying, "The sugar-house is the capital of the negro quarters . . ."[55] Indeed, the sugarhouse frequently rose at the terminus of the quarters axis like a capital building.

It was larger and more durably built than the slave cabins. Brick was preferred to wood for sugarhouse construction because of its fire resistance. The buildings could be as much as three hundred feet long to accommodate boilers, engines, rollers, and evaporators and the smoke and steam they exuded is said to have given them the appearance of New England factories.[56] By 1850, it is estimated there were 1,495 sugarhouses in Louisiana, 907 of which were powered by steam.[57]

Russell noted the "factory-looking chimney" of André Bienvenu Roman's large brick sugarhouse where he got to observe its use for slave socializing and dancing during the off season.[58] He recognized the contrast this scene would have with the grueling and dangerous labor of other months. Among those attending the dance were house servants Russell described as wearing white dresses with crinolines, pink sashes, and "gaudily colored" head scarves. For these young women, who otherwise worked in the house, visiting the sugarhouse must have been a very different experience than for those who regularly labored over the boiling vats. The latter would have been intimately familiar with the building and the heat, hard labor, and danger of its productive months, whereas the house servants would be somewhat of strangers to it, perceiving it perhaps with curiosity or with only the present social scene in mind.

Where cotton rather than sugar was the dominant cash crop, the cotton gin and press were the center of agricultural processing on the plantation. The processing requirements of cotton were less complicated and dangerous than those of sugar, and the gin house was likewise a less complicated structure. It was typically a large wood frame building, looking much like an ordinary barn but with a distinctively large roof structure to accommodate the gin. At the gin house, the cotton picked by each slave would be weighed at the end of the day, and so it served in part as place of judgment.[59]

A very standard part of larger plantation complexes were slave hospitals, but there is no evidence of a standard building form.[60] As mentioned earlier, in 1792 Destrehan Plantation in St. Charles Parish possessed two 11′ × 17′ "old hospitals" and Highland Plantation in West Feliciana Parish had a hospital added in the 1830s. The aerial of Uncle Sam Plantation shows the hospital as an approximately 50′ × 100′ building, possibly with a surrounding gallery, near the front road. At Cabanocey in St. James Parish, Sir William Howard Russell visited the hospital, which he indicated was within the quarters' fencing and supervised by "an old negress." He described that its "naked rooms contained several flocks of beds."[61] At Houmas, the overseer boasted of the hospital—using derogatory language regarding the enslaved—that once he "gets in there, he'd like to live there the rest of his life," upon which Russell quipped, "even shrewd Mr. Seal did not perceive the conclusion that was to be drawn from his testimony to its excellent arrangements."[62] At Waterloo Plantation in Ascension Parish, 1850s records reveal varying numbers in the double-digits of people in the hospital at any one time, with as many as eighty-six on the sick list for things such as cholera, dengue fever, influenza, and grippe.[63] Quite obviously, medical care of the enslaved was considered an operational necessity for the planter. On the other hand, it was another space that was primarily the domain of the enslaved African Americans, with elderly women placed in charge and only periodic visits by the doctor.

SMALL AND MIDDLING PLANTERS

It is impossible to discuss the plantation landscape of Louisiana without focusing on large slaveholders because of the domination described above. Nevertheless, 51.6 percent of Louisiana slaves belonged to holdings with fewer than fifty slaves in 1860 and many of their owners had properties along the Mississippi River.[64] These properties tended to consist of fewer buildings, more ephemeral buildings, and buildings that were not as likely to capture the attention of twentieth-century observers as were the grand—if decaying—main houses, so we have less visual documentation of their appearances. Likewise, owners of smaller plantations were less likely than large slaveholders to leave behind documentation of their own lives. Some records do exist, however, that help to establish an understanding of lesser known plantation landscapes. William Howard Russell again provides an evocative commentary regarding this category of plantation in 1861.

> The bank of the river below the large plantations was occupied by a set of small creole planters, whose poor houses were close together, indicating very limited farms, which had been subdivided from time to time, according to the French fashion; so that the owners have at last approached pauperism . . . It is among these men that, at times, slavery assumes its harshest aspect, and that the negroes are exposed to the severest labor; but it is also true that the slaves have closer relations with the families of the owners, and live in more intimate connection with them than they do under the strict police of the large plantations.[65]

Perhaps one of the most detailed and evocative accounts of the Louisiana small planter comes from Solomon Northup in *Twelve Years a Slave.* His experience between the years 1841 and 1853 actually occurred outside of the boundaries of this study in Avoyelles Parish, adjacent to Concordia and Pointe Coupée, but its close proximity to the study focus renders it relevant and its rarity makes it worth including here. As a free man in New York, Solomon Northup had experienced several types of living arrangements which contrasted greatly with the crude shelters he encountered in slavery. After marriage in 1829, he and his wife lived in the "Old Fort House" at Fort Edward, New York, a two-story, weatherboarded Georgian house which then operated as a boarding house. They then made arrangements to live in a "quiet farm house on the east side of the Hudson."[66] Finally, before Northup was kidnapped, he and his wife lived in a house in Saratoga Springs. From his writing it is clear that in all these places, his family lived in modest comfort and that his wife and children made each home. Northup had carpentry skills and as a slave, was often employed in construction work so he offers particularly good details regarding buildings. Avoyelles was a sugar and cotton growing parish, but it did not have the river frontage of its neighbors, nor the great many large plantations. Northup described a job of putting up ceiling boards with the comment, "a plastered room being a rare thing in the parish of Avoyelles."[67] After passing through the hands of a few owners, Northup ended up on the property of Edwin Epps, a cotton planter who leased his place from his father-in-law. As Northup described him, Epps was an uneducated, frugal, and relentlessly mean master with course manners who was prone to drinking.

Epps's own house, which Northup helped build, offers some architectural context for the associated cabins (fig. 5). A far cry from the colonnaded Greek

Revival mansions of wealthy planters, his wood-frame house looked much like a larger version of the common two-room slave dwelling. It is two rooms wide, with two front doors set close together and two flanking windows. A side gable roof shelters the engaged front porch. Its fanciest features were its beaded ceiling boards and beams.[68] This was the grandest big house men of Epps's means could afford.

Figure 5. Epps House, original location, vicinity of Holmesville on Bayou Boeuf, Avoyelles Parish. Sue Eakin Papers, Central Louisiana Collections, James C. Bolton Library, Louisiana State University at Alexandria, Alexandria, LA.

Of his quarters Northup said, "The cabin is constructed of logs, without floor or window. The latter is altogether unnecessary, the crevices between the logs admitting sufficient light. In stormy weather the rain drives through them, rendering it comfortless and extremely disagreeable. The rude door hangs on great wooden hinges. In one end is constructed an awkward fireplace."[69] For Northup, who had been wrenched from his own life and family, such a place would never come close to being a home.

Just below the large slaveholders—those owning fifty or more slaves—were the middling planters, whose associated architecture is not at all well documented in Louisiana. Oscar Ayraud of Ascension Parish owned forty-eight slaves in 1860, which puts him into this category. His Palo Alto plantation near Donaldsonville fronted on Bayou Lafourche rather than the Mississippi River, and its appearance was captured by Marie Adrien Persac in the 1850s in his typical detailed perfection. The big house, which remains today, is a one-and-one-half story, side-gable, four-room center hall with a full-width engaged porch. Its style shows the influence of the Greek Revival in the broad entablature over boxed Doric columns and the pointed lintels and ears of the door enframements. The interior likewise features Greek accents in its plasterwork. Connected to the house by a now enclosed breezeway is the originally detached, side-gable kitchen with center chimney and full-width porch. In the Persac painting described here, a smaller building that could possibly be a dairy, smokehouse, or other food-related structure is located just in front of the kitchen.

Just to the south (left) of these buildings the fields began. To the right of the house, the painting shows what appears to be a small *pigeonnier*. Further, the painting displays a white picket fence—a common feature of Persac's plantation depictions—extending along the bayou road with an open shelter set on the banks of the bayou and a three-bay, side-gable building sits just inside the fence. This is reported to have been a schoolhouse. In addition to all the other types of buildings, plantations sometimes had schoolhouses where the planter's own children and those of neighboring plantations, excluding slaves, could be educated by an instructor living on the property. Off to the right of the image, but closer to the bayou than the main house are the overseer's house and slave quarters. Both the overseer's house and the cabins seem petite in this rendering. The overseer's house faces the river while the cabins present their gable sides to it, as was common. Each cabin, of which seven can be counted, has a front porch, a steeply pitched roof, and a center chimney. In the distance, behind the big house, smoke puffs from the sugarhouse. This arrangement differs from the one discussed previously in that the sugarhouse sat at the end of the row of quarters; also, this sugarhouse was made of wood rather than the preferred but more expensive brick. Other documents indicate that the property also included a cotton gin, sawmill, and, by 1867, stables, a corn house, and corn mill. Persac's painting presents a picturesque scene of the planter's life as was his mode, and it appears every bit as refined as the big plantation, just on a smaller scale.

The many variations of small to middling plantation life between the cramped and crude settings described by Russell and Epps and the orderly complex portrayed by Persac can only be imagined. The associated buildings of small plantations are every bit as key to understanding the plantation landscape as those of the larger plantations and deserve expanded examinations.

MASTERLESS LANDSCAPES

Absentee ownership defined a distinct frontier of the plantation experience in the United States. Speaking of the driving economic forces, and with sharp critique of the results, W. E. B. Du Bois wrote that,

> the high price of cotton, and the rapidly increasing internal slave trade, was the beginning of a system of commercial slavery in the gulf states which will ever remain a disgraceful essay in American history. In its worst phase there was no Big House and cultivated master, only an unscrupulous, paid overseer, lawless and almost irresponsible if he only made the crops large enough . . . In the forests of Louisiana, the bottoms of Mississippi, and the Sea Islands of Georgia, where the Negro slave sank lowest in oppression and helplessness, the Negro home practically disappeared, and the house was simply rude, inadequate shelter.
>
> But whither went the Big House, when so entirely separated from the slave quarters? It moved to town and it moved with the house servants.[70]

Within the area represented by *Norman's Chart,* Concordia Parish represents the situation of absentee landownership best. In 1860, approximately 81 percent of land in the parish was owned by absentee landlords and 90.9 percent of the population was enslaved.[71] In 1860, J. W. Dorr wrote,

> Many of the planters who own and cultivate these lands are among the largest agriculturists in the State, and exercise the authority of ownership over estates as broad as some German principalities, and yielding far greater revenues. But very few of these lords of the soil reside on their estates, but have their residences across the river, on the hither but scarcely more pleasant lands of Mississippi—in Natchez or elsewhere.[72]

The large, absentee slaveholders were mostly concentrated on the eastern portion of the parish along the Mississippi River while the western side of the parish had more small, resident landowners.[73]

In the antebellum period, Concordia Parish's eastern landscape was one nearly devoid of big houses; instead, overseers' houses dominated the slave quarter complexes. In 1860, the census recorded 12,542 enslaved people in Concordia with 10,514 residing on one of ninety-five holdings with more than fifty persons.[74] The census taker for Concordia Parish was apparently particular about how he enumerated enslaved people and his notes indicate that he attempted to have slaves assemble at their individual dwellings but did not always receive cooperation from the overseers in this regard and was, instead, being given only a master list of names and counting of the dwellings. He was able to make a more detailed note of slave and cabin count at Rifle Point, about eight miles north of Vidalia, in Concordia Parish, where he wrote, "On this place are 70 Negro cabins 19 × 23 feet. There are 271 Negroes from 100 down to one month, which will give about four Negroes to each cabin."

The extensive plantation holdings that existed in Concordia in 1860 included 2,257 slave dwellings, which was more than any parish in the study area. Of this built landscape, Canebrake Plantation was the only overseer's house and quarters type complex to survive long enough—at least in part—to be documented.[75] When it was listed on the National Register in 1982, six of its slave cabins were still standing. In 1860, it was owned by Gerard Brandon of Brandon Hall near Natchez and 113 slaves were enumerated on the plantation with thirty-two slave dwellings.[76] The arrangement of Canebrake is striking in its departure from the arrangements of large plantations described above. It places the overseer's house at the front, directly facing the river, and the slave quarters are arranged on either side of an axis extending directly behind it. An early twentieth-century image gives a glimpse of this configuration and the house types, though some alterations had been made by that time. The overseer's house was an ample, raised, side-gable, three-bay house with a very wide entrance and unusual double-leaf, hinged doors that would have afforded much ventilation to the center passage (fig. 6). The slave quarters were typical two-room buildings with front porches and center chimneys.

As with the landscapes of the small planters and middling farmers, those of the overseer-headed plantations have been nearly eradicated. The slave quarters

Figure 6. Canebrake Plantation overseer's house, vicinity of Ferriday, Concordia Parish. Historic Natchez Foundation.

documented at Canebrake appear much like those of larger plantations where masters lived and not necessarily the "simply rude, inadequate shelter" Du Bois suggested to be the norm of the absentee owner situation. Other historic images of Concordia Parish also captured typical wood-frame, side-gable slave cabins. Beyond this, we have little to analyze actual circumstances as they existed in this part of Louisiana. The ratio of dwellings to enslaved persons was roughly the same as in other parishes and the one note of size at Rifle Point Plantation was consistent as well, but what were the actual spatial conditions? How well were the buildings maintained? To what degree did enslaved people have any control over their domestic spaces? What were the relationships between people sharing a dwelling space? How much stability was there in continued occupancy on a given plantation and in a specific building? To better understand the spectrum of the plantation experience across Louisiana, these are questions we need to ask, even if the answers remain elusive.

AFTER THE CIVIL WAR TO TODAY

Plantations did not completely cease to operate or be inhabited with end of the Civil War. Though the interpretation of history at plantation sites often stops with the war, a great many continued or resumed operations postwar with people living in the same big houses and in the same quarters and working the same fields, only under the different terms and nomenclature of tenancy, (token) wage work, and sharecropping. The promise of forty acres and a mule was never realized. Instead, property owners such as the incredibly wealthy John Burnside, a British subject, kept his plantations after the war. Many others—former Confederate soldiers included—did as well, and former slaves and descendants of slaves became more deeply attached to the plantations as they continued to live and work on the same places as previous generations. Slowly though, the built plantation landscape began to disappear as agricultural practices and economic structures changed. Some plantations that did not recover economically from the Civil War and Reconstruction sat vacant and deteriorating. Natural disasters (like the Great Flood of 1927), new infrastructure built to control forces of nature, and industrial expansion in the twentieth century took others like Cabanocey and Uncle Sam. The diminishing of Louisiana's vast collection of plantation architecture accelerated after the first quarter of the twentieth century.

The 1930s to 1940s were a pivotal time for Louisiana's plantations. Amid the rising threats to the plantation architecture, architects and photographers documented an extraordinary number of buildings in their last gasp. New Orleans architect Richard Koch was made the District Officer of Louisiana for the Historic American Buildings Survey in 1934. Working with nineteen other architects and draftsmen, plus photographers like Robert Tebbs, Koch led in the meticulous documentation of numerous plantation big houses.[77] Meanwhile, photographer Frances Benjamin Johnston was working throughout the South documenting historic architecture with grants from the Carnegie Corporation for the Carnegie Survey of the Architecture of the South. In 1937, she received a grant for the Lower and Gulf South states, including Louisiana. Clarence John Laughlin was hired by the Corps of Engineers to photograph buildings as they moved forward with a reworking of the Mississippi River levee. Published in 1948 as *Ghosts Along the Mississippi,* those and other images of grand plantation homes he captured left an indelible impact on the public impression of Louisiana plantation architecture, as is discussed in Jochen Wierich's essay in this volume.[78] All of this work spurred new interest in preserving the grand architecture of plantation big houses. Very rarely, however, did any of the photographers turn around to capture the stables, barns, sugarhouses, cotton houses, gin houses, well houses, loom houses, offices, school buildings, hospitals, or any of the hundreds of slave quarters. These buildings were largely left out of the documentation and also out of the interests and concerns of preservationists.

As changes in agriculture were ending life on plantations as it had been known, this visual material established a misconception that equated plantations with mansions. The growing interests in history and preservation which focused on the big houses brought new direction and sometimes abrupt changes to life on the plantations for people who traced their connections back generations. The transformation of Oakley Plantation into Audubon State Historic Site in West Feliciana Parish is one example of this. In the approach to historical interpretation of the 1940s, a museum site was not a place for people to continue living, even those whose family history ran deep on the property. When Oakley became a state historic site, the last descendants of slaves residing at Oakley were evicted.[79] In more controlled ways, descendants of slaves were sometimes made a part of the plantation revival. A circa 1940s image shows an African American woman dressed all in white, looking up from the bottom of the spiral staircase in the tourist wing of Afton Villa Plantation in West Feliciana Parish, which was opened to the public in 1945.[80] She was likely working as "historic" character to enhance the setting of the house in a manner consistent with period interpretation of plantation life, which was heavily influenced by the 1939 film *Gone with the Wind.* Another image from the same set of photographs shows an African American man in a top hat at the gate. In such roles, African Americans were employed not to interpret their own history on plantations, but to support a big house and master-centric narrative.

So much and yet so little truly describes Louisiana's built plantation landscape in the twenty-first century. We have a seeming abundance of plantations. Every year thousands upon thousands of visitors pour through the many plantations that are open to the public to see the architecture, the decorative furnishings, and to try to understand what plantations and American slavery were all about. Yet, it is challenging to accurately interpret existing plantations when so many of the buildings that made the plantations functional complexes are no longer there. Most of what we think of today as plantations consists only of a big house and a few, if any, ancillary buildings. This is exacerbated by the fact that distortedly genteel and master-centric portrayals of plantations such as those of Persac's map dominate period documentation. Big houses do serve well to help us understand a part of the plantation landscape; however, they are but one piece of their original matrix. The more than 14,000 slave dwellings and other outbuildings are mostly missing.

The few ancillary buildings seen on plantation tours are usually reconstructions or buildings moved from other plantations, as historical interpretations have begun to shift toward a somewhat more honest inclusion of slavery in the narrative. Rarely are they in historically accurate locations and they do little to recreate a real feel of the plantation complex with all of its working and living bustle, its hierarchy of countless buildings and fencing, and its complicated feelings of ownership and place.

In his seminal book, *Between the World and Me,* Ta-Nehisi Coates advised his son,

> Slavery is not an indefinable mass of flesh. It is a particular, specific enslaved woman, whose mind is active as your own, whose range of feeling is as vast as your own; who prefers the way the light falls in one particular spot in the woods, who enjoys fishing where the water eddies in a nearby stream, who loves her mother in her own complicated way, thinks her sister talks too loud, has a favorite season, who excels at dress making and knows, inside herself, that she is as intelligent as anyone . . .
>
> You must struggle to truly remember this past in all its nuance, error, and humanity.[81]

We often look to tangibles like buildings to help us connect to the past in this kind of intimate way. We cannot bring back the thousands of lost buildings, but we can bring them to the forefront of our imagination.

By thinking more specifically and inquisitively about the abundance of architecture that existed on plantations as described in this essay, we may more clearly reflect on the particular of the humanity. We can look out from the gallery or veranda of the big house and imagine, off at a little distance to the right or left, an entire neighborhood called the quarters. We can imagine a cluster or row of service buildings between us and the quarters and the movement of people and animals between. We can imagine how we might feel taking in that view and scene depending on our identity in this plantation community: our class, wealth, and condition of freedom; our gender; our age; and our race. We can walk out and down the lane between the fields and envision rows of houses and perhaps in so doing, we can imagine a particular, specific woman walking between those rows, taking in the view of whitewashed gables as the sun hits them and casts long shadows in front of the porches. We can imagine her attention redirected by a plume of smoke from the sugarhouse and a sudden chill she escapes by entering a cabin, where she sets to making a fire in the center fireplace. In this way, architectural history can augment the present reality and bring it into focus.

NOTES

The author extends great appreciation to all who so graciously assisted in obtaining images and permissions in the midst of COVID-19 limitations so that this essay could be the better through their use: Kevin Williams, Mimi Miller, Emily Ardoin, Michelle Riggs, and Bobby Ticknor. The author also thanks Tulane School of Architecture Graduate Research Fellows John Hausladen and Shelby Mitchinson for their research assistance.

1. Some of the earliest plantations were within the boundaries of present-day New Orleans. Outside of New Orleans, a substantial settlement developed on the west bank of the Mississippi River that came to be known as the German Coast. Many Germans immigrated there beginning in 1721, were concentrated there by 1723, and the population established a church at Karlstein (present-day Killona) in St. Charles Parish in 1724: see Mary Ann Sternberg, *Along the River Road: Past and Present on Louisiana's Historic Byway* (Baton Rouge: Louisiana State University Press, 2001), 8. A circa 1725 *Map of Louisiana near New Orleans showing various concessions* depicts the partial division of land up and down the Mississippi River from New Orleans into long lots by that time (1974.25.18.11, The Historic New Orleans Collection): see http://hnoc.minisisinc.com/thnoc/catalog/1/39213. The first slave ships arrived in Louisiana in 1719: see Daniel H. Usner Jr., "From African Captivity to American Slavery: The Introduction of Black Laborers to Colonial Louisiana," in *The African American Experience in Louisiana: Part A,* ed. Charles Vincent (Lafayette: University of Southwestern Louisiana, 1999), 45, first published in *Louisiana History* 20 (1979): 25–48.

2. For further analysis of the process of creolization in Louisiana and in architecture, see Nicholas R. Spitzer, "Monde Créole: The Cultural World of French Louisiana Creoles and the Creolization of World Cultures," *Journal of American Folklore* 116 (2003): 58; Jay Dearborn Edwards, "Architectural Creolization: The Importance of Colonial Architecture," in *Architectural Anthropology,* ed. Mari-Jose Amerlinck (Westport, CT: Bergin & Garvey, 2001), 83–120; Benjamin Maygarden, "Building in Colonial Louisiana: Creolization and the Survival of French Traditions," *International Journal of Historical Archaeology* 10, no. 3 (2006): 211–39; Carl Lounsbury, "The Dynamics of Architectural Design in Eighteenth-Century Charleston and the Low Country," *Perspectives in Vernacular Culture* 7, Special Issue (1997): 65.

3. Only Charles's first name is provided in the contract. Research published by Destrehan Plantation suggests he may have been a St. Charles Parish resident named Charles Pacquet. *A Brief History of Charles Pacquet: A Free Man of Color* (Destrehan, LA: Destrehan Plantation, 2000).

4. Ann M. Masson and Jean M. Farnsworth, eds., *The Architecture of Colonial Louisiana: Collected Essays of Samuel Wilson, Jr., FAIA* (Lafayette: University of Southwestern Louisiana, 1987), 370.

5. Ibid., 371.

6. Destrehan Plantation, "Slaves included in the 1782 sale of the Plantation by Guillaume Guignan to Robert de Logny" at http://www.destrehanplantation.org/uploads/files/SalebyGuillaume Guignan.pdf.

7. Masson and Farnsworth, ed., *Architecture of Colonial Louisiana,* 371.

8. For descriptions of various West African building techniques, see Susan Denyer, *African Traditional Architecture: An Historical and Geographical Perspective* (London: Heinemann, 1978) and Paul Oliver, ed., *Shelter in Africa* (New York: Praeger, 1971). For analysis of the origins of Africans brought to Louisiana, see Gwendolyn Midlo Hall, *Africans in Colonial Louisiana: The Development of Afro-Creole Culture in the Eighteenth Century* (Baton Rouge: Louisiana State University Press, 1992). Leland Ferguson makes the point that "Black men and women on the Georgia Coast in the 1930s, just one generation removed from slavery, reflected that their grandparents lived in small, thatched, clay-walled houses—in both Africa and America." See Leland Ferguson, *Uncommon Ground: Archaeology and Early African America, 1650–1800* (Washington, DC: Smithsonian Institute Press, 1992), 74–75.

9. Teresia R. Lamb, *Preliminary Archaeological Reconnaissance and Assessment of Destrehan Plantation, St. Charles Parish, Louisiana* (New Orleans: University of New Orleans, 1983). For more on the African origins of enslaved people in Louisiana and their cultural transfers, see Hall, *Africans in Colonial Louisiana.*

10. Abram Feltus Barrow Family Papers, Mss. 3696, 3745, Louisiana and Lower Mississippi Valley Collections, Louisiana State University Libraries, Baton Rouge; *The Louisiana Purchase: A Heritage Explored* (Baton Rouge: Louisiana Digital Library, 2011) at http://exhibitions.blogs.lib.lsu.edu/?p=115&page=3.

11. See the Louisiana Division of Historic Preservation, National Register of Historic Places nomination form for "Highland Plantation," Baton Rouge: Louisiana Division of Historic Preservation, 1983; Henry V. Taves et al., eds., *The Historic Architecture of Halifax County, North Carolina* (North Carolina: Halifax County Historical Association, 2010).

12. Louisiana Division of Historic Preservation, National Register of Historic Places nomination form for "Highland Plantation," Baton Rouge: Louisiana Division of Historic Preservation, 1983.

13. Fortescue Cuming, *Cuming's Tour to the Western Country (1807–1809),* vol. 4 of *Early Western Travels, 1748–1846,* ed. Reuben Gold Thwaites (Cleveland, OH: Arthur H. Clark, 1904), 336. The work was originally published in Pittsburgh by Cramer, Spear and Eichbaum in 1810.

14. Bennet Hilliard Barrow and Edwin Adams Davis, *Plantation Life in the Florida Parishes of Louisiana, 1836–1846, as Reflected in the Diary of Bennet H. Barrow* (New York: AMS Press, 1967).

15. Damian Akan Pargas, *The Quarters and the Fields: Slave Families of the Non-Cotton South* (Gainesville: University Press of Florida, 2010), 130.

16. Joseph Karl Menn, *The Large Slaveholders of Louisiana, 1860* (New Orleans: Pelican Publishing, 1964), 1.

17. Ibid., 2, 24.

18. Ibid., 2.

19. Ronnie W. Clayton, *Mother Wit: The Ex-Slave Narratives of the Louisiana Writers' Project* (New York: Peter Lang Publishing, 1990), 46.

20. J. Carlyle Sitterson, "The William J. Minor Plantations: A Study in Antebellum Absentee Ownership," *Journal of Southern History* 9, no. 1 (February 1943), 70–71.

21. Louisiana's French triangle of influence roughly encompasses an area between New Orleans on the east, Lake Charles on the west, and Natchitoches to the north, though, of course, the boundaries are not rigid.

22. Anomalies include the picturesque eclecticism of San Francisco Plantation in St. John the Baptist Parish and the Gothic Revival Afton Villa Plantation in West Feliciana Parish.

23. Lamb, *Reconnaissance and Assessment of Destrehan Plantation,* 36.

24. Donna Fricker, "Evergreen Plantation," National Register of Historic Places nomination form, Louisiana Division of Historic Preservation, 1991.

25. For discussion of the orchestration of space and movement on colonial Virginia plantations, see Dell Upton, *Holy Things and Profane: Anglican Parish Churches in Colonial Virginia* (Cambridge: MIT Press, 1986), 199–218. See also John Burkhardt Rehder, "Sugar Plantation Settlements of Southern Louisiana: A Cultural Geography" (PhD diss., Louisiana State University, 1971); John Michael Vlach, *Back of the Big House: The Architecture of Plantation Slavery* (Chapel Hill: University of North Carolina Press, 1993); and Clifton Ellis and Rebecca Ginsburg, eds. *Cabin, Quarter, Plantation: Architecture and Landscapes of North American Slavery* (New Haven: Yale University Press, 2010).

26. Clayton, *Mother Wit,* 46.

27. Tattler, "Management of Negroes," *Southern Cultivator* 8 (November 1850): 162–64, in *Advice among Masters: The Ideal in Slave Management in the Old South,* ed. James O'Breeden (Westport, CT: Greenwood Press, 1980), 121.

28. Edward J. Gay and Family Papers (Mss. 1295), Louisiana and Lower Mississippi Valley Collections Special Collections, Hill Memorial Library, Louisiana State University Libraries, Baton Rouge.

29. These quarters were documented by the WPA circa 1940, but no longer existed when the main house was listed on the National Register in 1982.

30. Quarter Bill, 1817, Plantation Record Book 36, Evans Papers, Louisiana State University, detailed in Ann Patton Malone, *Sweet Chariot: Slave Family and Household Structure in Nineteenth-Century Louisiana* (Chapel Hill: University of North Carolina Press, 1992), 128–31.

31. Malone, *Sweet Chariot,* 130.

32. Clayton, *Mother Wit,* 65.

33. Ibid., 99.

34. William Howard Russell, *My Diary North and South* (Boston: T.O.H.P. Burnham, 1863), 275.

35. L. P. Hartley, *The Go Between* (1953), as noted in David Lowenthal, *The Past Is a Foreign Country* (Cambridge: Cambridge University Press, 1985).

36. Andre Bienvenu Roman's brother Jacques Telesphore Roman owned the well-known Oak Alley Plantation in St. James Parish.

37. Russell, *My Diary,* 255.

38. Paling refers to fencing of pickets which in some cases were driven into the ground.

39. Menn, *Large Slaveholders of Louisiana,* 355.

40. Ibid., 256–57, 266.

41. This is equivalent to purchasing power of roughly $42,507,036 in 2018.

42. This is equivalent to purchasing power of roughly $24,289,734.94 in 2018.

43. This is equivalent to purchasing power of roughly $78,941,638 in 2018. All historic figures from Menn, *Large Slaveholders of Louisiana, 113.*

44. Ibid., 121, 353.

45. Russell, *My Diary,* 273.

46. Ibid., 275.

47. Barrow and Davis, *Plantation Life in the Florida Parishes,* 407.

48. In anticipation of legal cases that culminated in *Brown v. Board of Education* (1954), which brought a legal end to school segregation in the United States, there were initiatives in the South to improve school buildings for African Americans to justify segregation. South Carolina and Mississippi had official school equalization programs while Louisiana did not, but many new schools for African Americans were built in the state just before and even after the *Brown* ruling in 1954. For more on equalization schools, see Rebekah Dobrasko, "Equalization Schools in South Carolina 1951–1959" (Columbia: South Carolina Department of Archives and History, 2008) at http://nationalregister.sc.gov/SurveyReports/EqualizationSchoolsHistoricContext.pdf.

49. Ibid., 281.

50. Menn, *Large Slaveholders of Louisiana, 121.*

51. This is based on the dwellings on large holdings in these parishes recorded in Menn (13,802), rounded up to include some smaller holdings.

52. Roderick A. McDonald, "Material Culture in Louisiana," in *The African American Experience in Louisiana: Part A,* ed. Charles Vincent (Lafayette: University of Southwestern Louisiana, 1999), 289.

53. Garret Fesler, "Excavating the Spaces and Interpreting the Places of Enslaved Africans and Their Descendants," in *Cabin, Quarter, Plantation: Architecture and Landscapes of North American Slavery,* ed. Clifton Ellis and Rebecca Ginsburg (New Haven: Yale University Press, 2010), 27–49.

54. James Baldwin, *Giovanni's Room* (London: Penguin, 1991), 88.

55. Russell, *My Diary,* 273.

56. Vlach, *Back of the Big House,* 11, 128.

57. Rehder, "Sugar Plantation Settlements of Southern Louisiana," 199, 205.

58. Russell, *My Diary,* 257.

59. Solomon Northup, *Twelve Years a Slave* (1853; repr. New York: Soho Books, 2011), 79.

60. Vlach, *Back of the Big House, 144.*

61. Russell, *My Diary,* 257.

62. Ibid., 275.

63. Sitterson, "The William J. Minor Plantations," 67.

64. Menn, *Large Slaveholders of Louisiana,* 2.

65. Russell, *My Diary,* 278–79.

66. Northup, *Twelve Years a Slave,* 5.

67. Ibid., 47.

68. "Edwin Epps House," National Register of Historic Places nomination form, Louisiana Division of Historic Preservation, 1984.

69. Northup, *Twelve Years a Slave,* 80–81.

70. W. E. B. Du Bois, "The Home of the Slave," 1901, reprinted in *Cabin, Quarter, Plantation,* ed. Ellis and Ginsburg, 21–22.

71. D. Clayton James, *Antebellum Natchez* (Baton Rouge: Louisiana State University Press, 1968), 148; Menn, *Large Slaveholders of Louisiana,* 2.

72. J. W. Dorr, "A Tourist's Description of Louisiana in 1860," *Louisiana Historical Quarterly* 21 (October 1938), 1207–8.

73. "Kilkarney," National Register of Historic Places nomination form, Louisiana Division of Historic Preservation, 1999.

74. Menn, *Large Slaveholders of Louisiana,* 196–211.

75. "Canebrake," National Register of Historic Places nomination form, Louisiana Division of Historic Preservation, 1982. The Louisiana State Historic Preservation Office has surveyed the parish for historic standing structures and found a paucity of resources. The slave quarters no longer stand at Canebrake, although the overseer's house remains.

76. Ibid.

77. "Richard Koch," *Encyclopedia of Louisiana,* ed. David Johnson, at http://www/knowlouisiana.org/entry/richard-koch. HABS drawings and photographs of Louisiana plantations can be accessed online at http://www.loc.gov/pictures/collection/hh/.

78. Clarence John Laughlin, *Ghosts Along the Mississippi: An Essay in the Poetic Interpretation of Louisiana's Plantation Architecture* (New York: Bonanza Books, 1961).

79. Laurie A. Wilkie, *Creating Freedom: Material Culture and African American Identity at Oakley Plantation, Louisiana, 1840–1950* (Baton Rouge: Louisiana State University Press, 2000).

80. The house burned in 1963, so the image must predate that year.

81. Ta-Nehisi Coates, *Between the World and Me* (New York: Spiegel & Grau, 2015), 69–70.

THE PLANTATION LANDSCAPE

Spectres of an Unseen Imprint

SUZANNE TURNER

> Landscape is in truth nothing less than the complex, interrelated and unified material product of the geographical environment, a seamless totality in which the immemorial processes of nature and the much more recent activities of mankind interpenetrate. Society is not a supranatural category which creates cultural landscapes isolated from nature; rather it remains inextricably related to natural elements and forces, constraints and resources.
>
> —Paul Coones, "One Landscape or Many? A Geographical Perspective"

The mid-nineteenth-century place that Marie Adrien Persac documents in his 1858 *Norman's Chart of the Lower Mississippi River* is the product of over a century of experiments in settlement, and those experiments left marks that have lasted to the present. It is no wonder that the plantation landscape represented in this iconic map evokes complex reactions. On the one hand, it brings to mind images of natural beauty, wealth-producing land, and magnificent houses and gardens, but these elements existed in an unforgiving climate, an often threatening environment, and underscored by the ever-present reality of human bondage. A closer examination of the cultural processes that shaped this landscape, particularly the formative events of the eighteenth century, brings clarity to the contradictory landscape of *Norman's Chart.* Moreover, it makes the landscape as it exists today more legible and comprehensible.

For a century, visitors to this region have been seduced by the verdant order of sugarcane fields, the majesty of the architecture, and the popular literary and film depictions of place and time. The reality of the Louisiana plantation landscape is that there was much less romance, "moonlight and magnolias," to being alive. Instead, a series of landscape-altering interventions transformed what was essentially forest and wetlands to a managed agricultural entity, one that required tremendous financial investment, primarily in the form of enslaved labor. Only in peeling back the many imprints that have been made on this landscape can one comprehend the truth and duality of the human experience—Black and white.

ENCOUNTERING THE FATHER OF WATERS

> We arrived on the borders of the Mississippi, at which we were greatly rejoiced. We regarded this beautiful river with admiration, which is at least half a league wide at the place where we first saw it. About forty leagues from its entrance into the sea. The water is of a light color, very good to drink, and very light. The country, on its banks, appeared to be everywhere covered with splendid trees of every description, such as oak, ash, elm, and many others, the names of which we did not know. We encamped that night on the river's bank, under the trees, upon which a vast number of wild turkeys roosted. We killed as many of them as we wanted by moonlight . . . I can truly say, that I never saw turkeys in France as fat and large as these were.
>
> —M. Penicaut, "Annals of Louisiana from 1698 to 1722," in B. F. French, ed., *Historical Collections of Louisiana and Florida* (1869)

Early descriptions give us both a physical picture of this complex place of land and water and insight into the worldviews, priorities, and concerns of those responsible for these initial colonial encounters. To a greater or lesser degree, the land had already been traversed, occupied, cultivated, and cleared by the Chitimacha, Choctaw, and Houma nations, among others, but for arriving Europeans, first and foremost was the need to address the existing conditions according to their cultural priorities.

Numerous accounts of the lower Mississippi River emphasize its wildness. Records kept by the initial explorers reporting back to the sponsors of their expeditions on the conditions faced in the New World depict a range of reactions. Iberville viewed the landscape he saw as a place of natural wealth and resources, noting in 1699, "The beautiful countryside is blanketed by woods, containing all varieties of trees, except pines. I have seen a few wild apple trees and a few peach trees; there are neither strawberries, raspberries, or mulberries . . . The countryside is absolutely beautiful."[1] He also noted how inadequate his men's axes were in felling trees—taking an entire day to cut a single tree (oaks and pecans). His intention, as soon as clearing was complete and construction underway, was to assign "twenty-five men to sowing peas, maize, and beans."[2] For men such as Iberville, the landscape offered both an impediment and an opportunity: a backwoods of impenetrable vegetation and formidable wetlands and also incomparably fertile soil. The European encounter and exploitation of this fecund, mysterious, yet life-threatening landscape took literally centuries before it would achieve the orderly existence depicted in *Norman's Chart.*

Missionaries were often included on the expeditions, and they typically journaled as a part of their daily routine and religious discipline, so their accounts are extremely vivid, if slanted toward their aspirations for the souls of the area's indigenous peoples, or "savages," as they were often called. In 1727, Marie-Madeleine Hachard, one of the group of Ursuline nuns sent to Louisiana to assist in the religious and educational aspects of civilizing the new French outpost of New Orleans, described the scene as they sailed toward the new town: "There are no lands cultivated the whole length of the river, only great wild forests inhabited solely by beasts of all colors, serpents, adders, scorpions, crocodiles, vipers, toads, and others which did us no harm even though they came quite near us."[3] Her perspective is quite different from Iberville's. Hachard sees a place untamed, a "wild forest" full of "wild beasts." The reader can almost hear her knees trembling. On the other hand, Iberville's task was to create a secure French base that would serve as a trading post and administrative center. His tone is one of assurance that he can accomplish the challenge ahead. Both Iberville and Hachard faced issues of survival, but the nuns were at the mercy of those who were already residing in the young settlement; Iberville was master of his own fate. Yet for both, the ever-present landscape was their subject.

During these years, the colonists' perceptions of this watery New World evolved as they experimented with its topography. For Europeans from cities or small towns, surrounded by meticulously cultivated farmsteads, Louisiana's landscape could not have been more foreign in its composition and scale, and the task of establishing permanent settlement could not have been more daunting. Slavery historian Gwendolyn Midlo Hall summarized the challenges of settlement in colonial Louisiana: "The damp climate was unhealthy, the long summers very hot, the winters sometimes quite cold. The mortality rate was high. Hurricanes and floods regularly decimated settlements and fortifications. Land had to be ditched and drained, and flooding of the Mississippi River had to be controlled with dikes called *levees,* now levees in English."[4]

Not mentioned in this damning list of deficiencies was the intermittent shortage of food, requiring dependence upon small-scale exchanges with indigenous people and the enslaved. The French encouraged early settlement by offering colonists moderately sized tracts of free land, typically forty arpents deep with five arpents of river frontage (200 square arpents or 170 acres). Father Paul du Poisson described the phenomenon in 1727, noting the extreme modesty of initial settlements, as well as the relationship between crop diversification and security, as the planter moved from planting to live to planting to sell.[5]

These modest *habitations,* as they were called, would eventually stand in stark contrast to the plantation settlements that followed, and Fr. Poisson noted that the primary measurement of success in this evolution was the scale of a plantation's enslaved workforce. As planters' enterprises developed from subsistence farming to commercial production, plantations required a labor force to match the production scale for the world market, and the African presence became an increasingly notable one in the plantation landscape. Slave traders happily obliged by bringing soaring numbers of men and women across the Atlantic, especially from West Africa. Two-thirds of Africans trafficked to Louisiana in the 1720s came from the Senegambian region of West Africa. Experienced in the cultivation of rice, corn, tobacco, cotton, and indigo, the majority of these West African laborers were bought to work on plantations along the Mississippi River outside New Orleans.[6]

SHAPING THE SUGAR PLANTATION LANDSCAPE

> Invariably, and symbolically, the plantation homes faced the water streams, which, in the majority of instances, meant the great Mississippi. It was the bearer of their produce, their path to the outer world, the means by which their profit and power were realized, the sentient artery which tied them to the culture of France.
>
> —Clarence John Laughlin, *Ghosts Along the Mississippi* (1948)

Typically in French colonies, experienced architects, engineers, and surveyors relied on centuries-old formulas for planning and designing colonial settlements. These places were the products of intentional decisions applied to the site. For example, by the time the Ursulines arrived in New Orleans, the colonial town had been laid out by engineer and surveyor Adrien de Pauger. De Pauger arrived in New Orleans in 1721 with the reputation of being a "respected engineer."[7] His 1722 plan incorporated the best principles of site selection with regard to prospect, access to natural harbor, and breezes, with a grid that was adjusted to the bend in the river and centered with a *place* or square at the river's edge. The order that geometry and symmetry created was paramount.

Beyond New Orleans, however, the models for shaping the larger agricultural landscape—both *habitations* and larger plantations—were neither so obvious nor time-tested. In addition, variations existed depending on a plantation's particular crop. Tobacco plantations, for example, did not take the same form as rice plantations. From 1718 to 1742, agriculture in the Louisiana colony focused on indigo and tobacco. By the middle to late eighteenth century, however, a crop was introduced that drastically altered the plantation landscape: sugarcane.

Although there is disagreement on how the crop was initially introduced to Louisiana, the popular story is that Jesuits brought sugarcane stalks from Saint-Domingue to Louisiana in 1751. The climatic limit of the crop was always a concern. Planter Joseph Villars Dubreuil, whose plantation was on the east bank near New Orleans, recorded his observations on sugar cultivation on September 10, 1752:

> I am working now Monseigneur, in an effort to establish the sugar industry in this country, as sugarcane can successfully be grown below here and 12 leagues up the river. I sincerely believe that this culture will not cause any serious injury to the islands [French West Indies] from what I can see, we can make sugar only during two months; but as cattle are plentiful and cheap we can increase the number of mills. The sugar industry is still a good branch of trade.
>
> I have proof that sugarcane does not freeze in the ground during the winter if we cover the stalks that have been cut four inches from the ground; in the spring at the beginning of February, the cane sprouts and is ready to be cut in October. I hope Monseigneur, that your Highness will not disapprove of this culture, while I am actually undergoing all necessary expense to

> establish same, since I am certain the stalks will not die in winter if properly covered.[8]

Clearly, such testimony was accepted, the cane did not freeze, and over time the crop spread to its climatic limits in Louisiana and east and west to its soil limits by 1860.[9] In addition, the Haitian Revolution of 1791–1804 proved irrelevant Dubreuil's assertion that the crop would not "cause serious injury" to the French West Indies sugar business. The Revolution, if anything, provided the opportunity for Louisiana planters to fill a market void, and by 1795, sugarcane acquired enough resource commitment to become a commercial crop. Soon, hundreds to thousands of acres of sugarcane covered the lower Mississippi River valley, stitched into a system of ditches and paths that brought a rhythmic pattern to the landscape (fig. 1).

The process that transformed this unimproved land into vast areas of cultivated cropland is not as well documented as is the creation of an urban settlement like New Orleans, with its wealth of legal correspondence, surveys, and plans requisite of a military outpost and a royal colony. However, that is not to say there is a complete lack of material. Sugar planters kept journals and ledgers in which they recorded financial transactions, and a close read reveals they also included daily projects necessary to carve out a plantation and make it productive. One of the greatest tasks was the need to keep back the native vegetation which was thicker and faster-growing than most Europeans had ever experienced. The Company of the Indies sent Antoine-Simon Le Page Du Pratz to Louisiana with a formidable charge—to develop not one but several plantations simultaneously. In 1758, Du Pratz published his memoirs of his time in Louisiana and offered a solution for the clearing of forests and brush:

> Such as begin a plantation in woods, thick set with cane, have an advantage in the Maiz, that makes amends for the labour of clearing the ground; a labour always more fatiguing than cultivating a spot already cleared. The advantage is this: they begin with cutting down the canes for a great extent of ground; the trees they peel two feet high quite round: this operation is performed in the beginning of March, as then the sap is in motion in that country: about fifteen days after, the canes, being dry, are set on fire: the sap of the trees are thereby made to descend, and the branches are burnt, which kills the trees.[10]

Figure 1. *Gathering the Cane,* engraving from *Harper's New Monthly Magazine* (1853), vol. 9, p. 760, showing enslaved workers in foreground gathering cane, those in mid-ground cutting cane, horse carts hauling cane, and a manager or owner supervising. Available at Slavery Images.org.

This recommendation, perhaps learned from indigenous Americans, was ingenious and probably the most labor-conserving and practical suggestion available. It also indicates that preparing Louisiana land for sugarcane was not a task for the faint of heart. It demanded an individual who had capital, enslaved labor, and resolve.

Once cleared, the sugar plantation's architectural assemblage took shape (fig. 2). The center of each sugar plantation was the factory. This large structure

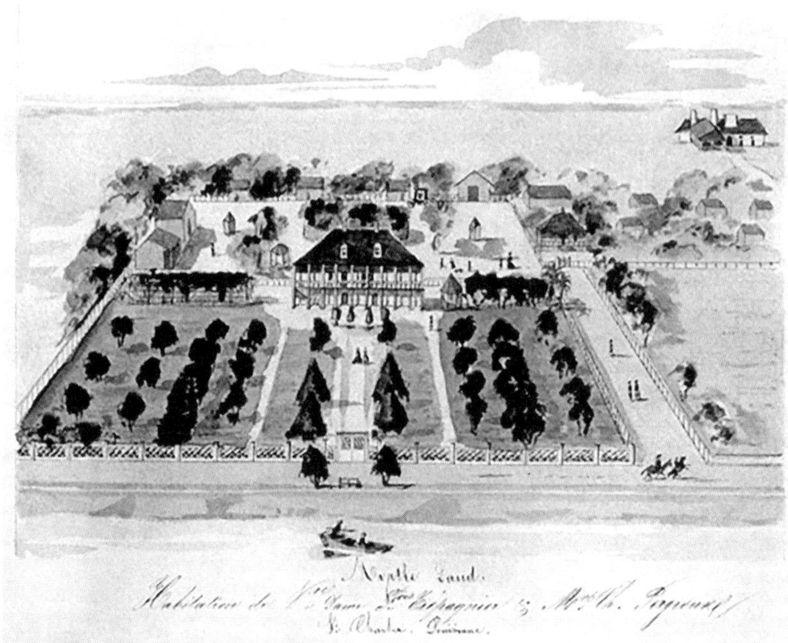

Figure 2. *Myrtle Land Plantation,* by Father Joseph Paret, watercolor, c. 1859. The scene illustrates the kind of formality planters of French descent typically used to organize their pleasure gardens (front of house, including arbors extending on either side of house, separating garden from work yard) and the entire site plan, including outbuildings, work yard (behind big house), quarters (to right of work yard), and roadways connecting the sugarhouse (extreme top right corner) to the rest of the "urban village." From *Plantations by the River, Paret's Myrtle Land Plantation,* St. Charles, c. 1859. Reproduced courtesy of Dr. Jay Edwards.

included a steam-powered mill where cut cane was crushed and juice extracted, a boiling house where the juice was boiled down to raw sugar and molasses, and the various chimneys and vents for releasing the smoke and vapors the process produced. The "mother" of these vertical points in the landscape was the called the stack, which sometimes bore the name of the plantation and became a landmark along the river and River Road, announcing ownership of each property. At the height of expansion of the sugar industry, sugar census-taker Champomier recorded 1,536 mills in Louisiana.[11]

The location of the big house was selected for both practical and symbolic purposes. The river was the connection to market, to culture, to supplies that could not be produced on the plantation, and to the world at large. The ideal site for the planter's residence was on a point of prospect, with easy access to the water yet with sufficient elevation and distance for protection from floods or levee crevasses. The fields for the production of the cash crop virtually engulfed the settlement, occupying the vast majority of the acreage, typically numbering in the thousands, and using the most fertile lands. The processing area—the sugar mill or refinery—was located away from the big house and within walking distance from the quarters, the dwellings of the enslaved labor force. The overall layout appeared much like an urban plan, a rectilinear grid positioned in relation to the sinuous curves of the river's course. The back swamp was beyond the sugarhouse and cane fields—that land that was too wet for cane, but it was the all-important source of timber to fuel the sugarhouse, to heat the big house, and to provide wood for fencing and building construction.

The sugar plantations of the lower Mississippi River valley may not have had the patterns and precedent that de Pauger used in designing the New Orleans landscape, but that does not mean they were haphazard. John Rehder, a cultural geographer whose career focused on the sugar plantations of Louisiana, identified three patterns of layout, with each linked to a cultural origin. The French Creole used a linear plan, and the Anglo Tidewater a "nodal block" plan (fig. 3).

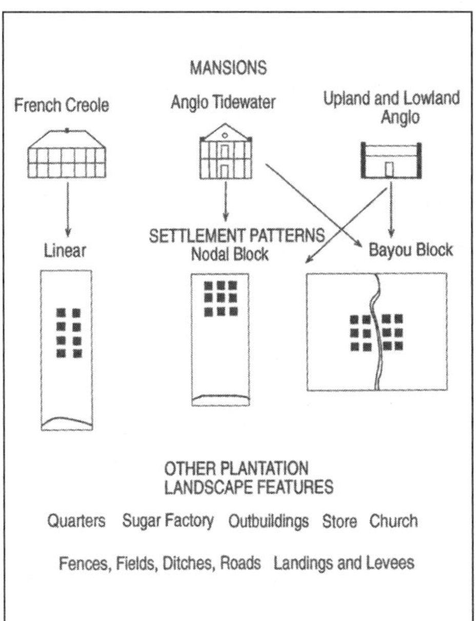

Figure 3. Diagram illustrating patterns linked to French, Anglo Tidewater, and Upland and Lowland Anglo cultural origin. The resultant layout of the quarters complex was either a single *allée,* an urban grid or "nodal block," or the grid arranged along both sides of a bayou. John B. Rehder, *Delta Sugar: Louisiana's Vanishing Plantation Landscape,* p. 63, fig 2.1. © 1999 The Johns Hopkins University Press. Reprinted with permission of Johns Hopkins University Press.

Along the Mississippi River near New Orleans, where some of the first sugar plantations developed, the linear plan was the logical choice, given the narrow and long shapes of the land holdings. On broader parcels as well as plantations with large enslaved workforces, planners employed the nodal block, akin to the form of an urban grid, making circulation throughout the virtual village more efficient than would be the case with one extremely long lane.

GARDENS AND LANDSCAPES OF THE GENTRY: *POTAGER,* PLANTATION GARDEN, PLEASURE GARDEN

> For several miles after leaving New Orleans, the eye reposes agreeably upon the shores, enriched with fine cotton and sugar plantations, and embellished with clusters of orange trees, from the midst of which rise the white and showy dwellings of the planters. By degrees the gardens and houses become more rare; but all the way to Baton Rouge, one continues to see fine and well cultivated lands. These plantations spread along the river, sometimes extending nearly a mile back to the thick forests, which serve as their limits.
>
> —Augustine Levasseur, *Lafayette in America in 1824 and 1825* (1829)

As sugar planters of the early nineteenth century ascended the economic ladder, less time was spent battling the environment and more time was dedicated to the kind of landscape shaping that expressed their personal and cultural aesthetic. Many planters were well-traveled as first-generation French immigrants or well-schooled French Creoles. It was a social class that had seen—or knew of—the great gardens of Europe and were educated in a curriculum that included botany, horticulture, and agriculture. Last, they owned the labor source necessary for any ambitious endeavor in ornamental gardening.

The spectrum of garden types on a prosperous sugar plantation included the *potager* or kitchen garden, the plantation garden, and the pleasure garden. The *potager* produced vegetables and fruit for feeding the planter's family and the numerous visitors and travelers who frequented the plantations. In the plantation garden, foodstuff for the enslaved population and for livestock were grown. Planters used the embellishment of the larger landscape—the entrance drive, the property boundaries, and often a delineated space in front of the big house that reached to the river landing—as an outdoor living space for the enjoyment of family and guests, as a display of their wealth and taste, and as an indication of horticultural prowess. The solutions developed by planters and their wives for each of these garden types were as varied as their individual personalities, but several characteristics were universal.

Kitchen and plantation gardens were ephemeral and do not survive on any plantation in the lower Mississippi River valley, but some documentation exists in archival references, period gardening manuals, and paintings, to give an idea of the size and methods of cultivating both the *potager* and the plantation garden. In his 1860 edition of the *Southern Rural Almanac, and Plantation and Garden Calendar,* the *Almanac* publisher and nurseryman Thomas Affleck wrote specific advice about the location and the layout of the kitchen garden:

> The location should be one convenient to the dwelling, that the ladies of the family may have easy access; the garden being usually under their exclusive care. . . .
>
> The shape should be an oblong square, that the plow and cultivator may be used as much as possible. One broad main walk up the centre, at least eight feet wide, with a gate at each end, wide enough for a cart or wagon to pass; with borders five feet wide next the fence, all around; and a walk inside of these borders, also five feet wide. Dwarfed fruit trees may be planted alongside of all of the walks . . . The less complication in the arrangement and laying off of the vegetable garden, the better. Shade and ornamental trees, flowers, &c., are out of place there.[12]

An 1861 painting, *Bois de Flèche Plantation,* in St. Martin Parish, by Marie Adrien Persac (1823–1873), provides a rare depiction of the *potager*'s appearance (fig. 4). It illustrates a series of square beds with paths and gates as prescribed by Affleck and what may be dwarf fruit trees shading the walks.

Most planters and their families traveled frequently between New Orleans and their plantations, depending on the season, as matters of needs to do banking and shopping and as social preference; many had a city residence in addition to the plantation. Houses in town were embellished with ornamental gardens almost from the outset in the form of *parterres, allées,* groves, and even more naturalistic patterns.

Remnants of the ornamental gardens of plantations sometimes survive in the form of live oak *allées* and vague lines in the landscape that may suggest the extent or boundaries of these gardens. Because of the passage of time, the

Figure 4. Gouache drawing of *Bois de Flèche Plantation,* by Marie Adrien Persac, 1861. The foreground of this image is a rare depiction of a Louisiana plantation kitchen garden, with a broad center walk, planted borders along the fence, and vegetables planted in rows filling the rectangular beds. Most of the plantings are shaded by what appear to be Affleck's prescribed fruit trees, as protection from the harsh summer sun. Collection of the Louisiana State Museum.

destruction of the postbellum era, the eventual division of large land parcels, and the lack of labor to care for such horticulturally elaborate and expansive planted areas, little else survives. Most of what we know about plantation gardens comes secondhand: travelers during the antebellum period often commented on the gardens that seemed most unusual or impressive. Family members included details of their horticultural trials and successes in correspondence with friends and relatives living away from the plantation. Often, the degree of survival of these large garden spaces was determined by the passion that the family, particularly the planter or his wife, had for the gardens and whether they maintained ownership through succeeding generations.

In creating these pleasure gardens, the designer, whether the planter, his wife, or a hired designer, looked to the current fashion not only in his or her "neighborhood" but also to what was *au courant* on the Eastern Seaboard, in gardening manuals, and most importantly, in France and, to a lesser extent, the rest of western Europe.

The makers of these pleasure gardens used two general approaches in their designs. Most often, they employed French formalism, not because it was "of the time," but because of the way that it ordered the garden, fitting into the rest of the gridded agricultural landscape, the series of drainage ditches, the lanes of the quarters, and the road system that connected the cane fields to the sugar mill.[13] The alternative was the picturesque, which especially gained traction by the middle of the nineteenth century. By 1841, New York horticulturist, author, and landscape designer Andrew Jackson Downing (1815–1852) had promulgated the tenets of the picturesque for middle-class Americans in his *Treatise on the Theory and Practice of Landscape Gardening* and in writings in his magazine, *The Horticulturist*.[14] Downing's writings were extremely popular, and the picturesque approach to landscape design spread rapidly.

Interestingly, as popular as formalism was in the lower Mississippi River valley, Persac selected Belle Grove (Iberville Parish, 1857) to illustrate the margins of *Norman's Chart*. One of the largest of Louisiana's antebellum plantation houses, Belle Grove's architecture and landscape design were a departure from the straightforward French big houses and *parterre* gardens that lined most of

Figure 5. HABS photograph of Belle Grove in White Castle, Louisiana, 1930s. The picturesque quality of the front garden can be deduced from the irregular placement of the trees and their varying sizes and types. Library of Congress Prints and Photographs Division, Washington, DC.

the Mississippi from New Orleans to beyond Baton Rouge. Belle Grove featured a landscape treatment in the picturesque mode, with groupings of exotic trees rather than *allées* of native trees and curvilinear roads and paths (fig. 5). Perhaps this was an artistic attempt to represent the progressive outlook of the southern planter.

St. James Parish planter Valcour Aimé, thoroughly French in his taste, was perhaps the boldest proponent of the picturesque on Norman's river corridor and drew directly from the French for his vision of the setting for his plantation house.

ST. JAMES REFINERY AND THE PLANTATION OF VALCOUR AIMÉ

> In the Aimé garden was a great collection of plants, trees, and shrubs, along with hothouses and ornamental buildings. Among the surprises to be seen at "le petit Versailles," as it was often called, was a miniature river, and a pagoda set on a mound covered with violets. But in all of these gardens the profligacy of nature in that subtropical climate produced results quite different from those originally intended.
>
> —Charles Van Ravenswaay, *A Ninteenth-Century Garden*

It is impossible to consider the plantation landscapes depicted in *Norman's Chart* without considering the plantation of Valcour Aimé. Born in 1798, Aimé owned the St. James Refinery in St. James Parish (fig. 6). There he became known for his extravagant lifestyle, keen interest in sugar production and experimentation, and a passion for horticulture. Although christened François Gabriel, according to legend a nurse called him "Valcour" and the name stayed.[15]

Both parents died when Aimé was young, leaving him and his brother in the care of their maternal grandfather, Michel Fortier II. At the age of sixteen, Aimé fought in the Battle of New Orleans, and in 1819 he married Josephine Roman. Following his mother-in-law's death in 1830, Aimé exchanged his plantation for the family estate, which he immediately began improving.

Aimé was an innovator in sugar production, having traveled to the Caribbean to observe local techniques. After his travels, he always seemed to return home with a new technology to test, as well as tropical plants. Fortunately for historians and Francophiles, Aimé was also a meticulous recordkeeper, and his

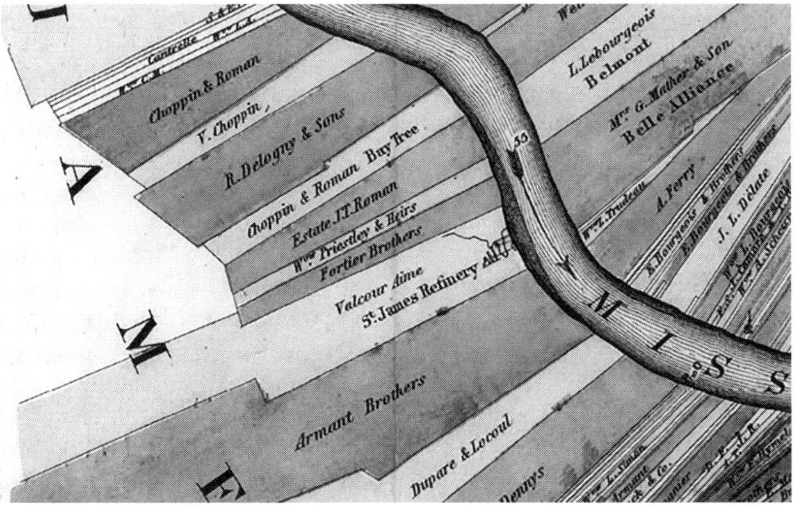

Figure 6. The land holding of Valcour Aimé, St. James Refinery (center of image). Note the nearby plantations of Aimé's relatives (the Fortiers) and his wife's family (the Romans). Detail from *Norman's Chart of the Lower Mississippi River,* by Marie Adrien Persac, Benjamin Moore Norman, and J. H. Colton & Co. (New Orleans: B. M. Norman, 1858). Available at https://www.loc.gov/item/78692178/.

journals (1823–54) were translated several times, first in 1878 by Albert Ferry, and later, a complete translation by the Works Progress Administration. The document is invaluable on many fronts, giving a clear picture of all activities associated with an operating sugar plantation.

Of primary importance here, however, is Aimé's garden, today referred to as Le Petit Versailles. Aimé was an avid horticulturist, but he was also interested in high-style design. He wanted his garden to reflect the latest fashion in France. He reputedly brought over a gardener trained at the Jardin des Plantes to build for him an English Park, a *jardin anglais.*

Not only was Aimé's garden based on the English picturesque model, which had quickly spread to France and was popularized as *jardin anglais,* but it was even more sophisticated in following the mode of what became known as *jardin anglo-chinois,* a refinement of the style fashionable in France and on the continent in the late eighteenth and early nineteenth centuries. Two French publications, *Le Jardin Anglo-Chinois* (1770–87), including engravings of the gardens of the Chinese emperor, and a folio of illustrations by Le Rouge, entitled *Recueil des Plans et des Vues des plus beaux Jardins de l'Europe Paris* (1774–78), contributed to the dissemination of this exotic garden type.

Based on the English romantic model of the pastoral landscape characterized by serpentine rather than straight lines, curving lakes, and clumps of mixed tree types, this variant of the style incorporated exotic architectural and landscape elements used as focal points to guide the user throughout the space, with new scenes unfolding around every curve in the path. The focal elements included rockeries, pagodas, Turkish tents, fantastic towers, and other imaginative sculptural features. Examples of this type of garden in France were the Desert de Retz (begun circa 1778 and still partially extant; fig. 7) and Parc Jean-Jacques-Rousseau at Ermenonville (1765–76).

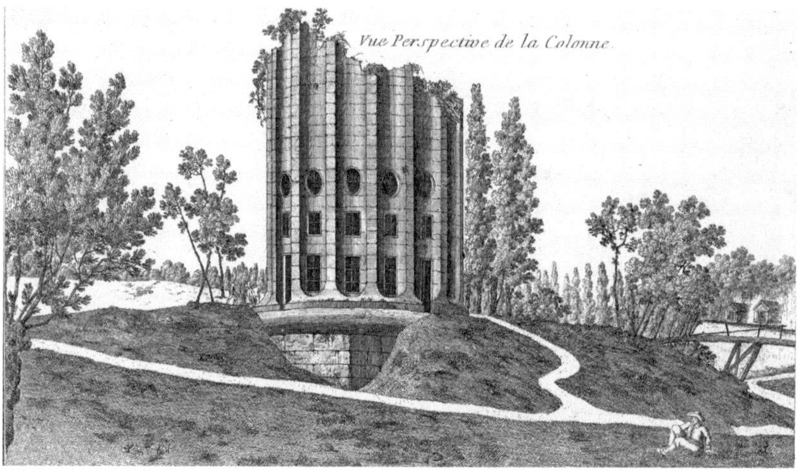

Figure 7. *Vue Perspective de la Colonne* (Desert de Retz), engraving from Georges Louis Le Rouge, *Les Jardins Anglo-Chinois,* 1785. The truncated Tuscan column, built as if in ruin, served to symbolize the primacy of nature over the achievements of man. The large folly served as the home of the garden's creator, de Monville. Courtesy of Sims Reed Ltd., London.

Aimé's garden concept employed a *rivulet* with bridges of varying styles as its organizing element, a small reflecting pond and fountain in front of the house that contributed to drainage of the swampy site, St. Hélène, a miniature rockery fortress named after the island upon which Napoleon was exiled, and incorporating a subterranean icehouse with corbel brick dome, purportedly topped by a Chinese pagoda. The imaginative garden was also a place in which to display the exotic plants from his several greenhouses. No doubt a playground for his grandchildren and their cousins, the garden was also a setting for Aimé's frequent and elaborate parties (fig. 8).

The first reference in his diary to this project is from September 1842: "From the 3rd to the 9th, prepared the ground for an 'English Park,' and dug a basin in front of the dwelling house, with one hundred and twenty hands."[16]

Figure 8. Undated photograph of one of several original bridges in the garden of Valcour Aimé, with the big house in the background. Each bridge was designed in a different architectural vocabulary. The Historic New Orleans Collection, Acc. No. 1979.215.1.

Aimé's work on the park fluctuated as he shifted his workforce based on the needs of the sugar crop. Almost a year later, to the day, Aimé reports on the project's progress: "Begun digging an artificial lake and the rivulet in English Park, on the 4th. On the 5th, rain occasionally. Through refining. Completed ornamental pond and rivulet on the 7th . . . From the 15th, working again in levelling ground, etc., in 'English Park.'"[17]

In October 1844, the Park was still under construction: "13th. Hauled to

'English Park' 1500 loads of manure, in one month, with two carts; with four carts and four loaders, hauled to 'English Park' one thousand loads of dirt in seven days . . . On the 21st, plantation hands say prayer in the newly built sugar house, and then give a ball. Begun cutting cane for the mill on the 23rd."[18]

An excerpt from October 1852 shows how Aimé industriously went about the work of managing the plantation as well as the garden, as if they were extensions of the same activity: "Repaired and strengthened part of the levee. Worked to the levees on each side of plantation railroad. 19th, began cutting cane for the mill. Pumped water from the river during three days, for sugar house ponds, and stream in the garden."[19]

But Aimé also recorded the details of his efforts at horticulture:

> Nov 1841 An orange from this garden measured fourteen and three-quarter inches in circumference. Another orange, in 1840, weighed one pound, less one-half of an ounce; both were produced by seed from Cuba.[20]
>
> . . .
>
> Nov 1843 A rose here called triomphe du Luxembourg measures five and a quarter inches in diameter.[21]
>
> . . .
>
> Feb 1851 Two bunches of bananas grown here, one having one hundred and ninety-five bananas, and the other two hundred and three bananas.[22]

Valcour Aimé's diary closes in 1854 when Aimé essentially retired from active life after the death of his only son Gabriel, who contracted yellow fever upon arrival in New Orleans after an extended stay in France. The garden had been Aimé's passion, but Gabriel had been his pride and joy, and without him Valcour had little interest in continuing his work—on his garden or plantation. This horticultural paradise sank into steady decline. The economic devastation of the Civil War, subsequent hurricanes, and trespassers accelerated the garden's demise. The house burned in the early twentieth century, and trespassers hunting treasure and rare plants accelerated the garden's demise. Today it survives as an archaeological site devoid of most of its plantings save a dense canopy of live oaks and invasive tree species. In a way, it presents a landscape not unlike that encountered by the first who visited the area—a network of impenetrable vines and full of water, snakes, and mosquitoes. What does survive bears testimony to the spirit and energy of a planter and garden-maker who created a virtual empire and who used his fortune and considerable imagination to build a garden that was to become an icon in the region.

GARDENING AND THE ENSLAVED COMMUNITY: IDENTITY AND CARE

> In America . . . the great houses followed the great crops . . . Supporting it all, a living foundation, like a great column of blood, was the labor of the slaves. The very bricks of which the walls of the famous houses are made were shaped by the hands of the Negroes. . . . The Negro is anchored to the soil; his way of life has changed hardly at all since the great debacle. He is the real owner of the land, despite all titular changes of possession. . . . The blacks are the weak and flexible backbone of this decapitated region of America.
>
> —Henry Miller, *The Air-Conditioned Nightmare*

The impulse to garden in this most perfect natural situation was an early hallmark of the region and today remains an essential component of its cultural landscape. However, it can be an elusive one. Surviving garden outlines such as Valcour Aimé's are rare, and even rarer are surviving plantings. Compounding this loss is the context that all gardens on a plantation existed within the plantation structure of planter and enslaved. As slim as material culture representing planter-defined gardens is, information about gardens cultivated by and for the enslaved laborers is even thinner, yet is crucial in understanding the plantation landscape.

When de Pauger wrote that "to have a garden . . . is half of life," he used the word "garden" in a universal sense, but probably foremost on his mind was the *potager,* where produce and fruit were grown for plantation consumption. Planters and enslaved people shared an important trait—they had all been raised in lands where agriculture was a central part of survival and success and had been for centuries. Knowing how to plant and grow food was as basic to their cultural identity as the desire for family, freedom, and happiness was to their psyches. Each group arrived with as much of their home place as possible, which in the case of the African enslaved was not much.

The enslaved may have arrived with nothing more than the shirts on their backs but the images and ideas they held in their minds' eyes were powerful reminders of the homes they had left and of the kinds of landscapes that would bring the comfort of "home" in a strange and sometimes foreboding place. Africans confronted the new landscape without the real option to recreate a semblance of their homeland, and yet the imprint of that place was, no doubt, equally strong. They brought ideas about the shape that gardens should have, and they were highly skilled in the culture of plants and gardens, both agricultural and horticultural.

Those who came to Louisiana from the Caribbean came with experience in cultivating and refining sugar, and they had exposure to both the culture and the technology necessary to process tobacco, indigo, and rice. Enslaved people with well-developed skills in gardening became gardeners in charge of kitchen gardens, pleasure gardens, or the care of planters' greenhouses, their expertise and ingenuity in servitude of another's vision. Those who could translated their skills onto the landscape in small personal ways, from "sweeping" the floor of their outside space to vegetable gardens; many Africans and enslaved people from Saint-Domingue cultivated dooryard gardens.[23]

For the enslaved, the impulse to shape a home place manifested in subtle ways, focusing on where they could exercise the most control: their quarters and surrounding area. Historian Garrett Kessler, in an essay from the 2010 volume *Cabin, Quarter, Plantation,* writes that

> A pervasive feature of African cultures throughout time is Africans' propensity to spend much of their daily life in the yards and other exterior spaces of their home site. For enslaved Africans . . . "The quarter extended beyond its walls. The space around the building was as important as the building itself." Whereas Europeans congregated inside their houses, closely bunched around the hearth, Africans spread out in the yard, segregating various activities in different zones around their home. . . .

In a sharp differentiation from their European owners, enslaved people put a large emphasis on their yards as a living space, an equal extension of the interior.[24] The enslaved spent their limited, personal time in their yards and gardens adapting these deeply inculcated traditions to their situation and environment.

> . . . enslaved people had a substantial bearing on their surroundings, that they reshaped the spaces they were obliged to occupy in ways not obvious to

> their owners. To return a fence in the yard, a slave master may have erected it to serve as a barrier or to restrict movement—controlling space—whereas enslaved Africans may have construed the fence as a familiar device that simply delineated a communal yard around a dwelling—making it a place.[25]

One such adaptation is the swept yard. In West Africa cooking was done outside, and the cramped, hot quarters assigned to an enslaved person in Louisiana supported the continuation of this tradition. As a result, the enslaved spent time shaping the landscape to accommodate this practice.[26] More than simply a space to cook, swept yards provided a place for families to socialize that was clean, vermin free, and perhaps most importantly, defined. In a world where they had no control over their situation as property, no control over their job, no control over their own family unit, shaping their landscape was a definitive expression of will and cultural identity.

These yards also contained plants, but they were not arranged like the slaveowners' gardens. "The Africans understood the niche each plant fit in the ecosystem, so they'd seek out places in their yards that fit the requirements of a certain plant. The phrase the West Indians have is 'Put them where they won't trouble each other.'"[27] Enslaved people from Saint-Domingue interpreted this tradition by cultivating dooryard gardens.

In addition to swept yards and dooryard gardens, enslaved men and women on plantations engaged in subsistence farming out of necessity. Planters doled out rations often consisting of dried fish, corn, etc., however, the portion and frequency varied according to the enslaver. Affleck, in his 1860 *Southern Rural Almanac,* recommends that for the diet of the enslaved, the plantation garden should be planted with potatoes, sweet potatoes, "Mustard, Turnips, Cabbage, Beets."[28] In addition, the realities of field slave activity on a sugar plantation demanded an enormous caloric intake. In short, slave subsistence farming was less a product of the largess of the enslaver and more a matter of survival. As a result, enslaved people filled these gardens with plants of their own gardening heritage: okra, yams, cowpeas, bottle gourd, amaranth, hibiscus, and watermelons.[29]

The process of creating a place where one feels connected to the larger universe of nature and the cosmos is emblematic of a culture's worldview. In shaping the yards surrounding their quarters and through sweeping and gardening, enslaved Africans pulled from the traditions of their ancestral homes in establishing "a semblance of stability and personal satisfaction, to groom their environment in a way that fit their cultural aesthetic."[30]

GARDENS AND THE MYTH OF THE PLANTATION SOUTH

> The foremost symbol of the mythos of plantation culture is, probably, the river . . . Soundless and uncaring, creator and destroyer, the river flowed on; through the night of the magnolia, whose scent gives the very darkness a body; through the night in day of the cypress clad in moss, whose thick web traps the light of the sun; through the days of glory and riches; the long night of war and disaster and irretrievable ruin.
>
> —Clarence John Laughlin, *Ghosts Along the Mississippi*

The myth of the plantation South is perhaps one of the most powerful of American myths. The region mapped in *Norman's Chart* became the subject of stories, novels, movies, and images that have essentially shrouded the plantations' realities in romantic and nostalgic narratives that in many ways were supported by the picturesque quality of the architecture, the gardens, and the broader cultural landscape that ties these places together. These twentieth-century mythologized versions of this place and time, however, distorted much of the reality of what occurred here.

Among the images that captured the imagination of Americans and Europeans, giving a "face" to the myth, was the work of photographer Clarence John Laughlin, particularly his photos in *Ghosts Along the Mississippi,* first published in 1948. Although its focus is southern architecture, *Ghosts* has been described as a "photography book that has achieved cult status among the photographic fraternity due to the elements of spooky surrealism."[31]

The plantation that perhaps most attracted Laughlin was the very same Belle Grove illustrated on *Norman's Chart.* In his book, Laughlin described it as "the greatest ruined house in the entire Mississippi Valley," and he was clearly taken by the house and its landscape, commenting, "Set in a garden, at once spacious and beguiling, it became the apogee of Louisiana majesty."[32] Vacant since 1925, the house had been allowed to decay until a fire in 1952 destroyed what remained (fig. 9).

Laughlin also photographed Uncle Sam Plantation. In *Temple to a Misplaced Past,* the subject is the south plantation office, one of the plantation's several

Figure 9. *Tragic Queen. Number Two,* by Clarence John Laughlin. Laughlin described the owners of Belle Grove mansion as being "forced to stand helplessly and despairingly by while time and the water conspired to bring about the ultimate ruin of the house." The Clarence John Laughlin Archive at The Historic New Orleans Collection, Acc. No. 1981.247.5.614.

outbuildings (fig. 10). The two offices contributed to a parade of classical temple facades of decreasing scale that formed the overall riverview of the planter's mansion. Of note is the matching southern magnolia trees flanking this little building and reinforcing the formal geometric composition of the architectural complex. In both his representations of "Louisiana Majesty," Laughlin's narrative is clear: here is a landscape of lost elegance, an elegance that once took shape in the plantation's gardens and architecture; their loss was a loss of something noble, something beautiful.

While there is the temptation to indulge in the drama and pathos of this mythical antebellum plantation, such myth-making ignores—not only the harsh realities of plantation operation—but also the cultural influences brought to the area by enslaved Africans. Louisiana is distinctive from other states in that the Company of the Indies had exclusive trading rights based on a concession in Senegambia dating back to 1664. From 1726 to 1731, thirteen slave ships

Figure 10. *Temple to a Misplaced Past,* by Clarence John Laughlin. Uncle Sam Plantation was demolished with the 1940 construction of the new levee. This photograph of an outbuilding captured the diminished, ghostly state and setting of the plantation in the years prior to its demolition. The Clarence John Laughlin Archive at The Historic New Orleans Collection, Acc. No. 1981.247.1.833.

arrived in Louisiana, with all but one of them from Senegambia. Senegambia is therefore significant for the African roots of the culture that shaped this landscape and its way of life.[33]

The Senegal valley, bounded by the rivers Senegal and Gambia, has been described as "inconceivably" productive, with outstanding soil made rich by the flooding of the rivers. This same area today appears decimated because of the natives' "emulation of European technology and world view, in which the traditional African reverence for all forms of life was replaced by the European drive to maximize production and conquer nature. . . ." Hall noted that this path "did not serve the land and its people well."[34] But according to Hall, the early Senegambians who came to Louisiana arrived with their ethos and agricultural expertise intact:

> . . . the first generation of creole slaves grew up in stable, nuclear families composed of African mothers and fathers and creole siblings. We have seen that almost all the black slaves either arrived directly from Africa between June, 1719, and January, 1731, or were descendants of these first slaves. Two-thirds of these Africans came from Senegambia from a limited number of nations living in a relatively homogenous culture area.[35]

In considering the development of the plantation landscape and later its associated mythology, it must be remembered that enslaved Africans' ideas about the cosmos, physical healing, and human relationships were in many ways counter to those of their European captors. Archaeologist Leland Ferguson described the significance of water in the imagination of some Africans: "The watery barrier, which in West and Central African cosmology separates the corporeal and spirit worlds, also found a weighty role in African American ideology."[36] He also cited scholar Melville Herskovits's comments on the idea: "In all these parts of the New World where African religious beliefs have persisted . . . the river cult or, in broader terms, the cult of water spirits, holds an important place. All this testifies to the vitality of this element in African religion."[37]

The strength of the many distinct African cultures—particularly Senegambian in the early eighteenth century—was such that its blending with the French culture was extremely potent, giving birth to a unique Creole culture. Hall summarized another effect: "the knowledge and skills of the African population, the size and importance of the Indian population throughout the eighteenth century, and the geography of lower Louisiana . . . All contributed to an unusually cohesive and heavily Africanized culture in lower Louisiana: clearly, the most Africanized slave culture in the United States."[38]

Central to the African mythos was the power of the imagination to determine one's destiny, to imagine one's home place, and to shape the landscape in support of the places seen in the mind's eye. Considering the more threatened a culture's mythology is, the stronger it holds, it could be argued that this contributed to the development of a landscape imbued with symbols and systems that held meaning for those enslaved; symbols and systems that were distinct and separate from those of their owners but by no means less influential. Laughlin may have given form to the plantation myth, but those who endured its reality were most certainly sustained by beliefs that not only shaped their interaction with the landscape but took hold as what we today consider Creole culture.

> Sugar plantations persistently dominated the rural landscape from 1795 until about 1970. But today's plantations are vanishing, and their dominance as cultural traditions is in danger of disappearing . . . It is a complete and genuine plantation landscape that evolved over two and a half centuries, a quarter of a millennium, on a flat, damp surface called the Lower Mississippi River floodplain in southern Louisiana. It is also the last place in the continental United States where a functional plantation landscape exists.
>
> —John B. Rehder, *Delta Sugar*

In 1900, William C. Stubbs, director of the Louisiana Sugar Experiment Station, wrote a essay in Henry Rightor's *Standard History of New Orleans* on the "Origin and Evolution of the Sugar Industry of Louisiana."[39] He observed in his closing remarks that,

> Taking a retrospective view of the sugar industry of Louisiana for the last fifteen or twenty years it can be said with truth that there is no industry in the world that has made such progress . . . Improved implements for breaking the soil and for the cultivation of cane, have been introduced and almost universally used. Improvement of soils and crops, both by scientific rotation of crops, involving the nitrogen gathering cow pea, and the extensive use of commercial fertilizers, whose purity and guarantee are sustained by chemical analysis made by official chemists, without cost, are everywhere in evidence. Tonnage has been increased, and the cost of growing cane materially reduced.
>
> Small sugar houses are fast disappearing, and enormous factories with every modern labor and fuel saving apparatus, are to be found in every section. The output of sugar, both per acre and per ton of cane, has been greatly increased. New lands are being opened and old plantations better drained and cultivated. In fact, "expansion" in the cultivation of sugarcane in Louisiana and other Southern States, and sugar factories in the "expansion," is

> the *only kind* favored by the sugar planters of the South. Thousands of acres of land well adapted to the growth of sugarcane, are available in Louisiana, Texas, and other Southern States. Capital alone is wanted to develop them and build the necessary factories.[40]

Stubbs acknowledged, however, in this somewhat defensive tome on the state of sugar at the turn of the century, that the huge amount of seasonal labor required to manually harvest the cane crop and the difficult and dangerous nature of this work remained a challenge for the industry. "The cane cutter or harvester has not yet materialized, although a standing prize of $2,500 by the Sugar Planters' Association awaits the successful inventor."[41] It would be more than three decades before that technological problem would be solved.

What would have been the hallmarks of the landscape that one would have seen sailing north on the Mississippi River during the antebellum period, traveling between New Orleans and Baton Rouge as depicted on *Norman's Chart?* The view on both banks would have revealed distinct areas of ownership, each with its big house; its sugar mill and tall stack inscribed with the name of the plantation; numerous workers' houses, all vernacular building types; and miles of cane under cultivation. Indeed, the names of the plantations typically reflected some aspect of the indigenous landscape (Mulberry Grove, Myrtleland, Bay Tree, Magnolia Mound, Live Oak, Oakland) or a family name (Louisa, Celeste, Felicité, Therriot).

More than two centuries later, the landscape still bears the mark of those original land grants, and sugarcane is still very much in evidence, although some acreage has given way to soybeans. Where fences no longer survive to mark property boundaries and divisions, the trees that grew up as fencerows mark early territorial lines. Very few of the stacks survive because of liability once a mill closed. The scene today along the same stretch of road is a collage of sugarcane fields, the occasional plantation house, numerous small vernacular houses of various periods, and massive petrochemical plants.

Sugar expert Stubbs could not have known that in January 1901, the year after he wrote his essay, near Beaumont, Texas, an oil well in a salt dome would strike oil, revolutionizing the way that Louisianans would think about the rich alluvial lands along the mighty Mississippi River. By 1909, Standard Oil of New Jersey had selected Baton Rouge for its first refinery location in the South and had begun processing the petroleum. From that day forward, sugarcane would share the rich banks of the Mississippi River with the great petrochemical conglomerates of the world, coexisting to utilize Louisiana's rich natural resources and the benefits of the river's access to world markets. When these corporations bought land for their plants, they did so according to the configuration of the original landholdings so that these megalithic refineries still conform to the pie-shaped, arpent-based divisions of this riparian landscape.

For years, Louisianans with ties to the sugar legacy of this landscape warned about its slow demise, attempted to apply preservation techniques like historic districts and scenic easements to the surviving fabric, and denounced the petrochemical industry as the culprit. Clearly, their pleas have fallen on deaf ears. Yet, it is too simple to say that the purely agricultural landscape is beautiful and good, and that the current landscape representing a diverse economy is ugly and dissonant, and therefore bad. As the petrochemical plants begin to be dismantled, there will be those who feel that this more recent layer must also be remembered, because it has now defined the state's economy and contributed to its culture for over a century. This will raise the need for creative interpretation and preservation exponentially.

The layers of cultural patterns in the plantation landscape of south Louisiana contain important threads of continuity, yet they also contain disturbing implications about human rights and the future of the environment. They bear a message about how generations have used natural resources, how changes in technology and the world economy have produced changes in the landscape, and how this land has shaped the lives of generations of people of many colors and origins. The view that change is unilaterally bad puts one in a very deep hole. The message is, indeed, seductive. Rapid change makes people dream of stopping time, of retreating. But it is incumbent on the stewards of this powerful and poetic landscape to decipher all of its imprints and to view it in all of its parts.

NOTES

1. Carl A. Brasseaux, trans. and ed., *A Comparative View of French Louisiana, 1699 and 1762: The Journals of Pierre Le Moyne d'Iberville and Jean-Jacques-Blaise d'Abbadie* (Lafayette: Center for Louisiana Studies, University of Southwestern Louisiana, 1979), 50–52.

2. Ibid., 72.

3. Myldred Masson Costa, trans., *The Letters of Marie-Madeleine Hachard, Ursuline of New Orleans, 1727–1728* (New Orleans: Laborde Printing Co., 1974), 43.

4. Gwendolyn Midlo Hall, *Africans in Colonial Louisiana: The Development of Afro-Creole Culture in the Eighteenth Century* (Baton Rouge: Louisiana State University Press, 1992), 11.

5. Daniel H. Usner Jr., "The Frontier Exchange Economy of the Lower Mississippi Valley in the Eighteenth Century," in *American Encounters,* ed. Peter C. Mancall and James H. Merrell (New York: Routledge, 2000), 228–29.

6. Michael T. Pasquier, "French Colonial Louisiana," in *64 Parishes,* www.knowlouisiana.org /entry/french-colonial-louisiana.

7. Mary Louise Christovich and Roulhac Bunkley, "Toledano," in *Garden Legacy* (New Orleans: The Historic New Orleans Collection, 2016), 45.

8. Henry P. Dart, "The Career of Dubreuil in French Louisiana," *Louisiana Historical Quarterly* 18 (1935): 286.

9. John B. Rehder, *Delta Sugar: Louisiana's Vanishing Plantation Landscape* (Baltimore, MD: Johns Hopkins University Press, 1999), 55.

10. M. Le Page Du Pratz, *The History of Louisiana* (Baton Rouge, LA: Claitor's Publishing Division, 1972), 164. The cane referred to is *Arundinaria gigantea,* a member of the grass family and the only bamboo native to the United States. Canebrakes or thickets were a dominant feature of the presettlement landscape. d'Iberville recounted in 1699 that, "These canes, which resemble bamboo, have roots extending three to four feet underground." This quote, which was translated by Carl A. Brasseaux, accounts for the settlers' difficulty in clearing the cane and explains the survival of this invasive species in parts of Louisiana to the present day (see Brasseaux, *A Comparative View of French Louisiana,* 44). "Maiz" refers to Indian corn, called "Turkey corn" in France.

11. Rehder, *Delta Sugar,* 55.

12. Thomas Affleck, *Southern Rural Almanac, and Plantation and Garden Calendar, for 1860* (Washington, MS, 1860), 95.

13. French formalism is a generic description of the style of garden layout and management made popular through the work of French designer Andre LeNotre. The landscape of King Louis XIV's palace Versailles, outside of Paris, is the exemplar of this approach to garden design.

14. Andrew Jackson Downing, *Treatise on the Theory and Practice of Landscape Gardening* (New York: Wiley & Putnam, 1841).

15. Roulhac B. Toledano, "Louisiana's Golden Age: Valcour Aimé in St. James Parish," *Louisiana History* 10, no. 3 (Summer 1969): 211–24.

16. Valcour Aimé, *Plantation Diary of the late Mr. Valcour Aimé* (New Orleans: Clark & Hofeline, 1878), 83. The 120 workers referred to here were enslaved people.

17. Ibid., 90.

18. Ibid., 98–99.

19. Ibid., 159.

20. Ibid., 77.

21. Ibid., 92.

22. Ibid., 143.

23. Clarissa Kimber, *Dooryard Gardens of Martinique* (Honolulu, HI: University of Hawaii Press, 1966), is the first study of these simple vernacular spaces surrounding the door of simple dwellings in many Caribbean and other tropical countries, in particular. They typically contain

a combination of fruit and plants mixed with ornamentals, some of which may have medicinal applications.

24. Garrett Fesler, "Excavating the Spaces and Interpreting the Places of Enslaved Africans and Their Descendants," in *Cabin, Quarter, Plantation: Architecture and Landscapes of North American Slavery,* ed. Clifton Ellis and Rebecca Ginsburg (New Haven, CT: Yale University Press, 2010), 31.

25. Ibid., 26.

26. Anne Raver, "In Georgia's Swept Yards: A Dying Tradition," *New York Times,* August 8, 1993, nytimes.com/1993/08/08/us/in-georgia-s-swept-yards-a-dying tradition.html?pagewanted =all.

27. Ibid.

28. Affleck, *Southern Rural Almanac, and Plantation and Garden Calendar, for 1860,* 22.

29. Michael Twitty, "Crops of African Origin or African Diffusion in the Americas," *Afroculinaria,* October 5, 2016, https://afroculinaria.com/2016/10/05/crops-of-african-origin-or -african-diffusion-in-the-americas/.

30. Fesler, "Excavating the Spaces," 33.

31. Richard Davies, "Mississippi Ghosts: The Photography of Clarence John Laughlin," Abe Books article at www.abebooks.com/books/features/ghosts-along-mississippi.

32. Laughlin, *Ghosts Along the Mississippi.*

33. Pasquier, "French Colonial Louisiana."

34. Hall, *Africans in Colonial Louisiana,* 2.

35. Ibid., 158.

36. Leland Ferguson, *Uncommon Ground: Archaeology and Early African America, 1650–1800* (Washington, DC: Smithsonian Books, 1992), 115.

37. Ibid., 115.-

38. Hall, *Africans in Colonial Louisiana,* 160.

39. Born in Virginia, William Carter Stubbs (1846–1924) fought in the Civil War before graduating from the University of Virginia in 1867. He served as professor of chemistry at Alabama A&M University (1872–1885) and as director of the Louisiana Sugar Experiment Station in New Orleans (1885–1905). Furthermore, Stubbs published numerous books and articles, including *Cultivation of Sugar Cane* (1901). http://snaccooperative.org/ark:/99166/w6f76qjd.

40. Henry Rightor, ed., *Standard History of New Orleans, Louisiana. . . .* (Chicago, IL: Lewis Publishing Co., 1900), 685.

41. Ibid., 681.

SEVERED HEADS TO STATEHOUSE

The Political Landscape of the Sugar Coast

CHARLES D. CHAMBERLAIN III

THE SUGAR COAST AS POLITICAL LANDSCAPE

In 1858, French artist and lithographer Marie Adrien Persac published *Norman's Chart of the Lower Mississippi River.* The illustrated map covered the frequently trafficked, largely agricultural stretch of the Mississippi River between Natchez, Mississippi, and New Orleans, Louisiana. The chart also celebrated the success of those men who defined the area with their enterprise, including plantation names and owners, small vignettes of cotton and sugar plantations, and a view of the number of cities included within its borders. This essay focuses on the

Figure 1. Sugar plantation. Detail from *Norman's Chart of the Lower Mississippi River,* by Marie Adrien Persac, Benjamin Moore Norman, and J. H. Colton & Co. (New Orleans: B. M. Norman, 1858). Available at https://www.loc.gov/item/78692178/.

lower section of the map, an area in Louisiana so heavily invested in producing sugarcane that it became known as "the sugar coast."[1]

At the time *Norman's Chart* was published, the sugar coast stood prominently at the center of political power in Louisiana. Persac's inclusion of planters' names allows the viewer to navigate his chart as a map of concentrated power. Planters—particularly those who owned property on the prestigious sugar coast—were often political leaders, and they adopted economic and social policies that benefited their class. These favorable policies allowed planters to expand their enterprises, increasing their wealth and securing their positions of power. Lawmakers fashioned the state constitution and voting requirements to maintain this extraordinary concentration of power in the Louisiana Senate throughout most of the nineteenth century.[2]

This essay examines the nature of early planter power, which was dominated by Creoles, and the way that post–Civil War planters used tenacity and lingering Creole influence to maintain a foothold in the political arena. Finally, at the close of the nineteenth century, industry professionalism replaced antebellum Creole status as a measure of influence along the sugar coast.[3]

Rather than a broad political survey, this essay offers concentrated points of study of individuals whose narratives reflect the larger movements. André Bienvenu Roman represents the Creole Whig politician at the peak of Creole political power when *Norman's Chart* was published. Jean Noël Destréhan and Jacques Villeré define the early Republican roots of planter power. Paul Hébert and Dick Taylor offer contrasting examples of the tenacity of the post–Civil War sugar planter—parlaying ideological flexibility or their planter status and Creole ties to retain a foothold in an unstable political landscape. Lastly, Duncan Kenner was a man whose influence and activity in both the sugar and political arenas ensured that those who dominated the sugar industry would control the political arena as well, and do so through the end of the nineteenth century.

CREOLE SUGAR NOBILITY

Standing on River Road in front of Oak Alley Plantation, one gazes on perhaps the most recognized plantation landscape in Louisiana. Located in rural St. James Parish, the large sugar plantation's Greek Revival home is framed by the gracefully intertwining branches of sturdy live oaks planted in two rows to form a long, straight, and grand approach to the Creole manor from the river, very much in the French landscape tradition of an *allée* of plane trees leading to a *château.*

Jacques Télésphore Roman and his wife Celina employed a crew of enslaved skilled carpenters and masons to construct the Greek Revival main house in 1839. Jacques's older brother André Bienvenu served as governor of Louisiana at the time, when Creole Whig sugar planters such as the Romans maintained oversized political influence while cultivating a lavish slavery-based lifestyle.

Jacques and André Bienvenu Roman did not descend from French nobility but fashioned themselves as a Creole aristocracy on the sugar coast. Their father leveraged his small Attakapas land concession on the prairies west of Bayou Teche into a large *vacherie* (cattle ranch) to purchase a large plantation on the Mississippi River in the more prestigious St. James Parish.[4] André Bienvenu (born 1795) and Jacques grew up in one of the newer families of more established Creole planters of French nobility granted concessions.

The young André Bienvenu graduated in 1815 from St. Mary's College, a Roman Catholic seminary and university in the Catholic-friendly state of Maryland. This immersive experience in the English-speaking world of the Chesapeake likely provided him with a familiarity of the Anglo-American character. Upon Roman's return from Maryland to Louisiana in 1815, he married Creole Aimée Françoise Parent and settled in St. James Parish, where he threw himself into politics and rose quickly through the ranks in Louisiana's assembly.

André Bienvenu Roman's success as a planter-politician from the 1820s to the 1850s defines an era when sugar and Whig politics wed one another. During this period, Louisiana's sugar coast stood out geographically as a Whig island in a sea of Jacksonian Democrats across much of the American South. For aspiring politicians like Roman, the state assembly served as the most direct path to power. He was first elected in 1818 at age twenty-three and the state body voted him speaker three years later, a position Roman served in for four years and then again in 1828–29 after taking off the two interim years to serve as judge in St. James Parish. With the special gubernatorial election of 1830, Roman emerged as a strong National-Republican (anti-Jacksonian) candidate for a party that promoted internal improvements and protective tariffs, two policies dear to sugar coast planters.[5] In this political landscape, Roman's victory in Louisiana unleashed a Whig sugar boom.

Under Roman's first administration, banking policies created a fever-pitch economic expansion in the state. Despite his objections, the assembly loosened economic regulations and banks increased from five to eleven.[6] As canal and railroad building boomed in the eastern United States, Roman and his fellow Whigs enabled infrastructure development in Louisiana, especially the southern part of the state where sugar plantations sought cheap transportation to New Orleans. On the 1858 *Norman's Chart,* artist Marie Adrien Persac prominently includes numerous canals and new railroads connecting plantations to the river and the port of New Orleans. Roman modernized the state's infrastructure and educational system. He approved the creation of the state civil engineers' office and a board of public works with a fund created for internal improvements. Roman also sanctioned the opening of the pass at the mouth of the river to improve shipping.[7]

In the merging of planters' political and physical landscapes, the dredging of the Barataria Canal lays out Whig planters' government-funded infrastructure and navigation projects, which they controlled and from which they stood to benefit. The canal was intended as an east-west barge shipping route connecting the western Teche and Lafourche sugar country to the Mississippi River and New Orleans. Act 38 of 1829 signed by planter and Whig governor Pierre Derbigny created the Barataria and Lafourche (B&L) Canal Company, in which the governor's son and company president Judge Charles Zenon Derbigny and Kentucky-born Walter Brashear owned the majority stock. Lower-river Creole sugar planter families LaBranche, Zeringue, LeBreton, and Fazende owned the remainder. The law, brazenly employing sugar planter nepotism and favoritism, included a state subsidy of $10,000 and enabled Governor Roman to appoint Charles Derbigny director, with (planter-dominated) Senate approval, to protect the state's investment. The B&L's maintenance costs ultimately proved too costly for the state to bear, however. Only after the Civil War did Louisiana sugar planters successfully cultivate federal funding and oversight for levee and canal maintenance in their districts.[8]

In 1858 Persac prominently showcased on *Norman's Chart* the overall Roman-Aimé family's multiple large plantations in St. James Parish, constituting their sugar empire that would soon collapse. Even as the Roman brothers' successful brother-in-law planter Valcour Aimé won the New York World Fair's top prize for sugar in 1853, the unexpected death of Valcour's son Gabriel during the great yellow fever epidemic of that year, followed by the death of his wife Josephine Roman in 1856, pushed the sugar seigneur to retire from the business of planting.[9]

Meanwhile, in retirement from his second term in 1843, André Bienvenu Roman played experienced Whig statesman in the state constitutional conventions of 1845 and 1852, the latter of which bolstered the representation of Whig planters in the sugar belt by counting slaves as citizens in apportioning representation.[10] Roman also secured the necessary finances that sustained his fellow Creole sugar planters. As with many agricultural enterprises, the Citizens Bank and the Consolidated Association of Planters (CAPL) was created to secure sugar planters deeper credit in Europe. Roman served as a valuable bilingual agent in their negotiations with both English and French banks. Such loans were crucial to Creole planter stability, for the landscape Persac depicted on his map of mighty Creole planters was a house of cards.[11]

Planters consistently overextended themselves by leveraging property holdings, including the aggregate value of their enslaved workers, as collateral for loans—even mortgaging the same piece of real estate or enslaved person with multiple banks. And in cases such as with CAPL, it was unlikely that their debts would be called in as planters, quite literally, owned the bank. André Bienvenu Roman, securing credit and loans in Europe for the sugar planter banks, disguised the fragility and subsequent weakness of their plantation-based power, the absolute dependency on slavery's existence.[12]

SEVERED HEADS

Creole planters' political power originated in the earliest years of the American period, when sugar first became profitable. Sugar planter-politicians Jean Noël Destréhan (1759–1823) and Governor Jacques Villeré (1761–1830) cultivated greatly concentrated power in the years following the Louisiana Purchase. As such, Destréhan and Villeré define the elite Creole planter-politician on the lower Mississippi River that shaped the sugar planters' influence in early American Louisiana. Their families had received land grants (seigneurial concessions) in the early 1700s, based on their nobility titles or service to the French crown. They then amassed additional large land holdings along the Mississippi River. As a class with outsized political influence, these Creole large landholders on the sugar coast paralleled the landed gentry of Virginia's Tidewater. With the United States' purchase of Louisiana, Creole planters shaped territorial policy, thus protecting slavery and fashioning a restrictive voting system in January 1811 through the state's first constitution.

The forty-five constitutional delegates meeting at the Tremoulet's Hotel in New Orleans to write the state's first constitution included prominent planters Jacques Villeré, Jean Noël Destréhan, convention president Julien Poydras, Joseph Bellechase, and Bernard de Marigny among some Tidewater-born planters and Creole merchants and lawyers. The resulting constitution, modeled almost verbatim on Kentucky's of 1792, solidified planter control of electoral politics. They included property qualifications for white male voters, the indirect election of governor, and the appointment of members of Congress, judges, and justices of the peace, all early Republican practices common at the time in the United States.[13] Kentucky had already revised its state constitution in 1799 to allow direct elections at the state level. But in 1811 Louisiana, the new state's political leadership preferred the politically restrictive language of twenty years prior.

While the new constitution addressed the planters' desire for political control, and the state delegation debated verbiage in New Orleans, an event took place upriver that affirmed the planters' second concern: the absolute continuation of slavery. The Deslondes slave revolt, or German Coast Uprising of 1811 led by Charles Deslondes, considered the largest in US history, erupted upriver in the town of LaPlace, where participants planned to march all the way to New Orleans and take the city. The revolt failed, however, and the response of Jean Noël Destréhan and the Creole planters' to the uprising speaks volumes about their position on slavery. The trial, led by local judge Pierre Bauchet St. Martin and five local planters, including Destréhan, concluded so quickly and with such grotesque enforcement that national news outlets outside of the South severely criticized the process and punishment.[14]

The speedy tribunal at Destréhan's home charged and executed forty-one persons in a gruesome and barbaric sentence, including Jasmin, Petit Lindor, and Gros Lindor from Destréhan's plantation. Those persons found guilty were decapitated, and their heads placed on pikes along River Road, the colonial-era public route connecting plantations along the river. The gruesome display gave an extreme warning that insurrection would mean death. The planters' power as politicians and as slaveowners was to be absolute.

Barely a year after the trial and execution, Destréhan and Jacques Villeré both ran for governor against Claiborne in the first gubernatorial election of 1812. With only 3,874 voters statewide, Claiborne crushed Villeré and Destréhan with 71 percent of the popular vote and 84 percent against Villeré in the general assembly vote. As consolation, Claiborne appointed third-place loser Destréhan as Louisiana's first US senator. Perhaps dreading time in the new capital city of Washington, DC, Destréhan resigned to serve closer to home in the Louisiana Senate. Governor Claiborne appointed Villeré justice of the peace of St. Bernard Parish, a logical appeasement for a military man who prioritized law enforcement, especially as a tool of slave control on the lower coast plantations undergoing the transition from indigo and tobacco to sugar. The St. Bernard planter's service as a major general in the state militia at the Battle of New Orleans elevated his local prestige further in the post–War of 1812 euphoria.[15]

Villeré had greater success when he ran for governor again in 1816, a victory that provided the first opportunity for Creoles to shape the state.[16] His governing priorities focusing on law and order using the state militia and bolstering the criminal code create a common thread of support among lower coast Creole planters. In part because of the high federal sugar tariff passed in 1816, Villeré's four years in office witnessed economic stability and growth as sugar became the most profitable crop in the state, driving the expansion of slavery on the lower river. In his patronage appointments Villeré selected majority English-speaking persons to state and local positions such as justices of the peace and judges. This gesture enabled Creole and American political bridge-building in a culturally and politically divided state, where the opposition (English-language) press portrayed Villeré and sugar coast planters as elitist and undemocratic.[17]

Villeré retired to his Conseil Plantation at the end of his term, but four years later the general assembly voted Villeré to serve as elector for John Quincy Adams in the controversial 1824 presidential election. Through Villeré's support, Adams won the sugar coast, setting the region apart politically from much of the cotton South. In the 1824 election, Adams and Jackson represented two different visions of the Democratic-Republican Party. Jackson gained support among small farmers and those supporting slavery and western expansion, whereas most of the cotton South opposed Adams because of his antislavery views and his reputation as an elitist. Yet, Adams won the sugar coast in 1824, and from the 1828 presidential election into the early 1850s, the sugar coast (and the Mississippi River valley generally) voted Whig, thereby distinguishing the commercial region from the small-farm and cotton South.

In a period of early party formation nationally, Villeré likely found appealing Adams's support for protective tariffs and state-funded internal improvements before the National-Republican and Whig Parties embodied the promarket policies favored by sugar coast planters in the 1830s. Additionally, Adams's language fluency and appreciation of French culture likely appealed to sugar coast Creoles.

The sixty-nine-year-old Villeré died in 1830 while running for governor in a crowded field of candidates including former planter Bernard de Marigny and the youthful twenty-six-year-old sugar coast planter André B. Roman, who won the election. The generation of Creole leaders in Louisiana's early statehood years transitioned smoothly into the American political system, under which they maintained their wealth, status, and political power over a largely disfranchised public and an outsized representation based on the inclusion of slaves in the population. Destréhan and Jean Étienne de Boré's promotion and experimentation with the sugar industry coincided with the migration of the slave-based industry from French colonial San Domingue to Louisiana's Creole sugar coast. In Louisiana's early American period from 1803 to 1830, sugar came to dominate the plantation economy along the river, shape political influence, and define the wealth and grandeur of the antebellum Creole sugar coast.

EMANCIPATED FROM WEALTH

The Roman-Aimé sugar empire failed to survive the loss of real estate value with emancipation in the early 1860s. At the call for secession in 1861, André B. Roman voted in the state assembly to remain with the Union. Many old Whig sugar coast planters like Roman did not see their economic interests and political future aligning with Democratic cotton planters outside of the Mississippi River valley. On the cusp of war in 1861, Roman reminded powerful state senator and sugar planter Duncan Kenner, "cotton states, most of which practice the institution of slavery, have no common interests with us, and on the contrary, are competitors for the commerce of the Valley of the Mississippi and Ohio."[18]

The Roman house of financial cards crumbled during the war. The loss of real estate value wealth with emancipation ruined the family financially. At the end of the war, Roman accepted an appointment as a recorder of deeds and mortgages in New Orleans, a long fall for the proud ninth governor of Louisiana. The seventy-year-old Creole died while walking through the Vieux Carré on Dumaine Street in January 1866. He was buried in a simple tomb in the St. James Cemetery of his home parish.

Roman's brother in-law "sugar king" Valcour Aimé, owner of the extravagantly landscaped Le Petit Versailles in St. James Parish, also lost all of his real estate wealth with emancipation. Returning home from Christmas mass in 1866, the recluse Aimé caught pneumonia and died shortly thereafter. The former sugar king's estate was forced to sell his beloved Le Petit Versailles to meet debts. In 1870, the Ireland-born sugar baron John Burnside, owner of Houmas House, bought Le Petit Versailles and came to own a total of twelve sugar plantations along the river in Ascension and St. James Parishes, making him and Duncan Kenner the largest landholders on the river after the war.

The sale of Aimé's plantation to an upstart sugar baron who already owned Houmas Plantation, one of the largest plantations in the United States, stood as a stark symbol of Creole property loss in the river parishes. Le Petit Versailles burned in the early twentieth century, and little remains (see Turner's essay). As for André Bienvenu Roman's Cabanocey Plantation, a brown state marker up from Oak Alley along the River Road marks the once prestigious plantation.

Although Oak Alley remains an incredible testament to the grandeur of the Roman antebellum sugar empire, following Jacques's death from tuberculosis in 1848, his widow Celina and son Henri struggled to make the operation sustainable. By 1866, Celina had died at age fifty, and the property was auctioned to John Armstrong—another symbolic American acquisition of a prestigious Creole icon.[19] The Roman family tale reflects the shortcomings of a Creole world that intended to preserve a proud way of life and culture by sanctioning marriages with other French-speaking families along the river. During these heady Whig years, not all Creole families maintained the strict attitude and cultivated relations with American sugar-planting families arriving from the mid-Atlantic Tidewater region to create a new gentry in the river parishes below Baton Rouge.

CREOLE AND AMERICAN MERGERS

On the 1858 *Norman's Chart,* a small plantation along the Bayou Goula ridge south of Plaquemine in Iberville Parish is simply referenced in brackets as "Gov.r P.O. Hébert." The sliver of land belonged to the retired Governor Paul Hébert, who served as the last French-speaking bilingual governor in Louisiana from 1853 to 1856, and who represented the younger generation of American-born French-speakers who intermarried with English-American planter families along the river.[20] Hébert was born and raised in sugar-rich Iberville Parish on a plantation first settled by his Acadian (Cajun) grandfather in the 1780s. His smaller plantation lay between the river and the Atchafalaya Swamp in an area settled by the more hardscrabble farmers and small Cajun planters, in contrast to those who settled the elevated riverfront plantations of the Creole sugar aristocracy. Even as Hébert grew up in the heart of Whig country during the 1830s and 1840s, he found political success as a proslavery Democrat in the 1850s.

Hébert's 1853 gubernatorial victory as a Democrat reveals Jacksonian democracy's impact on Louisiana's political landscape. Reflecting a national wave of voter expansion, Louisiana finally revised its constitution in 1845 and, for the first time since 1812, the state dropped property qualifications for white male voters and allowed direct elections of governor. Louisiana voter participation almost doubled from 22,767 voters in the 1846 election to an antebellum peak of 43,347 in the 1855 election for governor. In the 1850s, the Democratic Party in Louisiana found success at the state level as the defender of slavery, while the Whigs lost relevance and the Republican Party's free labor platform represented the opposition to slavery.

During the 1860s and 1870s, adapting to the radically transformed political landscape enabled Hébert's financial and political survival. In 1856 the retired governor had returned to his Home Place Plantation in Iberville Parish, and when war broke out, he served as a brigadier general for the Confederacy. With liberal Republicans in power after the war and African American men given the franchise after 1869, Hébert joined the Republican Party in 1872 and supported the reelection of his old Army buddy Ulysses S. Grant, whom Hébert knew well at West Point and through the Mexican War.

Grant parlayed Hébert's support into an appointment on the Mississippi River Commission, a federal commission created in 1879 to improve navigation and commerce, as well as to prevent destructive floods through levees and locks. As a commission member, Hébert argued (as he did in the 1840s as state surveyor) for federalizing the costs and maintenance of flood control throughout the Mississippi Basin. Hébert's use of his position to advocate for federal flood control funds to bankroll protection of valuable plantation lands through levees and locks represented both a continuum of older Whig platforms from the 1830s and 1840s and their evolution into modern professional sugar industry tactics of the Democrats in the Gilded Age.

After his death from cancer in August 1880, Hébert was interred in the family plot at the Saint Raphael Cemetery in Bayou Goula.[21] In the end, Paul Hébert represented the astonishing and rare native-born sugar planter-politician who supported liberal Republicans after the war while using this political marriage to further the goals of conservative Democrat sugar planters. His nimble maneuvering of a complicated political landscape and his flexible practical nature represents the most vivid example of uncommon Creole/Cajun adaptability in a time of political and economic transition and uncertainty.

AMERICAN BUYOUT

For some political families, lines of both formal and informal credit enabled them to withstand bankruptcy. The Fashion Plantation, home of Richard "Dick" Taylor and Myrthe "Mimi" Bringier in St. Charles Parish, was intended to represent the over-the-top grandeur and wealth typical of the 1850s. The son of President Zachary Taylor, Dick Taylor inherited Fashion Plantation in 1850 with his father's sudden death in the White House. One year later, the Yale graduate married into the wealthy Creole Bringier family, which, as indicated on *Norman's Chart,* had amassed an empire of sugar plantation holdings in Ascension and St. James Parishes by the 1850s. The marriage of the Kentucky-born Taylor and Bringier represented an important and symbolic Creole-American alliance in the river parishes, much like her older sister Nanine's marriage to sugar planter-politician Duncan Kenner twelve years earlier.

Fashion was vulnerably undergirded by slavery and credit, as was true for a majority of the sugar plantations. The freeze of 1856 took the entire sugar crop, and Fashion faced a debt crisis. Dick Taylor's marriage into the land-endowed Bringier family afforded him lines of credit within the family such that his mother-in-law, Aglae Bringier, rescued Taylor's Fashion with a large loan (gift). With the Union's conquest of the sugar coast in 1862, troops looted Fashion. Taylor eventually foreclosed to his brother-in-law Duncan Kenner, who gradually bought the bankrupt Bringier sugar plantation empire after the war.

In Ascension Parish on the east bank of the Mississippi River below the town of Plaquemine, Duncan Kenner's prominent Ashland Plantation home stands today as testament to the Virginia-born Episcopalian families that came to dominate the sugar coast after the Civil War. Kenner's success can be attributed to his joining one of the most important Anglo-Creole family alliances in the river parishes during the nineteenth century and remaining politically adept while embracing modernization of the sugar industry.

Norman's Chart of 1858 lists five large properties of the Kenner family stretching from Jefferson Parish upriver to Ascension Parish. Duncan's Virginia-born father, William Kenner, had immigrated to New Orleans from Natchez, Mississippi, during Louisiana's Spanish colonial period and had cofounded the Episcopal Church of Louisiana in 1803. The Kenner family sugar empire gradually expanded along the sugar coast throughout the first decades of the 1800s.

William Kenner's purchase of Linwood Plantation in Ascension Parish and Oakland Plantation in Jefferson Parish upriver from New Orleans during the 1810s made him one of the largest sugar producers in Louisiana. His four sons continued the expansion of their family sugar empire in the 1830s and 1840s. By the end of the youngest son Duncan's life in 1887, he owned ten of the largest and most important plantations on the Mississippi River while his brother Stephen Minor Kenner owned numerous others, including the site of present-day suburban Kenner.

Duncan grew up as a local Episcopalian Anglo in a Creole world, thereby enabling his ease with the French-speaking community. The family resided at their Oakland estate on the river in East Jefferson Parish and in New Orleans during the 1820s. Learning French at school in New Orleans underscored Kenner's ease with Creole culture. Kenner's courtship and marriage to Anne "Nanine" Bringier in 1839 further cemented a bridge between French- and English-speaking worlds in the river parishes.[22] The twenty-six-year-old planter-politician built a new Greek Revival manor house in 1841 to distinguish his Ashland Plantation as one of the grandest in Louisiana, fitting of his rise to sugar coast planter-politician aristocracy.[23]

Duncan Kenner began his political career in the 1830s, and spent the two decades before the Civil War establishing his reputation as an effective legislative leader representing sugar interests. He initially served in the Louisiana House as a Democrat, given his familial social ties to both Thomas Jefferson and Andrew Jackson. With the negative national political backlash against Democrats following the Panic of 1837, Kenner emerged as a Whig leader in the state, more fitting with his planter interests of protective tariffs and state-funded internal improvements. The 1841 naming of his Ashland Plantation after the estate of Whig leader Henry Clay marks the political shift.

As a Whig state senator in the 1840s and early 1850s, Kenner shaped the Louisiana state constitutions in 1845 and 1852 to sustain or enhance planter power. In both conventions. Kenner argued for representation proportional to total population (free and enslaved persons), giving sugar planters in the majority-slave areas an oversized political representation. Even though the 1845 Constitution expanded the vote to all white men, the 1852 constitutional convention, at which Kenner served as convention president, apportioned senatorial representation on the total population, including enslaved persons, guaranteeing the sugar planters dominance of the upper chamber.[24]

Duncan Kenner's remarkable adaptability to a new economic and political environment on the same sugar coast political landscape provides a clear lesson on how successful planters survived the Civil War and then thrived in the postwar marketplace. By 1861, Kenner switched back to the proslavery Democratic Party, leading the call for secession and serving in the Confederate Congress as a minister plenipotentiary to England in France. When the war ended, he immediately took the oath of loyalty to the United States and received a presidential pardon from Andrew Johnson on his return in October 1865. Having his property seized by federal authorities, he regained control of his assets to leverage future acquisitions of prominent plantation properties on the sugar coast.[25]

Kenner's survival during the war, in part through his acceptance of emancipation and his moving immediately into paid labor, enabled him to use his assets to purchase the foreclosed properties of his in-laws and amass a fortune based on sugar, real estate, and other investments. Politically, he worked with Republican politicians and administrations during Reconstruction, recognizing that strategy as the one most likely ensuring financial survival. He embraced Black suffrage as a means of relieving the South of the federal military occupation. But with the return of Democrats to power in Louisiana in 1877, Kenner wasted no time in running for and winning the state senate seat, using 257 Carondelet Street in New Orleans, and not his Ascension Parish plantation home, for his residency. As a state senator, Kenner shaped the Louisiana state constitution of 1877 and stressed the policies of local or limited government, no-tax Democrats—a far cry from his Whig days of the 1840s. In truth, however, modern Democrat planters like Kenner welcomed federal flood control and tariff policies that benefited the sugar coast plantations directly.[26]

Kenner's efforts to modernize the industry ushered in a new era of more professional political representation. With Democrats firmly in power, he cofounded and served as first president of the Louisiana Sugar Planters Association (LSPA). The founding of the LSPA in 1877 provided a central organization in which the largest two hundred planters in Louisiana could channel modern political and economic strategies. The LSPA emerged as a lobbying organization for commercial sugar interests; at the same time, the newly created federal Mississippi River Commission (MRC) provided an influential planter voice for state-funded navigation and flood-control projects that benefited the sugar coast. The overall marriage of Kenner's LSPA with the new MRC reflected the professionalization of political influence in the post–Civil War sugar coast landscape amidst a decline in Creole family names, influence, and capital.

Even though Kenner's retirement from politics in 1879 left him time for socializing and his true passion of horse-racing, he masterfully used the organizing power of the LSPA to ensure sugar protections when he served on President Chester Arthur's tariff commission. Although a true sugar man, Kenner also presided over the committee organizing the 1884 World's Industrial and Cotton Centennial Exposition, an event celebrating New Orleans' reemergence as an international agricultural commodities trade center.

At the time of seventy-four-year-old Kenner's death in July 1887, the political landscape in Louisiana was shaped largely by conservative modern planters like himself. Yet even his sugar and real estate empire was not impervious to economic failure. Living and dying by the sword of sugar finance, Kenner had borrowed money against a bad crop in the exceptionally harsh winter of 1886–87, and within years his family sold the numerous holdings in New Orleans and along the river to meet Kenner's debts.[27]

THE INDUSTRIAL LANDSCAPE OF 1900

By the end of the nineteenth century, the political and economic influence of the Destréhan, Villeré, Roman, Hébert, and Taylor-Bringier families had ended. Sugarcane was declining in economic importance, and with the discovery of oil in 1901, mineral rights and production introduced a new era. By 1910, the Destréhan–de Boré family sold Destréhan Plantation to the Mexican Petroleum Company, which built a refinery and a company town around the historically significant Creole home, now a tourist site.

The Destréhan sale reflects the initial industrialization of River Road plantations and the emergence of a newly diversified economy for the sugar coast, encompassing oil, manufacturing, refining, shipping, and tourism. The plantation survived the Civil War as a federal Freedmen's Bureau experiment until 1866, and then resumed as a working plantation under Judge Emile Rost, the grandson of Jean Noël Destréhan. By 1910, however, the Destréhan–de Boré family would sell the grand West Indies-style home and plantation to international corporate investors.

By 1900, much of Louisiana's political power base emanated from the Lafourche and Teche sugar country to the west. In the twentieth century, the river parishes shifted more toward manufacturing and petroleum-based industry and, in the process, lost the allure of the noble sugar coast. Farther west in the more remote rural parishes, Anglo sugar planters emerged as the prominent and powerful politicians. On the lower sugar coast of St. John the Baptist Parish, French immigrant Leon Godchaux built cane railroads and the largest sugar refinery in the United States during the 1890s. The completion of the massive Domino sugar refinery in St. Bernard Parish in 1906 further reflected a shift in production and ownership toward larger, well-capitalized operations.

The rise and fall of the Destréhan–de Boré family, similar to other members of the Creole plantation aristocracy, belies the overall ability of sugar planters as a class and political force to maintain their power. Through the arc of the nineteenth century, sugar planters viewed themselves as a special group and consistently organized politically to maintain and enhance their standing. These businessmen actively sought restriction of political participation as a means to secure power and concentrate their influence. In the antebellum period, they maintained an oversized representation through the sadly ironic inclusion of enslaved people as constituents. Jacksonian democracy may have awakened the franchise of propertyless white men in Louisiana after the state constitution of 1845, but sugar planters deftly reduced their voice and impact in 1852.

Whereas the Civil War may have led to the demise of many older Creole family empires, it only strengthened the hands of larger sugar planters able to adapt to a new economy. Duncan Kenner's founding of the Louisiana Sugar Planters Association in 1877 and Edward Gay's cofounding of the New Orleans Sugar Exchange in 1883 reflected modern Democratic planters' consolidation of political and economic worlds. During the 1880s and 1890s, the LSPA successfully lobbied to protect sugar tariffs and federalize the south Louisiana levee systems. By 1898, the planter-derived new state constitution resurrected political exclusion reminiscent of the sugar coast's white racial and political domination under the politically restrictive state constitution of 1812.

All in all, the successful nineteenth-century planter-politicians of Louisiana's sugar coast provide a master lesson in consolidating social, racial, and economic power through the mechanisms of Republican Democratic political rule. The political landscape by 1900 defined the sugar planters' desire for stability and control. The state constitutional convention of 1898 engineered a political transformation that once again placed more control into the hands of powerful planters.

But sugar would not remain the base of planter wealth. The 1901 discovery of oil in Louisiana ushered in the new industrial era of minerals and mineral rights, and some sugar planters exploited this new source of wealth. The old sugar coast attracted corporate investors who brought down many of the antebellum homes while adapting the land to industrial use. After 1900, the sugar coast gradually transformed into an industrial landscape coexisting with a romanticized antebellum plantation tourism for those historic homes that remained.

NOTES

1. The sugar-growing parishes in this region stretch from Pointe Coupée Parish south to St. Bernard Parish.

2. The 1845 Louisiana Constitution is considered a reflection of the Jacksonian Democratic reform in that it removed property qualifications for white male voters for the first time since 1812.

3. Recognizing the multiple colloquial and scholarly definitions of the word *creole* (and its variations *criollo/criolo/kreyol*), in this essay "Creole" simply refers to Louisiana-born persons who identified as French-speaking Roman Catholics in contrast to the English-speaking American Protestants who migrated to Louisiana in the 1800s.

4. By 1803, French prefect Pierre-Clément de Laussat lauded the older Roman as one of the prominent visitors from Attakapas, where the Creole's land "was covered with his herds; he raised the finest cotton in Louisiana and had grown rich after thirty-six years of work and diligence." Pierre-Clément de Laussat, *Memoirs of My Life,* trans. Agnes-Josephine Pastwa, ed. Robert D. Bush (Baton Rouge: Louisiana State University Press, 1978), 22.

5. Joseph G. Tregle Jr., "André Bienvenu Roman." In *Encyclopedia of Louisiana,* ed. David Johnson, at http://www.knowlouisiana.org/entry/andre-bienvenu-roman.

6. Walter Greaves Cowan and Jack B. McGuire, *Louisiana Governors: Rulers, Rascals, and Reformers* (Jackson: University Press of Mississippi, 2008), 71; Leslie Murray Norton, "A History of the Whig Party in Louisiana" (PhD dissertation, Louisiana State University, 1940).

7. Joseph G. Dawson III, ed., *The Louisiana Governors: From Iberville to Edwards* (Baton Rouge: Louisiana State University Press, 1990), 110–11.

8. Thomas Becnel, *The Barrow Family and the Barataria and Lafourche Canal: The Transportation Revolution in Louisiana, 1829–1925* (Baton Rouge: Louisiana State University Press, 1989), 46–50.

9. R. Eric Platt, "Valcour Aimé," *Encyclopedia of Louisiana,* ed. David Johnson, at http://www.knowlouisiana.org/entry/valcour-aime.

10. Cowan and McGuire, *Louisiana Governors,* 81.

11. Edward Baptist, "Toxic Debt, Liar Loans, and Securitized Human Beings: The Panic of 1837 and the Fate of Slavery," *Commonplace,* http://commonplace.online/article/toxic-debt-liar-loans/https://www.common-place-archives.org/vol-10/no-03/baptist/.

12. Dawson, *The Louisiana Governors,* 112; Baptist, "Toxic Debt."

13. Eberhard L. Faber, *Building the Land of Dreams: New Orleans and the Transformation of Early America* (Princeton, NJ: Princeton University Press, 2016), 103–7, 190–200, 304–5; Laussat, *Memoirs of My Life,* 22–23, 51–70; Villere Family Papers, MSS 57, The Historic New Orleans Collection. Many leading Creole families in Louisiana adapted their French titled names to an American version: d'Estrehan/Destréhan, de Villeré/Villeré, des Londes/Deslondes, d'Herbigny/Derbigny.

14. Albert Thrasher, *On to New Orleans! Louisiana's Heroic Slave Revolt* (New Orleans: Cypress Press, 1996); Daniel Rasmussen, *American Uprising: The Untold Story of America's Largest Slave Revolt* (New York: Harper Perennial, 2012); Faber, *Building the Land of Dreams,* 297–311.

15. Faber, *Building the Land of Dreams,* 209–11; Dawson, *The Louisiana Governors,* 86–90; Jacques Villere Papers, MSS 14, The Historic New Orleans Collection.

16. Cowan and McGuire, *Louisiana Governors,* 64.

17. Dawson, *The Louisiana Governors,* 90.

18. André Bienvenu Roman to Duncan Kenner, Louisiana State University, Special Collections, Louisiana and Lower Mississippi Valley Collections, Hill Memorial Library, J-4, W: 91–92.

19. William Kauffman Scarborough, *Masters of the Big House: Elite Slaveholders of the Mid-Nineteenth-Century South* (Baton Rouge: Louisiana State University Press, 2006).

20. Faber, *Building the Land of Dreams,* 138–39.

21. Albert Leonce Dupont, "The Career of Paul Octave Hébert, Governor of Louisiana, 1853–1856," *Louisiana Historical Quarterly* 31, no. 2 (April 1948): 491–552; William H. Adams, "Paul Octave Hébert," *Encyclopedia of Louisiana,* ed. David Johnson, at http://www.knowlouisiana.org/entry/paul-octave-hebert.; Reeves, *The Governors of Louisiana,* 61–63; Dawson, *The Louisiana Governors,* 130–34; Cowan and McGuire, *Louisiana Governors,* 81–82.

22. Craig Bauer, *A Leader among Peers: The Life and Times of Duncan Farrar Kenner* (Lafayette: Center for Louisiana Studies, University of Southwestern Louisiana, 1993), 32–36, 82–83.

23. Bauer, *A Leader among* Peers, 100–101; Craig Bauer, *Creole Genesis: The Bringier Family and Antebellum Plantation Life in Louisiana* (Lafayette: University of Louisiana at Lafayette), 35–40, 55. Marie "Rosella" (born 1814) married Virginia-born neighbor Hore Browse Trist of St. James Parish. Myrthe "Mimi" (born 1834) exchanged vows with Richard Taylor in St. Charles Parish, while Anne (born 1839) wed Marylander Allen Thomas of Ascension Parish.

24. Bauer, *A Leader among* Peers, 98–111.

25. Bauer, *Creole Genesis,* 119–42; Bauer, *A Leader among Peers,* 242–44.

26. T. Michael Parrish, *Richard Taylor: Soldier Prince of Dixie* (Chapel Hill: University of North Carolina Press, 1992), 458–60; Bauer, *A Leader among Peers,* 275–82; Bauer, *Creole Genesis,* 130–33.

27. Bauer, *A Leader among Peers,* 82–83, 256–57, 284–85.

PLANTATIONS AS LANDSCAPES OF MEDICINE

CHRISTOPHER D. E. WILLOUGHBY

> At all events, we are certain of one fact; namely, that [the enslaved's] services are not only altogether essential to the southern, but to the whole civilized world. Without his aid the spindles and looms of Manchester, of Lowell and of all the large manufactories must in a great measure remain idle; the fertile plantations of the South and West must go uncultivated and our extensive forest must remain as they now are the storehouses of malaria and the dens of wild beasts and hissing serpents.
>
> —J. P. Bonner, student at the Medical College of the State of South Carolina, 1850

Claiming that God had "created one white, the other black," in 1860, Peter L. Horn explained that this initial, divine act preordained the underlying science of plantation health for both the enslaver and the enslaved. In his MD thesis for the Medical College of the State of South Carolina, Horn explained that the bodies of African descendants were perfectly suited to labor in Louisiana's sugar plantations given their supposedly ingrained capacity to resist tropical diseases. Horn's thesis focused on yellow fever, an urban disease, and he wrote in Charleston, more than five hundred miles from the lower Mississippi River valley and its regional capital of New Orleans. Still, Horn found reason to mention Louisiana's cane fields. Like Louisiana's sugarcane plantations, South Carolina's rice plots were infested with malaria, and the local ports were struck regularly with yellow fever epidemics. During the first half of the nineteenth century, Horn and other physicians almost unanimously agreed that people of African descent had an inherited immunity to malaria and yellow fever, thus supposedly making them well-suited laborers for the large-scale sugar and cotton plantations. Physicians such as Horn drew attention to the growing sense that medicine needed to be localized and that internationally accepted medical theories should be tailored to local climates. While different in many respects from the rest of the South, the Carolina Lowcountry and Louisiana's cane-planting regions shared a great deal in common in terms of disease environment and the high-mortality rates of enslaved workers. Plantations on the Carolina and Louisiana lowlands shared similar traits such as standing water, debilitating humidity, and a need for a large agricultural population, and Horn described African descendants as ideally suited for such conditions. Even as the plantations on and around the Mississippi River from New Orleans to Natchez were defined by distinct cultures and peoples compared to much of the South, these differences were more of degree than kind. The region shared many of the health problems that were typical of the modernizing plantation systems of an Atlantic World serving global trade networks and slowly but surely adopting scientific approaches to agriculture.[1]

This imagined plantation landscape filled with African descendants healthy and well-suited for slave labor was more fantasy than fact. Contradicting antebellum physicians, twenty-first-century science reminds us that inherited yellow fever defenses do not exist. Doctors' presumptions about African descendants' inherited immunity had some logic, as enslaved workers who suffered from the illness in their youth often acquired immunity to the virus, thus appearing immune as adults. That being said, physicians selectively applied this logic to African descendants, as whites who survived the illness as children also acquired immunity, yet no prominent physician claimed that whites had inherited an immunity to yellow fever. Likewise, while some West African slaves likely had genetic defenses to certain strains of malaria, resisting the parasite has nothing to do with race. Many enslaved people suffered and died from malaria and yellow fever, even though physicians during this period imagined them as protected against those diseases. Simultaneously, doctors shaped an ideological landscape of the plantation through concepts of race and health, just as the needs of cash crops, slavery, and global trade altered the physical landscape to the detriment of enslaved workers' health along the lower Mississippi River valley plantations.[2]

During the nineteenth century, physicians molded new meaning for the human landscapes of Mississippi River plantations south of Natchez, creating arguments for the fitness of enslaved workers' bodies for unhealthy climates, theorizing about the health and architecture of slave housing, and defining the geographies of health within the plantation. Plantation practice also molded the physician. As workplaces, trade entrepôts, and residences, the typical Mississippi River plantation represented myriad health problems for the enslaved and enslaver alike. Here, physicians delivered infants, treated global epidemics such as cholera and yellow fever, and amputated arms caught in cotton gins or crushed in sugar mills. Through changes to the land necessary for plantation agriculture, enslavers also affected the disease environment, tailoring the land to support certain ailments. Standing water on Louisiana sugar plantations provided breeding grounds for *Anopheles* mosquitoes, the main vector for the malaria parasite. Along similar lines, trade along the Mississippi River brought the 1849 cholera epidemic directly to the doorsteps of many plantations up to Natchez before reaching Memphis and beyond.[3]

Despite their rural geography, the health problems of large-scale sugar and cotton production in the nineteenth-century were those of an increasingly capitalistic world shaped by global commerce and industrialization. Residents of Louisiana plantations contracted cholera from epidemics first reported by British colonials in India in 1817 that then traveled through the trade roots of empire to Europe. More than a decade later, on anything from a ship seeking Mexican silver in Veracruz or Mississippi cotton in New Orleans, cholera crossed the Atlantic to disastrous consequences in 1832 and, eventually, the disease traveled up the Mississippi River in flotillas and other craft seeking the region's sugarcane and cotton plantations. In addition to global pandemics, enslaved workers suffered accidents more associated with urban, industrial workplaces than with the rural plantations of historical memory. Increasingly mechanized, the processing of cotton and sugar required machines that could be quite dangerous. Also the consequence of an increasing push westward, plantations were borderlands between agricultural expansion and what whites saw as untouched forest. While Native Americans had cultivated and curated these forested lands prior to the arrival of Europeans to the region, as with African diasporic knowledge and technology, antebellum white commenters rarely saw the marks of Indian environmental agency. These nearby wooded areas and swamplands were inhabited by poisonous snakes, black bears, and alligators, making an enslaved person's escape perilous. Similar to other stories of westward movement, lower Mississippi River valley plantations were landscapes of expansion and modernization, and physicians had to grapple with the complex health problems of such a society.[4]

Just as plantations were growing, so too was the region's medical community. During this period, two medical schools were founded in New Orleans, helping mold a class of physicians with shared knowledge and experiences, ready to interpret and reshape the region's medical landscape. Likewise, while not all in operation concurrently, during the antebellum era, New Orleans was home to three medical journals: *Southern Medical Reports* (*SMR*), the *New Orleans Medical and Surgical Journal* (*NOMSJ*), and the *New Orleans Medical News and Hospital Gazette.* Physicians in the lower Mississippi River valley, like the rest of the southern medical profession, were in the first throes of a move to professionalize. In the introduction to the first volume of his journal *SMR* in 1849, New Orleans physician-reformer Erasmus Darwin Fenner captured the feeling of professionalization among physicians in New Orleans and the rest of the South.

Many historians depict this movement—often called State's Rights Medicine—as a medical enunciation of southern nationalism during the lead-up to the Civil War. Instead, Fenner explained, "In our earnest endeavors to arouse the ambition and energies of Southern Physicians, far be from us the desire to see developed any *sectional feeling* beyond the strict proprieties of a laudable competition." The leading reformers in the area, often educated in the North or Europe, hoped to modernize the local profession, not create a medical confederacy. Fenner even described southern practitioners as "indebted to our brethren of the Northern States and of Europe."[5]

Mississippi River valley plantations were simultaneously different from and similar to plantations in the rest of the South. The region's complicated relationship to the rest of the South was particularly true in the case of health and medicine. The most obvious unique feature of the lower Mississippi River valley was sugarcane planting, yet many of the injuries of sugar planting resembled those of other southern plantations. Likewise, the main diseases of the lower Mississippi River valley plantations, including malaria, dysentery, and cholera, were common throughout the South, as were injuries related to hard labor. These plantations of the lower Mississippi River valley, however, were connected directly to New Orleans, the most active port in the South, thus making them highly susceptible to pandemics. In short, the lower Mississippi River valley represented a heightened version of the negative symptoms of the plantation system's connections to global commerce.[6]

An examination of the material and imagined features of plantations' health landscapes underscores the degree to which various aspects of nineteenth-century capitalism, including global trade, industrialization, and the creation of race as science, deeply affected the plantations of the lower Mississippi River valley. The plantation represented both a physical and metaphorical landscape of health. First, on the metaphorical side, just as they responded to the illnesses common to plantations, physicians enunciated biological theories of racial difference and the health relationship of enslaved laborers to the plantation landscape. They argued that enslaved African descendants were created for the labor and environment of sugar and cotton plantations, were improved physically and morally through hard work, were naturally comfortable in sweltering heat, and were immune to the worst of local scourges. Moreover, these ideas emerging on plantations inspired many problematic racial concepts in twentieth-century tropical medicine, physical anthropology, and genetics. All the while, by arguing for white supremacy, physicians marketed their profession by responding to the need for new defenses of slavery. However, the reality of sick and debilitated enslaved laborers constantly undermined this imaginary landscape of healthy, happy workers, forcefully revealing the brutal reality of plantation health and enslavers' roles in creating an unhealthy environment. In treating enslaved laborers, physicians managed the "natural" landscape, treating snakebites and nonindigenous epidemics. Moreover, changes to the land and global trade contributed to the development of the worst illnesses on local plantations, as few of these diseases were indigenous to the Americas. Finally, throughout the first half of the nineteenth century, physicians contended with the ailments of an increasingly industrialized plantation, one with large machinery and overworked bodies. Physicians also dealt with gynecological and maternal ailments related to intense reproduction quotas. In total, physicians in the lower Mississippi River valley battled the diseases inherent to the physical landscape and large-scale agriculture, but they also engaged in a national debate over the rectitude of slavery, commerce, and the future role of African Americans in the United States republic. In this sense, many medical professionals understood the success of the lower Mississippi River valley's diseased plantations as married to the health of African Americans. Finally, the lenses of health and medicine work to reorient popular perceptions of plantation landscapes more generally. Attention to enslaved people's health and how such was affected by enslavers' efforts to modernize their agricultural systems and commercial integration provides a damning blow to popular historical memory's association of the plantation landscape with the architecture of the big house. Rather the features of the plantation landscape that most readily defined the material existence of most of the plantation's residents were sites of labor and commerce, and these sites had profound, negative health effects on the bodies of the enslaved workers who populated plantation landscapes.[7]

RACIAL SCIENCE, MARKETING MEDICINE, AND THE PLANTATION LANDSCAPE

Just as the means of production were mechanizing on lower Mississippi River valley plantations in the first half of the nineteenth-century, physicians in New Orleans and elsewhere were redefining race. Not just a proslavery plot, ethnologists, also known as racial scientists, held professorships in elite universities throughout the United States and Europe. As evidence of this national trend, in his 1857 thesis, Tully S. Gibson, a Mississippi medical student studying at the University of Pennsylvania, argued for polygenesis, that is, that each "race" was a separate species. Rather than just making science speak to the crass needs of slaveholders, Gibson believed his ideas put him on the Academy's intellectual forefront. Mississippi medical students such as Gibson served as an important reminder of the mobility of physicians in the lower Mississippi River valley. While many were educated in New Orleans, many others traveled elsewhere for their education. Deeply influenced by the famous Swiss naturalist and Harvard professor Louis Agassiz (1807–1873), Gibson argued that God had created each race separately. Like other species of animals, God suited each race for the specific climate and geography where they were first formed. Thus, Black people were created in and for the tropics. According to polygenists, this initial choice by God shaped the course of Black health and labor for eternity. Gibson explained, "A black skin seems best suited for a hot climate; and for this reason, we may suppose that a special creation of black races took place in Africa. The strictly white race live mostly in the temperate zone, where they flourish best; and they certainly deteriorate physically and mentally when transferred to a hot climate." Gibson continued, "The Negro, like the Lion and the Elephant, though he may live in other latitudes thrives best in hot countries." As the sugar and cotton plantations of the lower Mississippi River valley were some of the hottest and most humid in the United States, these arguments rang particularly true for local physicians. Moreover, like many other contemporary doctors, Gibson understood health as rooted in deep questions about the origins of the human races. In these discourses, each race could only remain in optimal health in their native environment, and the subtropical plantations of the Mississippi River were an ideal space for white and Black people, blending the torpid with the temperate (fig. 1).[8]

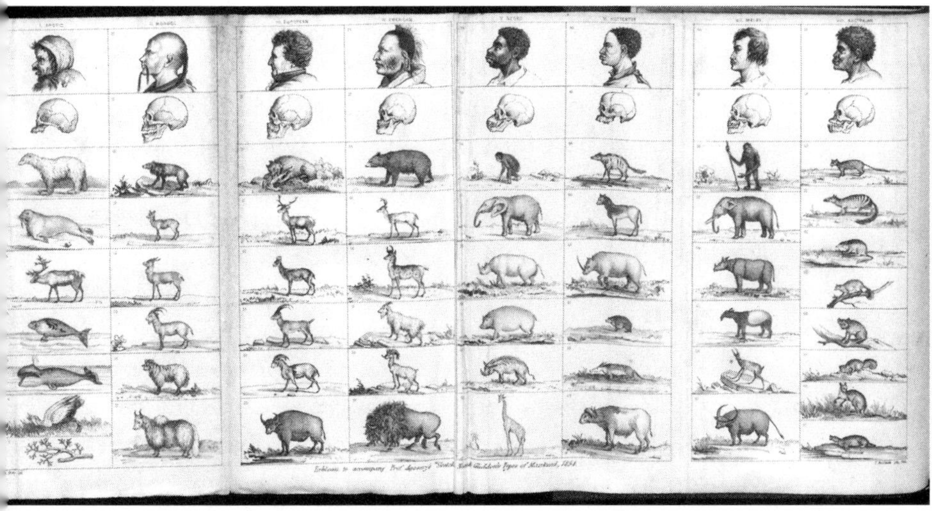

Figure 1. *Natural Provinces of the Animal World and Their Relation to the Different Types of Man,* by Louis Agassiz. This image is meant to illustrate how each human race along with other animals was created for specific climates and regions. From *Types of Mankind,* ed. George Gliddon and Josiah Nott (Philadelphia: Lippincott, Grambo, & Co., 1854), plate LXXVII.

Proslavery politicians used these scientific positions to their advantage. When seceding from the Union in January 1861, Mississippi's representatives sounded eerily like Gibson and other physicians of the period. Specifically, the Mississippi Secession convention asserted that both African bodies and the local cash crops were built for warm weather. As Gibson and Mississippi's leaders evidenced, in Mississippi and Louisiana, antebellum medical, political, and racial worldviews were connected deeply.[9]

Through medical defenses of slavery, physicians marketed themselves as indispensable to the slaveholding elite. While physicians certainly lent their expertise to the proslavery cause, the forms that their arguments took were more complicated than doctors merely bending science to the political needs of Mississippi River enslavers, not to mention enslavers in much of the rest of the South. Instead, changes in proslavery theory tracked alongside the medical profession's evolving beliefs about health and climate. Gibson wrote his thesis at the University of Pennsylvania, far from the radical secessionists who led Mississippi, Gibson's home. Yet, Gibson's northern professors schooled him on the supposed biological meaning of race and its connection to climate. Josiah Nott and Samuel Morton, two of the most influential ethnologists of the period, served as professors at the Medical University of Louisiana (now Tulane University) and the Pennsylvania Medical College. Likewise, less famous but still prominent ethnological writers such as Charles Caldwell (Transylvania University and University of Louisville), James Lawrence Cabell (University of Virginia), and Jeffries Wyman (Hampton Sydney College and Harvard University) all held positions at medical schools. Just these few examples covered medical schools in states including Alabama, Kentucky, Louisiana, Pennsylvania, Virginia, and Massachusetts. The link between the national medical profession and the production of racial science was simply profound, a fact that has often been overlooked in favor of a focus on racial science and the proslavery movement. Moreover, historian Mark Harrison has noted that during this same period, British colonial physicians in India were beginning to see Indians' bodies as inherently linked to the local climate, evidencing the global appeal of these medical constructs of race. While slavery and empire certainly influenced medical thinking, the same was true of the corollary. In defending slavery, local physicians used widely accepted medical theories to depict racial difference.[10]

In the first half of the nineteenth century, physicians in southern Louisiana and Mississippi formulated theories of race and its connections to the land as a part of a larger effort to professionalize and legitimize the medical trade. Following the increasingly capitalistic nature of local plantation society, physicians even saw racial expertise as a route to gaining legitimacy and, by extension, customers. The medical ideas undergirding slavery in Louisiana, Mississippi, and much of the rest of the South were shaped through a larger set of global processes, such as changes in medical theory internationally, the emergence of a medical print culture, and global networks of trade. Understanding the local history of race and medicine in the lower Mississippi River valley, then, requires considering a set of changes taking place around the world. The global influence of the belief that African descendants were biologically suited for hard labor in hot weather highlighted how racial theorists and physicians local to southern Mississippi and Louisiana utilized improved transportation, communication, and print technologies to gather and disseminate ideas. While physicians in south Louisiana and Mississippi lived a life often defined by their local communities, they also were connected deeply to intellectual networks that spanned the world through medical journalism.

Another important piece of this story is how physicians in the lower Mississippi River valley claimed expertise over the Black psyche. Speaking to the needs of local cotton and sugarcane planters, doctors argued that they were not only experts on the diseases of plantation landscapes, but they were also supposed experts on African descendants' minds. Medical journalism allowed for local experiences to be distributed widely among the profession and incorporated into a larger cannon of evidence and ideas. And as much as local racism shaped medical practice in the lower Mississippi River valley, medical training and internationally prominent professors influenced the racial basis of local proslavery thought.

It was through the dual prism of local and global scientific communities that physicians such as Tully S. Gibson of Vicksburg and others shaped their notions of race and the plantation. During the last two decades of the antebellum era, *NOMSJ* printed two book reviews that highlighted how a larger national and transnational conversation about race, health, and the environment influenced local medical practice and racial ideas. First, in 1848, William Martin Berry or "W. M. B." reviewed George B. Wood's two-volume tome *A Treatise on the Practice of Medicine.* By this period, Wood was the highly influential Professor of the Theory and Practice of Medicine at the University of Pennsylvania, the nation's leading medical program. Largely uninterested in race, Wood geared his text toward a medical audience, one more absorbed in general practice than the politics of slavery. But that did not mean that Wood never mentioned race, and in his review, W. M. B. honed in on a single passage from Wood's text that suited local needs. W. M. B. quoted Wood:

> It is a singular fact, that the negro, though not entirely exempt from miasmatic fever, is much less liable to it, and when attacked, suffers less from it,

> as a general rule, than the white. Hence the coast of Africa, which is so fatal to persons of our color, is favorable to the negro; and the latter lives and works in the rice fields of Carolina, at a season when a single night spent among them would be fatal to his master.[11]

Wood trained thousands of physicians—hundreds from Mississippi and Louisiana alone—during his tenure at the University of Pennsylvania from 1835 to 1860, and this passage evidenced the mutual influence of medicine and racial thought throughout the nation. In the actual text, Wood also noted his belief that people of African descent were inherently predisposed to tetanus. Wood displayed how racial difference was in many ways an unquestioned aspect of medical thinking, and W. M. B. highlighted the hunger of lower Mississippi River valley physicians to see concepts of ingrained racial difference being adopted by the wider profession. This review evidenced how medical constructions of race were influenced by a broad array of forces, and while geographically remote from the United States' scientific capital of Philadelphia, local physicians in the lower Mississippi River valley were connected to an expansive library of thinkers through medical journals. While local practice inspired racial approaches to yellow fever and malaria, these ideas were broadly accepted and reproduced throughout the medical profession. While physicians across the United States learned racial medicine as part of their schooling, physicians from slaveholding states incorporated experiential knowledge from local practice into their racial worldview. Conversely, physicians in the lower Mississippi River valley, such as Samuel Cartwright, regularly published essays in medical journals in the North.[12]

Racial theorists from Europe also influenced medical thinking in the lower Mississippi River valley. In 1851, *NOMSJ* published a review of the Scottish anatomist Robert Knox's polygenist text *The Races of Men: A Fragment.* Knox (1791–1862) was a widely read anatomist whose career was marred by his involvement in the Burke and Hare murders in Edinburgh in the late 1820s. In his review, "W. H. P." generally praised Knox's text, seeing many of the Scottish author's racial beliefs as transferrable to the United States. Specifically, W. H. P. confirmed Knox's trust in the superiority of pure races. Speaking "from observation and ample experience," W. H. P. added, "every planter prefers a jet-black negro for enduring service." Bringing this evidence, W. H. P. bolstered Knox's ideas with commonly held local belief. Knox's text applied to the local context because his work spoke to the primacy of race and the fitness of Africans for hot climates. He also added European legitimacy to ideas most often associated with slave-state physicians. While Knox more often focused on disparaging the Irish than discussing plantation slavery or even colonization in Africa or India, W. H. P. believed Knox's framework was relevant to plantations along the Mississippi River. As with local plantation practitioners, British imperial physicians conceptualizing race and the expansion of the British Empire considered there to be some limits on the mobility of each race because of climate. While W. H. P. disagreed with Knox on some points, he firmly recommended *The Races of Men,* asserting that it "should be in the library of every physician." These reviews shed light on the deep interconnections between the south Louisiana medical profession and the wider world. In addition to everyday practice, racial ideas about the plantation were shaped through an emerging medical print culture wherein local authors influenced the European and national medical programs and vice versa. Just as with the lived experience of plantation health, medical theories of race were molded by the same forces of exchange that imported diseases, underscoring that, in the first half of the nineteenth century, global exchanges in ideas and pathogens shaped local medical practice.[13]

While physicians of the lower Mississippi River valley existed within Atlantic intellectual networks, they also produced their own scholarship on race and the plantation environment. In the same year as the review of Knox, *NOMSJ* and *SMR* published New Orleans physician Samuel Cartwright's famous "Report on the Diseases and Physical Peculiarities of the Negro Race." Before moving to New Orleans in 1848, Cartwright had spent much of his adult life in Natchez. The "Report" came out of Cartwright's work as the Chairman of the Medical Association of Louisiana's committee "meant to investigate the diseases and peculiarities of our Negro population." While Cartwright depicted African Americans as anatomically, physiologically, and psychologically suited for slavery, he also argued that maintaining their health required a deft hand in shaping the plantation environment. In his discussion of pulmonary ailments, Cartwright mixed environmental determinism with common sense. On the determinist side, Cartwright noted that "the negro's lungs . . . are very sensitive to the impressions of cold weather." Despite this racist gloss, in this case, Cartwright's actual advice to enslavers was sound, prescribing well-insulated quarters, ample blankets, and readily available firewood. That Cartwright had to include this diction about well-built quarters and extra supplies during winter meant that some enslavers did not provide adequate shelter for the enslaved. Returning to racial determinism, Cartwright asserted his belief that African descendants were exceptionally vulnerable to gastrointestinal ailments. Evidencing the influence of climatic determinism on the etiology of local ailments, Cartwright explained that he had "never seen a negro die with black vomit," which was the mostly clearly identifiable symptom of yellow fever. Through discussion of pneumonia, gastrointestinal diseases, and yellow fever, Cartwright depicted the health of the plantation as at the behest of supposed racial peculiarities of African Americans and their treatment by enslavers. While enslaved people supposedly survived warm weather diseases such as yellow fever, they were particularly vulnerable to winter ailments. The opposite was true of whites. And as much as Cartwright was representative of the extremes of the racial-determinist wing of medical approaches to the plantation, even he contended that slaveowners who neglected the conditions of enslaved workers were responsible for their ill health. Cartwright clearly enunciated a supposed expertise of physicians when it came to slave management. Coming out of the local professional organizations' standing committee, "The Report" unveiled local physicians' desire to colonize racial knowledge as their own, making the physician indispensable to the enslaver regime.[14]

Beyond managing the health of enslaved workers, physicians also played a role in regulating their behavior, which also was defined by their supposedly innate dispositions. The most famous enunciation of this impulse was Cartwright's slave diseases that he argued caused enslaved workers to run away, behave poorly, or become depressed. While little evidence exists to support the notion that Cartwright's diagnoses were widely adopted, during this period physicians began to see advice on plantation management as a key portion of their practice. Echoing authors like Cartwright, Medical College of the State of South Carolina student R. McMillan asserted in 1843 that it was in the enslavers' best interests to provide enslaved workers with a healthy diet and treat them well, while encouraging "cheerfulness and good humor." McMillan argued that enslaved people should be permitted to dance and frolic at night. In McMillan's racist worldview, a happy slave was a healthy slave, and if allowed these privileges, enslaved workers were "not so prone to fall sick." McMillan advised restraint among enslavers while he reinforced the delusional image of the plantation as the residence of joyful forced laborers. Writings by students such as McMillan serve as a reminder that while Cartwright and others wrote for the lower Mississippi River valley medical profession, they also engaged in a wider conversation among their colleagues encompassing the entire South. Thus, understanding the local medical culture on antebellum lower Mississippi River plantations requires looking beyond just local doctors, enslavers, and medical institutions but instead examining local physicians' connections to a national and international profession.[15]

Local physicians also believed that controlling the "peculiar" emotional state of enslaved people during illness was central to treating them. In an 1850 article in *NOMSJ* on treating cholera, the author noted that it was important to treat slaves psychologically during epidemics, as "cholera creates a panic, which powerfully predisposes them to the disease." Cartwright made a similar point in his 1850s writings on cholera and dysentery. Beyond the specific therapeutics, the importance of these ideas resided in how they reinforced physicians' control over enslaved workers' minds and bodies, while at the same time doctors bolstered their claims to being experts on racial differences.[16]

While ideas about race, psychology, and disease were hardly universal among American physicians, doctors during this period strove, but often failed, to create a shared medical enunciation of a supposedly ingrained Black psyche. Thus, even within the lower Mississippi River valley, doctors disagreed about the best manner in which to treat the bodies and minds of African Americans. Contrasting with Cartwright, Dr. William A. Booth, writing about cholera in Bayou Lafourche for *NOMSJ,* argued that the problem was not the effects of panic but rather apathy toward obtaining treatment. Where the anonymous author in *NOMSJ* depicted enslaved workers as frightened children in need of management, Booth described enslaved people as only seeking treatment for cholera due to enslavers' compulsions. According to Booth, "all negroes are fatalists, and this fact renders the idea that they are scared into cholera perfectly ridiculous. *The worse it rages, the less they regard it.*" Booth, McMillan, and Cartwright highlighted how constructing a modernized conception of racial difference based in science and medicine was more a goal than a completed project. These antebellum physicians laid the foundation for Jim Crow and eugenics era physicians to claim authority on racial difference.[17]

When theorizing about disease and racial difference on the plantation, physicians in the lower Mississippi River valley utilized local observational experience and internationally influential racial science. Through these prisms, physicians constructed an image of African descendants' bodies as inherently fit for slavery. While antebellum doctors claimed that people of African descent might be more susceptible to cholera and pneumonia than whites, they also asserted that people of African descent were, supposedly, biologically protected from the worst plantation scourges of malaria and yellow fever. Nevertheless, even overtly proslavery theorists such as Samuel Cartwright argued for slaveowners' responsibility to provide for enslaved workers. However, by connecting enslaved people's bodies to certain diseases, physicians more often than not alleviated enslavers' responsibilities for the high mortality rates among the enslaved. In Cartwright and others' frame, unclean and overcrowded quarters were only part of the problem, as they believed African descendants' biology increased enslaved people's likelihood of contracting cholera. Likewise, depressed and morbid enslaved people were allegedly not reacting reasonably to harsh conditions and deadly diseases. Instead some physicians contended that enslaved people were either innately irrational or predisposed to morbidity.

The need to create such diagnoses seemed to contradict the paternalist depictions of enslaved adults as joyful children. As is true of all racial ideologies, antebellum racial medicine was rife with contradiction. African descendants' bodies were ideally suited for the plantation, yet supposedly predisposed to plantation ailments such as pneumonia, typhoid fever, and dysentery. Enslaved workers were built for plantation labor and contented when treated well, yet they were a depressed and morbid lot. While racial medicine was constructed beyond the immediate needs of the local slave system, it contained many of the same contradictions as typical defenses of slavery. As a result, physicians around the world had embraced seemingly delusional constructions of racial difference emerging from imperial and enslaver medical discourses. The racial constructs of the lower Mississippi River valley were part of international trends, and these local physicians had allies in Philadelphia, Edinburgh, and Bombay (Mumbai). As with the importation of diseases and incorporation of machinery, antebellum plantation medicine was a part of a larger shift taking place around the world. Instead of a plantation outside of time, the health landscapes, both imagined and real, of the lower Mississippi River valley were modernizing.

CONNECTING THE LOCAL AND GLOBAL ECONOMIES

In May of 1847, a tornado blew through the town of Woodville, Mississippi, located just north of the Louisiana border and about forty miles east of the

Mississippi River. The storm "prostrated much timber" and destroyed homes. Not just a blight on the environment, built and natural, according to a local physician, the storm also "crippled some negroes." Writing to *NOMSJ,* Woodville's local physician "A. R. K." gave stunning insights into the practice of a rural physician in the lower Mississippi River valley. The local health problems, caused by disease, disaster, and labor, were myriad. Just the month before in April, A. R. K. cared for an enslaved infant with hydrocephalus. A. R. K. noted the child's symptoms of fever, constipation, and convulsions before the child ultimately perished from the condition. After death, the doctor conducted an autopsy on the infant's corpse, diagnosing the disease. A. R. K.'s short letter highlighted the complex task of the plantation physician, especially one invested in professional improvement. In examining the child postmortem and reporting about the health of his town to a medical journal, A. R. K. displayed his investment in improving medical practice. Pathological anatomy and medical journalism along with medical schools were the hallmarks of the antebellum American medical profession's attempts to make their understanding of diseases more rigorous and universal. By reacting to national trends of modernization, physicians in the lower Mississippi River valley grappled with the health problems of a landscape defined by expansion into new and uncleared terrain, as well as diseases imported through global networks of trade. In short, even when treating ailments created by the natural world, such as storms, snakebites, and parasitic illnesses, physicians like A. R. K. wrestled with the health effects of modernity and global capitalism.[18]

The health of the plantation was produced by the interactions between humans and the natural world. While it can be tempting to conceptualize disease, floods, and animal attacks as outside the realm of human agency, interventions in the physical landscape, such as clearing of land and controlling of waterways for cotton and sugar production, shaped local health outcomes. The relationships between human agency and ill health were most apparent in the importation of "southern" diseases. While often physically distant from the great port cities of the South, southern plantations were tied intimately to an increasingly transnational form of capitalism that inextricably linked them through commerce to a whole host of diseases. Nowhere was this larger southern trend more obvious than in the plantations lining the Mississippi River. Close to New Orleans, the South's largest and most diseased port for much of the period, local plantations were struck regularly by global pandemics.

Furthermore, plantations in the lower Mississippi River valley represented the advanced front of enslavers' push westward into environments susceptible to "natural" disasters. Through trade networks and expansion, plantations suffered the health problems of both metropolitan ports and rural outposts.[19]

Plantations were complex biomedical landscapes, defined by reshaping the land for agriculture, yet they also constantly abutted forest. In *Twelve Years a Slave,* Solomon Northup's narrative of slavery in south-central Louisiana, he noted just such a relationship. After an attack from the plantation overseer Tibeats, Northup fled the plantation, yet no sooner found himself in another form of danger. During his flight, Northup regularly confronted bayou "monsters" such as alligators and water moccasins, an indigenous poisonous snake. Describing the local swamps and forests, Northup stated,

> For thirty or forty miles it is without inhabitants, save wild beasts—the bear, the wild-cat, the tiger, and great slimy reptiles, that are crawling through it everywhere. Long before I reached the bayou, in fact, from the time I struck the water until I emerged from the swamp on my return, these reptiles surrounded me. I saw hundreds of moccasin snakes. Every log and bog—every trunk of a fallen tree, over which I was compelled to step or climb, was alive with them.

Northup's story highlighted how the plantation represented an outpost of enslaver rule. Bordering on uncleared forest, Northup's flight from the plantation carried its own dangers. Likewise, Northup's account displayed how African descendants that escaped slavery shaped national understandings of Louisiana's plantation environments.[20]

In 1831, a medical student from outside Charleston, South Carolina, reinforced this intimacy between plantation and natural world further, reporting four different cases of snakebites on enslaved people and two on dogs in his neighborhood. The student described the symptoms of an enslaved child bitten on the thumb by a water moccasin. The child's entire arm became swollen, suffering considerable pain, and the symptoms lasted for days. The proximity to wildlife represented a day-to-day aspect of health on the plantation. Even though the local poisonous serpents were rarely deadly, they disrupted the labor and rhythm of plantation life. While far from Louisiana or Mississippi, this student's account, combined with Northup's testimony, highlight how snakebites were most likely a common medical problem on Mississippi River plantations and in the surrounding bayous.[21]

Like other floodplain agricultural societies, the need in this region to control the Mississippi River's flow for agricultural purposes seriously threatened the health of people and animals on local plantations. In 1850, physician Andrew R. Kilpatrick of Trinity, Louisiana (located in Concordia Parish, west of Natchez), complained that when the Mississippi's levees broke that year, it caused devastation. During the flood, thousands of "cattle, hogs, sheep and horses are starved to death or drowned." That year, Kilpatrick also treated intestinal worms, measles, and the global pandemic of cholera that had reached the town. For the small town of Trinity and its surrounding plantations, Kilpatrick noted, "1850 will be long held in memory as one pregnant with misfortune."[22]

On a similar note, disease influenced the built landscape through shaping commercial and residential patterns. Historians of medicine, the environment, and the South have given considerable attention to the histories of yellow fever and malaria. In many ways, this stems from these illnesses' deep ties to the slave trade. Both emerged early on as forces for change in the South and other parts of the Americas. For example, malaria certainly played a significant role in decimating certain Native American communities. Likewise, yellow fever became a regular scourge in New Orleans until the end of the nineteenth century, regularly disrupting both commerce and community.[23]

Because of yellow fever, some physicians even called for quarantining the port (a regular point of debate during nineteenth-century epidemics), which would halt trade, an untenable option for many in the region. Unlike *Anopheles* mosquitoes' preference for the rural environment, *Aedes aegypti* were urbanites. As environmental historian Urmi Engineer Willoughby explains, *Aedes aegypti* "seem to have a unique preference for man-made containers," and they "can breed in any crevice holding a small amount of water, causing them to prefer urban environments." Complaining of the importation of yellow fever into his small hamlet Petit Gulf Hills (located just north of Natchez) in 1853, physician A. P. Jones pushed for quarantine, citing his belief that this urban disease had traveled up the Mississippi River from New Orleans to his town, killing thirty people "of all ages, sexes and colors." Jones noted that the spread of yellow fever into the country would become only worse with the construction of more railroad tracks in the region, a prophecy that came true in the terrible epidemic of 1878. Despite yellow fever and malaria's central position in the region's health history, other diseases provided different lessons about the modernization of Mississippi River plantations and their deep imbrication in global trade.[24]

Like malaria and yellow fever, cholera revealed the deep embeddedness of plantations in the structure of the global economy. Cholera pandemics served as a reminder that globalization during this period had a profound health effect. In the early nineteenth century, American physicians diagnosed many different gastrointestinal ailments as cholera, but the disease that contemporary physicians classify as cholera often was referred to as "Asiatic" cholera due to its perceived Asian origin. In 1832–33 and 1848–49, the United States, like much of the rest of the world, suffered greatly from cholera pandemics. While physicians during this period often saw cholera as the product of the local environment or personal sin, the disease was undoubtedly imported in the bowels of agents of commerce.[25]

In the 1849 volume of *SMR,* two physicians' essays revealed the bacteria's spread throughout the region. Writing about cholera in St. Mary's Parish, local physician James B. Duncan asserted that few whites were struck by the disease, but it took an "erratic course" through the plantations, with one plantation "loosing ten or twelve slaves" while its neighbor remained unscathed. Reporting on cholera in one plantation near Natchez, physician C. H. Stone noted that "among 239 negroes, 129 were attacked, of whom fourteen grown ones and nine children died," or just shy of ten percent of the enslaved population. Cholera could quickly devastate a plantation's labor force.[26]

While physicians had not yet come to understand the cause and treatment for the bacteria, and enslavers could by no means completely prevent the spread of the disease, their treatment of enslaved workers likely aided in cholera's spread. As few plantations had privies for their quarters, most enslaved residents used the woods and areas surrounding their homes to dispose of feces, making plantations highly unhygienic landscapes. Large amounts of human waste surrounded the quarters, and because enslaved people lived in overcrowded homes, diseases were passed interpersonally. On some plantations, human feces even were used as fertilizers. This made the plantation a petri dish for the growth of intestinal diseases such as dysentery, typhoid fever, and cholera. Through their use as fertilizer, cholera-laced feces could infect the soil, which might then contaminate a local stream or groundwater, causing the further spread of the bacteria. This relationship between sanitation, crowding, and the plantation landscape explains why physicians found the widespread practice of moving the enslaved out of the quarters during outbreaks of intestinal ailments beneficial. Outside of the crowded quarters, the enslaved were less likely to be exposed to the disease through interpersonal communication or consumption of tainted food, and they even might collect water from a different source. While physicians believed that they were removing slaves from a "vitiated" atmosphere, this treatment might have unintentionally limited the disease's spread.[27]

As could be seen through common ailments, the health landscape of the plantation in the lower Mississippi River valley provided a meeting space for the rural South and global commerce. Physicians had to grapple with a medical landscape shaped by global trade, proximity to swamps, and control of water. The poor health of the period often was exacerbated by obstinate enslavers, who invested little in the sanitation of their enslaved workers' homes or the best location for the disposal of the feces of a large labor force. As much as the health of south Louisiana and Mississippi was defined by seeming natural causes such as disease, animal attacks, and weather, through westward expansion, water management practices, and trade, local enslavers, due to ignorance or neglect, created many of the underlying problems that contributed to the deadliest ailments of their plantations. As attractive as it may be to remember antebellum-era plantations as stately manors, these estates were largely sites of labor and production whose main goal was to supply sugar, cotton, and other goods to a growing population of middle-class consumers in Europe and the United States. The health problems of rural plantations shared much with other parts of the nineteenth-century industrial economy, as became apparent with the introduction of large machinery to the plantation in the first half of the nineteenth century. Nowhere was this relationship truer than on the large-scale sugar and cotton plantations of the Mississippi River between Natchez and New Orleans.

OCCUPATIONAL HEALTH AND INDUSTRIAL PLANTATIONS

In addition to native snakes, periodic storms, and deadly diseases imported from around the world, physicians on plantations in the lower Mississippi River valley grappled with ailments commonly associated with industrialized labor. Throughout the antebellum era, sugar planters slowly adopted steampowered sugar mills over ox-driven predecessors. Likewise, outside of the sea-island cotton varietal planted in select environments, cotton production only became profitable after the invention of the cotton gin in 1794, serving as a literal *deus ex machina* for the Atlantic textile industry. Thus, the introduction of large machinery enacted a total transformation of the plantation economy in the lower Mississippi River valley. It fueled westward expansion for cotton planting and increased the rate of sugar production. Through adopting industrial technologies and forms of labor, enslavers also shaped the plantation landscape and its health. Historians of slavery and capitalism have emphasized how, in addition to the introduction of new machinery, enslavers sought to increase the yields of their laborers, resorting to maddening labor quotas and intense implementation of corporeal punishment. The harsh, mechanized regimes of large-scale cotton and sugar plantations created many health problems as well as new challenges for local physicians. During the antebellum period, physicians treated industrial accidents, overwork-induced debilities, and gynecological problems caused by malnutrition, working while pregnant, and excessive births. Unlike disease, injuries of efficiency required surgical solutions, a legitimate realm of innovation among antebellum physicians. The need for innovation in the mechanical and labor output on plantations thus spurred improvement in the skills of local surgeons; therefore, in terms of ailments and treatments, the mechanization of plantation agriculture modernized the health of Louisiana and Mississippi's cotton and cane worlds.[28]

Nearly every aspect of cotton production—from transporting the picked product to crop scales to ginning it—had potential to harm enslaved laborers. In his 1860 thesis on cotton, George Halsey Peets, a medical student at the University of Pennsylvania from Wilkinson County, Mississippi (located at the southwestern corner of the state, just north of the Louisiana/Mississippi border and south of Adams County), detailed the backbreaking process of cotton production in the lower Mississippi River valley. Enslaved laborers first planted cotton in April, and the crop became available for picking in August. In the process, enslaved laborers risked life and limb each year to bring the cotton crop to market. The picking season lasted for months, sometimes going from August into December. Daily, laborers were expected to pick an average of 200 pounds of cotton, emptying their baskets twice a day, at noon and night. In short, enslavers demanded high yields and hard work, leading to many occupational injuries. Agricultural journalist Thomas Affleck of Washington, Mississippi (just east of Natchez), explained in *SMR* that the process of carrying picked cotton from the field to the scales represented one of the most dangerous activities during production. Affleck became famous in the South for his pioneering *Plantation Record and Account Book* which, quickly after its publication in the late 1840s, revolutionized how enslavers managed their slaves. Affleck's influence among enslavers was evidenced by the wide reprinting of his articles and the many editions printed of his account book.

In the process of picking cotton, the enslaved, Affleck described, wielded upon their heads "a load of 100 to 150 pounds pressing upon the skull, neck and back-bone, [and] when the muscles are relaxed by fatigue, [it] cannot but be injurious." The seemingly simple act of picking, packing, and carrying cotton caused serious injury on plantations. By weighing the cotton daily, enslavers also could gauge an expected yield for each hand, and certainly, if these quotas were not met regularly, the enslaved could expect some form of corporeal punishment. Like sugar production, cotton slavery demanded brutal, physical labor. From carrying mammoth loads to stooping to the plant's buds, many enslaved workers must have managed spinal and back injuries due to the means of cotton production.[29]

In addition to ailing backs, shoulders, and necks, malnutrition and the harsh labor regimes of enslavement abetted in the creation of significant gynecological ailments. Compounding on their roles as laborers in the house and/or field, enslaved women also were responsible for birthing slaves and as many as possible. Historian Deborah Kuhn McGregor explains, "By the early nineteenth century, slave women were clearly recognized as so-called breeders." Like cotton and sugar, enslavers understood enslaved people to be one of their most valuable commodities. While enslavers never possessed total control over slave reproduction, the need for more enslaved workers coupled with high infant-mortality rates meant that enslavers certainly encouraged women to birth many children during their lifetime, with only a fraction surviving. Unsurprisingly, enslaved women experienced high rates of complications to their pregnancies. Historian Deirdre Cooper Owens even notes that the Haitian émigré-surgeon François-Marie Prevost "pioneered" the cesarean section surgery "in Louisiana solely on enslaved women." While tempting to view complicated births as simply resulting from the poor state of medicine or ignorance, enslavers' neglect of nutrition and aggressive promotion of enslaved reproduction played a significant role in the rash of gynecological ailments on plantations.[30]

Gynecological complaints resulting from multiple or difficult pregnancies such as vesico-vaginal fistulas and prolapsed uteri were tied deeply to the combined rigors of slavery and maternity. Vesico-vaginal fistula is a tearing in the vaginal wall, thereby causing general incontinence. Sufferers embarrassingly could not control their urine flow, causing putrid smells and stained clothes. The sheer volume of births coupled with hard labor through the second trimester were bound to cause significant health problems, but the leading cause of fistulas was probably rickets. Caused by malnutrition, among other conditions, rickets often lead to a contracted pelvis, resulting in protracted and strenuous births. In short, gynecological ailments could not be solely chalked up to a society with a poor understanding of diseases and health. Instead, inattention to diet, hard labor, and too many pregnancies certainly contributed to the rash of humiliating fistulas on plantations. Fistulas also highlighted the circular relationship between ill health and surgical innovation. J. Marion Sims of Alabama perfected a surgical cure for vaginal fistulas during this period, conducting dozens of painful, experimental surgeries on enslaved women before successfully curing the injury in 1849. Thus, physicians were a necessary feature of the plantation landscape, and their business was increased by the negative health outcomes that resulted from enslaved people's poor treatment. Moreover, Sims became a famous and ultimately wealthy physician through perfecting his surgical fix for fistulas, made possible by the high rates of their incidence on plantations.[31]

Controlling reproductive labor also represented a point of enslaved women's expertise and ingenuity. Pregnant enslaved women unwilling to birth a child into bondage used an "infusion" of cotton seed oil to induce abortions. Enslaved women's knowledge of and skill in producing these herbal abortive concoctions drew attention to long streams in African diasporic medical and intellectual history. Enslaved healers, herbalists, and midwives had a profound (if less visible) impact on the health cultures of many southern plantations.[32]

In reporting on local ailments in his practice in St. James Parish, Louisiana, physician L. Lefevere reported a case of stillbirth, in which rickets almost certainly contributed to the infant's death. Attending to a birth overseen by a Dr. Bernard, Lefevere noted that the child could not be saved due to the size of the child's head and "the diminished size of the pelvis."

In this same period of practice, Lefevere conducted a cesarean and treated a case of a swollen uterus. Like other classes of ailments on local plantations, gynecological complaints represented a mix of both foreseeable and unforeseeable consequences. They were also the result of a capitalistic plantation society that valued Black women's bodies both for their manual and reproductive labor.[33]

Like injuries caused by childbirth and overwork, the needs of efficiency and high agricultural yields led to industrial accidents. Once the cotton had been dried it would be ginned, making it marketable but exposing enslaved workers to health problems resulting from the mechanical process. The cotton gin was essential to the profitability of cotton production. As Peets, the medical student from Wilkinson County, explained, before the gin, "the seeds were separated from the limb or fibre, by means of the fingers, which was a most tedious process." Much of the westward expansion of this period is clearly attributed to the gin's invention in 1794, as before that the labor costs were simply too high to make the crop profitable. The gin spread quickly to the plantations of the lower Mississippi River valley, and local mechanics continually improved upon the machine throughout this period. In Wilkinson County in 1795, Peets explained, an enslaved mechanic built the area's first gin at the behest of a local enslaver. This anecdote serves as a reminder that when forced to by profit motives, enslavers saw their enslaved laborers as highly skilled components of the plantation economy. By 1860, enslaved workers using a gin could remove the seeds from four to six bales per day, each bale representing 400 pounds of seedless cotton. Cotton gins were powerful machines. They transformed the regional (and global) economy, universally making cotton a viable cash crop along with sugar. They also caused significant industrial accidents, creating hosts of enslaved people with disabilities.[34]

Also worth noting, while sugar had long been a viable cash crop in the Latin American tropics and the Caribbean, its wide cultivation in Louisiana came about almost simultaneous to the rise of cotton. Widespread sugar cultivation was primarily the result of the successful granulation of sugar in New Orleans in 1795 by Jean Étienne de Boré, who was also the first mayor of New Orleans after the Louisiana Purchase. Thus, the American sugar industry, like cotton, relied on industrial and mechanical innovation for its success.[35]

Physicians commonly amputated or operated on smashed or shredded limbs, all the while improving their technique. Discussing the frequency of ginning accidents in his 1857 medical thesis at the Medical College of the State of South Carolina, J. A. Hewell of Tuscaloosa, Alabama, noted, "We can scarcely find a cotton plantation of any size but has one or more 'hands' maimed by one of these machines, most generally, too, by the loss of a finger, hand, or forearm." Hewell went on to assert that amputations related to industrial accidents provided for "nine tenths of the surgical practice" of plantation physicians. Following these broader statements, Hewell examined a case that had occurred in New Prospect, a town in north-central Mississippi, where a ten-year-old enslaved child "got his hand caught" in the gin, the claws then pulling in his arm up to the humerus and slashing the child's chest. Hewell's description of the child's limb was nothing short of lurid. The gin cut "his fingers literally to pieces, diving through and through the palm of the hand injuring the metacarpal bones, injuring the wrist slightly, but tearing the skin from three fourths the circumference of the fore arm for its whole length, splitting the muscles into thin, slender strips, cutting into the bones at many points." Hewell's thesis drew attention to important yet often forgotten features of antebellum plantations, the health effects of industrialized labor and the proximity of children to these machines. Numerous other examples abound of the harmful effects of cotton production on children and mothers on the plantation. On a cotton plantation in south Alabama in 1845, a daughter of an enslaver died by being crushed by a bale of cotton while playing hide-and-seek. While Hewell's examples occurred in western Alabama and central Mississippi, it is safe to assume that similar accidents occurred on the cotton plantations of the lower Mississippi River valley. Likewise, Hewell's lurid prose captured the sheer horror of these accidents, creating a poignant reminder that plantations were primarily busy workplaces rather than peaceful residences, and the labor regimes of Mississippi River cash crop plantations posed profound health risks to the enslaved workers as well as nonenslaved residents.[36]

In many ways, plantations were unique in their tripartite landscape of impoverished residences of the enslaved, labor camps, and estates of the wealthy. The brutal reality of the injuries of cotton production acted as a stark juxtaposition to the stately big houses of the region. Underneath these towering homes, enslaved laborers were brutalized by the daily grind of cotton production and its reliance on both human strength and mechanical innovation. In short, the ill health of plantation labor coupled with enslavers' wealth created a landscape rife with contrasts and serves to remind that geography and types of labor wrought significant health determinants in the antebellum lower Mississippi River valley.[37]

Industrialization had a similar effect on local sugar plantations, maiming the enslaved yet offering gruesome opportunities to improve physicians' amputation techniques. Historian Richard Follett explains, "The constantly moving cane carrier and flywheels required highly attentive workers to keep an ever-watchful eye on the turning belts and spinning gears that raced along at breakneck speed." Moreover, historian Sasha Turner notes that the design of these new steam sugar mills increased the likelihood of accidents (fig. 2). During this period, plantation laborers became accustomed to both agricultural and industrial labor, while suffering the injuries and ailments of both. In a letter to *NOMSJ,* physician R. H. D. of Pattersonville, Louisiana (now called Patterson, located on Bayou Teche in St. Mary's Parish) noted the neighborhood's general health in the winter of 1847, excepting three surgical cases, two of which were related to milling sugar. Sugar mills provided multiple dangers to limbs as can be seen in R. H. D.'s letter, which covered a mere two months of practice. In the first case, an unknown worker's hand was "caught with the cogs" and "mashed and lacerated." Given other possible outcomes, this first case was relatively mild, as R. H. D. only had to amputate the middle and index fingers. In the second injury, a presumably enslaved worker's hand became "entangled in the rollers of a sugar mill and crushed to pieces." Less fortunate than the previous patient, the worker lost his entire hand and forearm, up to above the elbow.[38]

Figure 2. Steam-powered sugar mill, c. 1830. Reproduced from *The Nature and Properties of the Sugar Cane,* by George Porter (London: Smith Elder, 1830), Rare Book Collection, LSU Libraries, Baton Rouge, LA.

Plantations were not simply genteel and paternalist estates. During their daily lives, enslavers, physicians, and enslaved workers lived or witnessed the brutal realities of industrialized agriculture. Thinking about plantation landscapes as the sum of the people, built environments, and the natural world, the mechanization of cotton and sugar production were nothing short of transformative of plantation scenery. Enslaved bodies, maimed by whippings, childbirths, malnutrition, disease, and amputations, resided on cotton and sugar plantations. The people and machines producing cash crops were a sharp contrast to the stately big houses that projected enslavers' aristocratic self-conceptions. An injured and exploited workforce populated the massive fields, gin houses, and sugar mills. Likewise, the great metal machines themselves seemed to contradict the antimodernist stance claimed by some enslavers and their self-fashioning as distinct from the industrial overlords of cities in Europe and the North.

Centering the enslaved population as a group that was overworked, malnourished, maimed by industrial machinery, and suffering from preventable ailments reminds us that not only were romanticized versions of plantation slavery inaccurate, they were also delusional. In contrast to this harsh reality of an agricultural society defined by forced labor and industrialization, physicians in Louisiana and Mississippi during this period aided in the construction of the enslaver's delusion. The physicians discussed here should serve as a reminder that doctors' imagined plantation landscapes of healthy and contented slaves existed in a sharp tension with the actual labor that physicians performed. As shown in R. H. D.'s letter to *NOMSJ,* in one sentence, a physician would praise the health of the plantation system and in the next paragraph would recount two amputations. In short, the nineteenth-century plantation's medical landscape existed at two levels, one based in material existence and the other in a mass, racial imaginary. On the first plane, the health landscape was dotted with scarred bodies, feces, malnutrition, and rundown slave quarters. In this second landscape, however, enslaved bodies were perfectly suited for the plantation's ailments, remaining a happy and contented labor force. This second landscape, rather than the first, helped southern enslavers attempt to maintain moral authority during the antebellum era as the British and French empires along with numerous independent nations in Latin America abolished slavery. This imagined estate even lingered on well into the twentieth century, infecting subsequent narratives of racial science along with plantation life and landscapes.

Yet it is in the medical landscape of plantation life, in the contradictory, even dual, planes of observation and practice by physicians of the time, that we can see a more accurate imaginary of the whole of plantation life.

In discussing infant mortality and treatment of enslaved workers in *NOMSJ,* "expert" in slave management Thomas Affleck of Washington, Mississippi, described with surprising clarity the corporeal brutality of the health norm of enslavement. Among other features, Affleck noted the startlingly high mortality rates among enslaved infants, reminding readers that natural reproduction of the slave population was contingent upon birthing a large volume of children. Affleck asserted, "The mortality of negro children is as two to one when compared with the whites, depending solely on locality and care. Quarters are often badly located; children allowed to be filthy; are suckled hurriedly." Moreover, Affleck projected that a large proportion of infants died in under ten days, and of those that survived birth, half did not make it to a year old. Another tenth of those children did not live to the age of five. As an advocate for the scientific management of plantations and a slaveowner, Affleck's class bias would have been toward depicting the plantation as an effective labor site rather than a graveyard, thus the thrust of his depiction of child mortality rang true. While *NOMSJ* often represented a factory for proslavery racial theory, medical commentators often found it difficult to keep the imagined plantation separate from the harsh reality of the lives of the enslaved in the lower Mississippi River valley.[39]

More than anything, the medical landscape of the lower Mississippi River valley was crafted through human hands and minds, and the lived landscape existed in sharp tension with the imagined plantation created by physicians. Global capitalism resided at the heart of the need to imagine the plantation as salubrious, to create transnational trade networks, and to mechanize the plantations' means of production. Colonization and global trade allowed for the importation of terrible scourges to the Americas, including malaria, yellow fever, smallpox, and cholera, to name just a few. The need for more fertile land to plant cotton and sugarcane meant plantations were always expanding into nearby woods and swamps, where the enslaved lived in dangerous environments. Through the common use of human feces for fertilizer and the almost constant existence of standing water locally, agriculture encouraged encroaching epidemics. In the service of profit and global trade networks, the lives of enslaved people were constantly at risk on the plantations dotting the banks of the Mississippi River.

Likewise, enslavers also sought to make the labor regimes of slavery more efficient and thus able to bring more crops to market. Higher yields meant harder work and more strain on the bodies of enslaved laborers. Due to late antebellum innovations like Affleck's *Plantation Record and Account Book,* enslavers could track the rate of slaves' production, using punishment to enforce efficiency. Inattention to diet, many births throughout their lives, and labor during pregnancy was a recipe for squeezing the most profit out of enslaved women as well as for high rates of gynecological complaints. On the large plantations of the lower Mississippi River valley, mechanization of crop production meant a quicker transition from planting to market as well as gruesome accidents that resulted in a workforce with many disabilities.

This brutal reality existed in a constant tension with the political need to justify slavery as healthy and humane. As the essay's opening quote from medical student J. P. Bonner illustrates, cash crops fueled the global economy as well as local profiteers, making slavery's survival a global concern. Influenced by this need for great profits, physicians aided in the construction of a fantasy plantation landscape where happy and healthy slaves lived with paternal masters. Capitalism and globalism constantly shaped the local landscape of plantations in the lower Mississippi River valley, both how it was imagined and how it was lived. At the forefront of these local responses to global trade were physicians. Using available medical knowledge and techniques, they treated global pandemics, amputated limbs, and clumsily mended genitals in order to keep the enslaved workforce productive. In undeniable tension, all the while doing the daily tasks to treat a sick society, many physicians claimed that slavery was healthy for the enslaved. Physicians worked to heal enslaved bodies, while minimizing the actual conditions that they treated daily, putting the health of the plantation system over those of enslaved African Americans.

NOTES

1. Peter L. Horn, "An Inaugural Dissertation on the Subject is Yellow Fever Contagious" (MD thesis, Medical College of the State of South Carolina, 1860), n.p., Waring Historical Library, Medical University of South Carolina, Charleston, SC.

2. For the best recent monographs on the environment, slavery, yellow fever, and malaria during this period, see Urmi Engineer Willoughby, *Yellow Fever, Race, and Ecology in Nineteenth-*

Century New Orleans (Baton Rouge: Louisiana State University Press, 2017), and Peter McCandless, *Slavery, Disease, and Suffering in the Southern Lowcountry* (New York: Cambridge University Press, 2011). Likewise, Kathryn Olivarius's recent article on yellow fever in New Orleans should remind us that whites in this period were intimately aware that the disease mostly struck new European immigrants, who did not have the opportunity to acquire immunity to the virus as children, rather than yellow fever targeting all whites. Kathryn Olivarius, "Immunity, Capital, and Power in Antebellum New Orleans," *American Historical Review,* 124, no. 2 (April 2019): 432–33. There is no shortage of great works on health, race, and the environment in the South. See also Conevery Bolton Valenčius, *The Health of the Country: How American Settlers Understood Themselves and Their Land* (New York: Basic Books, 2002), and Margaret Humphreys, *Yellow Fever and the South* (Baltimore, MD: Johns Hopkins University Press, 1992).

3. While this story will be explored in greater depth later in the essay, for more information, see, C. H. Stone, "Report on Epidemic Cholera in the Vicinity of Natchez," *Southern Medical Reports* 1 (1849): 359–71; and Lewis Shanks, "Report of the Commencement, Prevalence, Fatality, Treatment, &c. of Pestilential Cholera, in Memphis and its Vicinity; with the Prominent Facts Bearing upon the Unsettled Question of its Imported or Domestic Origin," *Southern Medical Reports* 1 (1849): 382–97.

4. Christopher Hamlin, *Cholera: The Biography* (New York: Oxford University Press, 2009), 44–47; W. Fitzhugh Brundage, *The Southern Past: A Clash of Race and Memory* (Cambridge, MA.: Belknap Press of Harvard University Press, 2005), 201–5. For more on land clearance for plantations in the lower Mississippi River valley, see Mikko Saikku, *This Delta, This Land: An Environmental History of the Yazoo-Mississippi Floodplain* (Athens: University of Georgia Press, 2005), 106–10. For a discussion on memory, see W. Fitzhugh Brundage, ed., *Where These Memories Grow: History, Memory and Southern Identity* (Chapel Hill: University of North Carolina Press, 2000). For more on slavery, expansion, and the American borderlands, see John Craig Hammond, "Slavery, Sovereignty, and Empires: North American Borderlands, and the American Civil War, 1660–1860," *Journal of the Civil War Era* 4, no. 2 (June 2014): 264–98; Walter Johnson, *River of Dark Dreams: Slavery and Empire in the Cotton Kingdom* (Cambridge, MA: Belknap Press of Harvard University Press, 2013); and John Craig Hammond, "Slavery, Settlement, and Empire: The Expansion and Growth of Slavery in the Interior of the North American Continent, 1770–1820," *Journal of the Early Republic* 32, no. 2 (Summer 2012): 175–206.

5. Fenner was a highly influential physician in New Orleans, having written an important tract on the 1853 yellow fever epidemic in the city, serving as President of the Louisiana State Medical Society, and cofounding the Medical College of New Orleans in the 1850s. Erasmus Darwin Fenner, "Introductory Address," *Southern Medical Reports* 1 (1849): 11. See also, Erasmus Darwin Fenner, *History of the Epidemic Yellow Fever, at New Orleans, La. in 1853* (New York: Hall, Clayton & Co., 1854).

6. Locally, sugar plantations were much larger than cotton plantations. For example, in St. Mary's Parish, in 1850, cotton planters possessed an average of 130 acres of cleared land versus 230 on sugar plantations. By 1840, the average sugar plantation housed seventy-six enslaved workers. Richard Follett, *The Sugar Masters: Planters and Slaves in Louisiana's Cane World, 1820–1860* (Baton Rouge: Louisiana State University Press, 2005), 23–25, 32–33.

7. For a detailed analysis of one such physician, see Christopher D. E. Willoughby, "Running Away from Drapetomania: Samuel A. Cartwright, Medicine, and Race in the Antebellum South," *Journal of Southern History* 84, no. 3 (August 2018): 579–614.

8. Tully S. Gibson, "An Essay on Plurality of Origin of the Races" (MD thesis, University of Pennsylvania, 1855), 2–6 (quote 1 on 5 and quote 2 on 6). For more on how slavery encouraged racist comparisons between enslaved African descendants and animals, see Karl Jacoby, "Slaves by Nature? Domestic Animals and Human Slaves," *Slavery & Abolition* 15, no. 1 (1994): 89–99.

9. The secession convention argued that cotton and sugar were "peculiar to the climate verging on the tropical regions, and by an imperious law of nature, none but the black race can bear exposure to the tropical sun." "A Declaration of the Immediate Causes Which Induce and Justify the Secession of the State of Mississippi from the Federal Union," 1861, Yale Avalon Project, https://avalon.law.yale.edu/19th_century/csa_missec.asp.

10. Mark Harrison, *Climates and Constitutions: Health, Race, Environment and British Imperialism in India* (New York: Oxford University Press, 1999), 16–20. For more on racial science in northern medical schools, see Christopher D. Willoughby, "'His Native, Hot Country,'" 328–51. For more on climate and race in the South, see Mart A. Stewart, "'Let Us Begin with the Weather?': Climate, Race, and Cultural Distinctiveness in the American South," in *Nature and Society in Historical Context,* ed. Mikuláš Teich, Roy Porter, and Bo Gustaffson (New York: Cambridge University Press, 1997), 240–56.

11. W. M. B., "Review, *A Treatise on the Practice of Medicine.* By George B. Wood," *New Orleans Medical and Surgical Journal* 4, no. 6 (May 1848): 716. George B. Wood, *A Treatise on the Practice of Medicine,* 2 vols., 4th ed. (Philadelphia: Lippincott, Grambo, and Co., 1855), 2: 789.

12. Based on Daniel Kilbride's data, approximately 371 students from Mississippi and Louisiana graduated from the University of Pennsylvania's medical department between 1831 and 1861. Wood taught there from 1835 to 1860, and enrollments from these states were at the highest at the heart of Wood's tenure, making it safe to estimate that Wood taught over 300 medical students from Mississippi and Louisiana. This represented a small but notable fraction of the 7,898 graduates of the University of Pennsylvania's medical school from 1831 to 1861, and a majority of those graduates were southern. Daniel Kilbride, *An American Aristocracy: Southern Planters in Antebellum Philadelphia* (Columbia: University of South Carolina Press, 2006), 84–85. For more on Cartwright and his publication record, see Willoughby, "Running Away from Drapetomania," 579–614.

13. W. H. P., "Review, *The Races of Men; a Fragment* by Robert Knox, MD 1850," *New Orleans Medical and Surgical Journal* 7, no. 5 (March 1851): 670 (quote 1); Robert Knox, *Races of Men: A Fragment* (Philadelphia: Lea & Blanchard, 1850), 210; W. H. P., "Review, *The Races of Men; a Fragment* By Robert Knox, MD 1850, Continued," *New Orleans Medical and Surgical Journal* 7, no. 6 (May 1851): 776–77 (quote 2 on 777).

14. Black vomit and jaundice were perhaps the most iconic symptoms of yellow fever. Samuel Cartwright, "The Report on the Diseases and Physical Peculiarities of the Negro Race," *New Orleans Medical and Surgical Journal* 7, no. 6 (May 1851): 691–701 (quote 1 on 691, quote 2 on 699, and quote 3 on 701). One vocal critic of Cartwright's report recommended that slaves be housed in light-framed quarters. "Review of Cartwright *On the Diseases and Physical Peculiarities of the Negro Race,"* Part 1, *Charleston Medical Journal & Review* 6 (November 1851): 839.

15. Cartwright, "The Report," 706–14. R. McMillan, "An Inaugural Dissertation on General Prophylaxis" (MD thesis, Medical College of the State of South Carolina, 1843), 16–17.

16. "Review, *On the Treatment of Cholera on Plantations.* By Dr. C. B. New," *New Orleans Medical and Surgical Journal* 7, no. 2 (September 1850): 212; Samuel Cartwright, "Remarks on Dysentery among Negroes," *New Orleans Medical and Surgical Journal* 11, no. 2 (September 1854): 155; Christopher D. Willoughby, "'His Native, Hot Country,'" 328–29. Peculiar is a reference to Cartwright's "The Report on the Diseases and Physical Peculiarities of the Negro Race," and it also represented a common phrase in antebellum medicine to describe medical, racial differences.

17. Bayou Lafourche is located about thirty miles southwest of the Mississippi River. Emphasis in original. Wm. A. Booth, "On the Cholera of Lafourche Interior," *Southern Medical Reports* 1 (1849): 215.

18. A. R. K., "American Medical Intelligence from A. R. K., June 16, 1847," *New Orleans Medical and Surgical Journal* 4, no. 1 (July 1847): 137–38. For more on dissection and the professionalization of medicine, see Michael Sappol, *A Traffic of Dead Bodies: Anatomy and Embodied Social Identity in Nineteenth-Century America* (Princeton: Princeton University Press, 2002). For more on medical journalism and professionalism, see James H. Cassedy, *Medicine and American Growth, 1800–1860* (Madison: University of Wisconsin Press, 1986).

19. For more on the relationship between commerce and disease in world history, see Mark Harrison, *Contagion: How Commerce Has Spread Disease* (New Haven, CT: Yale University Press, 2012).

20. While there were certainly no tigers roaming Louisiana swamps, large predator cats such as the eastern cougar and the Florida panther were not yet extinct or endangered in the South. Solomon Northup, *Twelve Years a Slave* (Buffalo, NY: Derby, Orton, and Mulligan, 1853), 138–40 (quote on 139).

21. Thomas Eveleigh, "An Inaugural Essay on the Properties of the Xanthum Stumanium or Common Sheep Bur as an Antidote to the Poison of Venomous Serpents" (MD thesis, Medical College of the State of South Carolina, 1831), n.p., Waring Historical Library.

22. Andrew R. Kilpatrick, "Report on the Medical Topography, Meteorology, and Diseases of Trinity, La., and its Vicinity, During the Year 1850," *Southern Medical Reports* 2 (1850): 157–58 (quote 1 on 158 and quote 2 on 157), 170–85.

23. It was not until 1881 that Cuban epidemiologist Carlos Finlay posited that *Aedes aegypti* mosquitoes transmitted yellow fever, and this conclusion was not confirmed until 1900. For more on yellow fever at the turn of the twentieth century, see Mariola Espinosa, *Epidemic Invasions: Yellow Fever and the Limits of Cuban Independence, 1878–1930* (Chicago: University of Chicago Press, 2009).

24. A. P. Jones, "Yellow Fever in a Rural District, August to December, 1853," *New Orleans Medical News and Hospital Gazette,* no. 9 (July 1, 1854): 205–9 (quote on 205). Urmi Engineer Willoughby, *Yellow Fever,* 16, 113–15 (quote on 16). Urmi Engineer Willoughby also discusses Jones's prediction in her essay about the centrality of railroads to the spread of yellow fever during the 1878 epidemic.

25. Hamlin, *Cholera,* 19–21, 35–41; Harrison, *Contagion,* 139–43; Harrison, *Climates & Constitutions,* 18–20.

26. James B. Duncan, "Report on the Topography, Climate and Diseases of the Parish of St. Mary, La.," *Southern Medical Reports* 1 (1849): 192. C. H. Stone, "Report on Epidemic Cholera, in the Vicinity of Natchez," *Southern Medical Reports* 1 (1849): 363.

27. Todd L. Savitt, *Medicine and Slavery: The Diseases and Health Care of Blacks in Antebellum Virginia* (Urbana: University of Illinois Press, 1978), 57–63. "Review of C. B. New, 'On the Treatment of Cholera on Plantations,'" *New Orleans Medical and Surgical Journal* 7, no. 1 (July 1850): 212 (last quote).

28. Follett, *The Sugar Masters,* 23–24, 91–92. Johnson, *River of Dark Dreams,* 255–56. Baptist has received considerable attention and criticism for his somewhat myopic depiction of corporeal punishment as at the core of pushes for efficiency in this period. It was more complex, as enslavers looked toward machinery, plant breeds and other agricultural innovations, and managerial schemes to increase crop yields. That being said, corporeal and other forms of punishment were certainly tools that enslavers used readily to enforce quotas. Edward E. Baptist, *The Half Has Never Been Told: Slavery and the Making of American Capitalism* (New York: Basic Books, 2014), 116–35. John E. Murray, Alan L. Olmstead, Trevon D. Logan, Jonathan B. Pritchett, and Peter L. Rousseau, "Roundtable of Reviews for *The Half Has Never Been Told,*" *Journal of Economic History* 75, no. 3 (September 2015): 919–31.

While numerous historians have written about the lives of slaves with disabilities, far less has been said about the treatment and the accidents that caused disability on the plantation. For more on disability and enslavement, see Jennifer L. Barclay, "Cripples All! Or, The Mark of Slavery: Disability and Race in Antebellum America, 1820–1860" (PhD diss., Michigan State University, 2011); Dea H. Boster, *African American Slavery and Disability: Bodies, Property, and Power in the Antebellum South, 1800–1860* (New York: Routledge Press, 2013); and Jeff Forret, "'Deaf & Dumb, Blind, Insane, or Idiotic': The Census, Slaves, and Disability in the Late Antebellum South," *Journal of Southern History* 82, no. 3 (August 2016): 503–48.

29. George Halsey Peets, "An Essay on Gossypium Herbaceum" (MD thesis, University of Pennsylvania, 1860), 9–10, Kislak Center for Special Collections, Rare Books, and Manuscripts, Van Pelt Library, University of Pennsylvania, Philadelphia, PA; Thomas Affleck, "On the Hygiene of Cotton Plantations and the Management of Negro Slaves," *Southern Medical Reports* 2 (1850): 434; Caitlin Rosenthal, "Slavery's Scientific Management: Masters and Managers," in *Slavery's Capitalism: A New History of American Economic Development,* ed. Sven Beckert and Seth Rockman (Philadelphia: University of Pennsylvania Press, 2016), 63–68; Baptist, *The Half Has Never Been Told,* 116–35. See also Lake Douglas, ed., *Steward of the Land: Selected Writings of Nineteenth-Century Horticulturalist Thomas Affleck* (Baton Rouge: Louisiana State University Press, 2014).

30. Deborah Kuhn McGregor, *From Midwives to Medicine: The Birth of American Gynecology* (New Brunswick, NJ: Rutgers University Press, 1998), 40–41; Deirdre Cooper Owens, *Medical Bondage: Race, Gender, and the Origins of American Gynecology* (Athens: University of Georgia Press, 2017), 26; Savitt, *Medicine and Slavery,* 118–19. For more on infant mortality, see William Dusinberre, *Them Dark Days: Slavery in the American Rice Swamps* (Athens: University of Georgia Press, 1996), 237–42.

31. McGregor, *From Midwives to Medicine,* 42–43, 111–13; C. A. Evens, "A Dissertation on Prolapsus Uteri" (MD thesis, Medical College of the State of South Carolina, 1855), 1, Waring Historical Library.

32. Peets, "Gossypium Herbaceum," 11–13. For more on enslaved healing in the United States and Atlantic World, see Sharla Fett, *Working Cures: Healing, Health, and Power on Southern Slave Plantations* (Chapel Hill: University of North Carolina Press, 2002); Pablo F. Gomez, *The Experiential Caribbean: Creating Knowledge and Healing in the Early Modern Atlantic* (Chapel Hill: University of North Carolina Press, 2017).

33. L. Lefevere, "Gangrenous Inflammation of the Arm—Amputation—Metastatic Fistulas—recovery. Caesarian operation performed with Success. Engorgement of the Uterus, attended with Ascires and anasarca," *New Orleans Medical and Surgical Journal* 7, no. 3 (1850): 336–39 (quote on 337).

34. Peets, "Gossypium Herbaceum," 11–13 (quote on 11); Sven Beckert, *Empire of Cotton: A Global History* (New York: Vintage Books, 2014), 102–4. For more on the proportion of enslaved people with disabilities, see Forret, "'Deaf & Dumb,'" 510–15.

35. Follett, *The Sugar Masters,* 17–18.

36. New Prospect was located in north-central Mississippi. J. A. Hewell, "The Question of Amputation: A Thesis" (MD thesis, Medical College of the State of South Carolina, 1857), n.p., Waring Historical Library. Samuel Forwood to D. Stump, February 11, 1845, William Stump Forwood Papers, Southern Historical Collection, Louis Round Wilson Special Collections Library, University of North Carolina, Chapel Hill, NC; Peets, "Gossypium Herbaceum," 25. MUSSC student Wiley J. McKain also discussed the use of cotton seed for abortions; see Wiley J. McKain, "An Inaugural Dissertation on Indigenous Plants" (MD thesis, Medical College of the State of South Carolina, 1844), 30–31, Waring Historical Library.

37. This juxtaposition between plantation as dangerous worksite and paternalist estate was observed in the antebellum period by antislavery writers, but it should be most jarring to twenty-first century readers. Much of our romantic conception of plantations derives from twentieth-century southern tourism and fiction like Margaret Mitchell's *Gone with the Wind.* Brundage, *The Southern Past,* 183–85.

38. Follett, *The Sugar Masters,* 107; R. H. D., "To the *New Orleans Medical and Surgical Journal,* Pattersonville, La. December 17, 1847," *New Orleans Medical and Surgical Journal* 4, no. 4 (January 1848): 543; Sasha Turner, *Contested Bodies: Pregnancy, Childbearing, and Slavery in Jamaica* (Philadelphia: University of Pennsylvania Press, 2017), 80.

39. Affleck, "Hygiene of Cotton Plantations," 435.

LANDSCAPES OF EMANCIPATION

Plantations and African American Liberation

WILLIAM HORNE

On March 24, 1900, Raymond Breaux, editor of the *St. Landry Clarion,* reprinted an article from the *East Feliciana Columbian.* The *Columbian* article invited its readers, "us Democrats, the white people, to pause and glance backward at some of the scenes enacted under the Republican regime." The essayist cautioned that "it is still within the memory of man when John Gair, a negro, was our state senator; when Bob Ray, a negro, was in the state legislature as member from East Feliciana . . . with Tony Clark, a negro clerk of court." "Magistrates and constables were negroes," the *Columbian* complained, and threatened to be so again if readers voted Republican. The writer celebrated the impossibility of this outcome. "No more will it be necessary for the white men to break up a court of justice," he wrote, "and drive judge, sheriff and all from the land." Even a quarter of a century later, the tenure of Gair, Ray, and Clark in office troubled the minds of white supremacists in East Feliciana. The memory of these Black officeholders, whose race was their primary shortcoming, apparently motivated white voters decades after they drove them from the parish under the threat of death.[1]

The experiences of John Gair, Robert Ray, and Tony Clark point to the need to understand the political landscape that emerged during and after Reconstruction, a landscape defined by its occupants' common goal of freedom and shared strategy of active political mobilization.[2] The *Columbian*'s discomfort with the men was not simply an expression of loyalty to their own race but a reaction to the fact that these men and hundreds of other local African American officeholders challenged the superiority of their former enslavers. Tony Clark had almost certainly been owned by East Feliciana Parish planter Benjamin F. Clark, while local carpenter James Gair had probably enslaved John Gair. Their trajectory from enslaved workers to postwar politicians grew from a web of kinship alliances founded in slavery. The relationships they formed in slavery had provided support and, in the wake of emancipation, formed the basis of African American political organizations. As a result, postwar plantations were not simply sites of labor but also provided the backdrop for grassroots organizing and resistance. From this perspective, postwar plantations were highly contested spaces—at once fetishized by former slaveowners who hoped to regain their antebellum elite status and weaponized by their formerly enslaved workers to throw off the yoke of oppression. This essay examines the landscape of political activity through which African Americans articulated a radical rejection of the established political topography. Together, they transformed the postwar plantation landscape and destroyed the efforts of former enslavers to resurrect slavery.[3]

THE ANTEBELLUM PLANTATION LANDSCAPE

Louisiana's antebellum plantation labor camps were sites of brutal exploitation. Many of those who worked Louisiana's plantations were victims of the so-called Second Middle Passage—the domestic slave trade through which enslavers in long-established slave states, especially Virginia, Maryland, and Delaware, sold Black men, women, and children into the Deep South. Some were also descended from Africans who were in St. Domingue during the Haitian Revolution. These forced migrants were the backbone of Louisiana's plantation landscape. They built its levees, cleared and tilled its fields, harvested its crops, and loaded its steamers. Their bodies were far and away the most valuable assets in the region and it was through them that plantation owners secured their wealth. The proximity of New Orleans—the vortex of the antebellum slave trade—also meant that slaves lived in constant fear of losing friends and family to sale, either as punishment or as a consequence of plantation mismanagement. Both were common enough to warrant concern. Even under "normal" circumstances, slavery was brutal and dehumanizing. Men, women, and children were forced to work in the planter's home, blacksmith shops, cooperages, barns, and sugar and cotton fields. Field slaves primarily labored in gangs and were the most vulnerable to overseer and driver abuses. Especially at the hands of those—such as an overseer—who had no personal investment at stake, punishments often left victims incapacitated for several days. Put briefly, slave life in Louisiana's plantation labor camps was dangerous, strenuous, and short.[4]

Enslaved people resisted exploitation and, when war broke out after many of the slaveholding states seceded in 1860, forced the Union to make emancipation one of its wartime goals. Nonetheless, popular images of emancipation in films like *Lincoln* (2012) often depict the president as a benevolent father-figure who was primarily responsible for emancipation. While historian James Oakes has more recently shown that it is possible to support this claim by looking at Lincoln's writings and life, the image remains deeply misleading and supports the convenient myth that slavery's demise was widely recognized or inevitable. Lincoln, for example, supported colonization—the idea that free African Americans should be resettled outside the boundaries of the United States—late into the war and longer than most of his advisors.[5] More important, however, we get an entirely different image of the enactment and adoption of emancipation as official Union policy by looking at the testimony of enslaved people themselves. Men and women took matters into their own hands, rejecting slavery when they saw the opportunity, reinforcing the end of slavery as a central feature of the Union war effort. In fact, this merely encouraged an action rooted in the antebellum plantation. Enslaved people had often fled southern plantations when the circumstances made it seem possible. The most significant wartime difference was that now, emancipation was en masse.

Self-emancipation and resisting oppression were enmeshed in plantation slavery. This was true on a smaller scale before the war as enslaved people sought resources and protection beyond overseers' view on the swampy margins of cleared sugar and cotton plantations. Resistance of this kind became a mass strategy, however, after Louisiana seceded in 1861. For example, Octave Johnson fled from S. Cantrelle's plantation in St. James Parish, just upriver of New Orleans, in 1861 and hid in nearby swamps for a year and one-half as a "maroon" before joining the Union Army.[6] As he later testified, he fled because "one morning the bell was rung for us to go to work so early that I could not see, and I lay still, because I was working by task." Working by "task" meant that it did not matter how much time Johnson spent working, but only that he accomplished the tasks for the day. "For this the overseer was going to have me whipped," he recalled, "and I ran away to the woods." Johnson hid out roughly four miles from the plantation and survived by stealing livestock and bartering with the enslaved workers. He was eventually joined by roughly *thirty men and women* as slavery became increasingly untenable after the Union liberation of New Orleans. Johnson and his comrades hunted and traded meat with those still bound on the plantation—a significant risk that left them vulnerable to recapture even as it was key to their survival. They were changing for themselves an environment of bondage into a landscape of agency, action and, subsequently, of uncertain freedom.[7]

While running away was a possibility, it was a considerable risk that not every person was able to take, even after the Union secured Baton Rouge in May 1862. Some slaves instead sought to reshape their current environment rather than seeking a new one and made demands of their enslavers that attempted to transform the plantation from a landscape of subjugation to one of negotiation. On Black Water Plantation in West Feliciana Parish, for example, enslaved men and women made a bargain with the manager of the plantation in 1863 after their owner died and the remaining white overseers fled the plantation. According to Luke Camey, workers agreed "not to go over to the Yankees but to remain and take care of [the plantation] and they should have all they could raise on it." The men and women on Black Water upheld their agreement with the managers of the estate, raising cotton for wages through the end of the war in 1865. Nonetheless, the estate managers, Jed Smith and Edward Converse, reneged on the deal. They returned to the plantation after the war, sold the cotton, and refused to give Camey and his coworkers the cash for its sale as agreed. Such open defiance of the established plantation structure was not common before the war because enslavers wielded total control over local government and vigilance committees. During the war, enslaved people understood the changing political and social landscape gave them new opportunities to seize their value in relation to the plantation. No laborers meant no crops, and in the case of Black Water Plantation, those laborers used that reality to rewrite their working environment. And though the managers had apparently never intended to honor the agreement, which he later denied having ever made, the Freedmen's Bureau eventually forced them to comply with its terms.[8]

If self-emancipation served as the precedent for postwar political activism, an important component was the war that created a window of opportunity for immediate action by enslaved people. Secession, in the most extreme of ironies, created multiple avenues of mobilization for enslaved Louisianans. That thirty men and women could escape slavery with Johnson and live just four miles from their plantation would have been unthinkable, at least in scale, in south Louisiana prior to secession. But with the massive outflux of young white men leaving to join the Confederate army, enslaved people seized opportunities of owner absenteeism in the lower Mississippi River valley. As historian W. E. B. Du Bois famously put it, when Edmund Ruffin "fired the first gun at Fort Sumter, he freed the slaves."[9] Even the Confederacy acknowledged this, making the "20 Negro Law" part of its 2nd Conscription Act, declaring that a white male must remain on plantations of twenty slaves or more. In a very real sense, Ruffin's shot and the war it began uprooted the very landscape of subjugation and immobility it sought to preserve.

POSTWAR TRANSFORMATION

Self-emancipating slaves and the Union Army transformed the postwar lower Mississippi River valley.[10] The bastion of slavery and a landscape of ordered subjugation had given way to uncertainty as former slaves mobilized to become active representatives of their own welfare and former slaveowners feverishly worked to regain their supremacy. Planters maintained overt slavery outside areas of direct Union control in direct defiance of the Emancipation Proclamation, prompting Major General Gordon Granger to enact it by force in Galveston, Texas, on June 19, 1865. His General Order No. 3 forced enslavers to concede emancipation, an event still celebrated in African American communities as Juneteenth. Unfortunately, these former slaveowners rejected equality as the product of emancipation, forcing African Americans to demand the rights of free people on their own.[11] Enslaved people had already struggled mightily for freedom and, even without Army intervention, would have been unlikely to accept a rebirth of antebellum slavery. Planters instead turned to limiting the impact of emancipation, creating the infamous Black Codes to limit Black workers' mobility and civil rights.[12] Army records and planter letters are replete with examples of this wave of resistance to African American liberty, a point they openly admitted at the time, and only glossed over decades after Reconstruction.

Black Louisianans refused to accept the Black Codes.[13] They regularly complained to Bureau agents about unfair practices and reported employers who threatened, beat, or kidnapped them into unfree labor. In West Feliciana, for example, Black worker Bat Henryham told Army officers that Charles Barrow, his employer and former enslaver, "bea[t] me with a sword" for going to a political meeting in 1865. Though Henryham could not vote in 1865, attending meetings was important to him and so was protesting the treatment he received as result of his political participation. Experiences like Henryham's revealed the reality of postwar violence, which was rooted less in misunderstanding than in competing visions of postwar society (fig. 1). Barrow's actions demonstrate the lengths to which some planters went because they were willing to do almost anything rather than accept equality as the consequence of emancipation.[14]

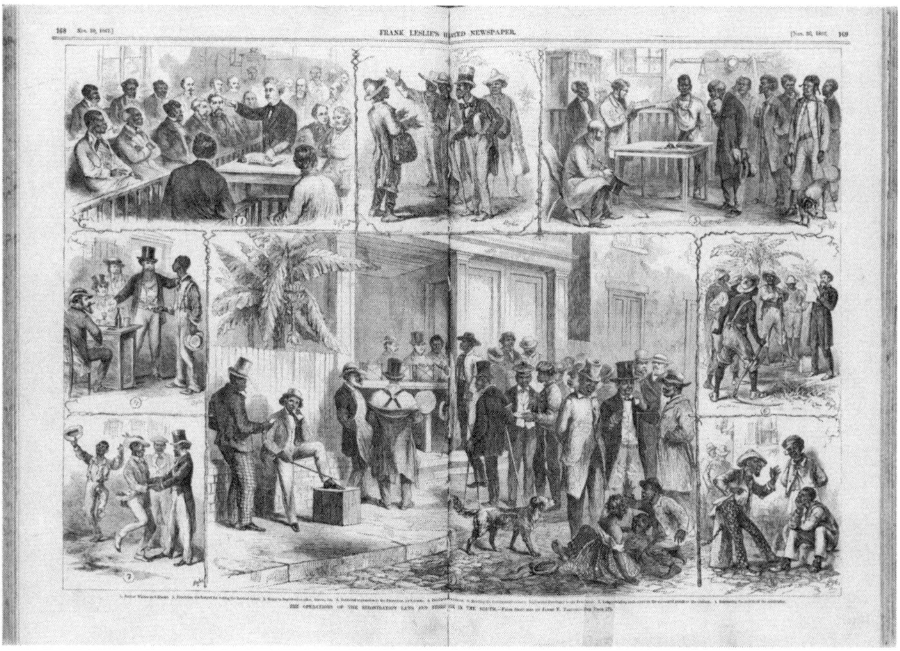

Figure 1. *The Operations of the Registration Laws and Negro Suffrage in the South,* sketch by James E. Taylor, in *Leslie's Illustrated Newspaper,* November 30, 1867. Planters used their exclusive control of land to try to keep Black Louisianans from voting and to force them to work for lower wages. Library of Congress Prints and Photographs Division, Washington, DC.

Louisianans like Henryham lobbied for expanded political rights, which they viewed as essential to realizing emancipation, particularly in the wake of the Black Codes. It was a political landscape marked by clear intent and determined action. On July 30, 1866, an interracial group of Republicans sought to force a change to the Louisiana Constitution of 1864 to recognize the citizenship and voting rights of persons of color. The effort was probably already doomed to failure because of the parliamentary procedures of the Louisiana legislature, but Democrats, under the leadership of former-Confederate mayor John T. Monroe, organized a devastating response. The New Orleans Police Department, along with the city's firemen and a mass of Confederate veterans, attacked the members and their supporters at the Mechanics' Institute. Surprised and unarmed, the convention's participants and its supporters ran. Some hid inside convention halls, only to be dragged out and killed by the police. Others sought refuge in nearby shops and yards. Vigilantes chased them down, killing participants and leaving ex-governor Michael Hahn for dead. The city's police, firemen, and white supremacists continued their killing spree for two and one-half hours, eventually killing at least thirty-eight members of the convention and its supporters and wounding 184. Though the attackers denied premeditation and avoided criminal and civil charges, they clearly came prepared to annihilate the group of unarmed activists.[15]

If Monroe and his mob were hoping their actions would stifle the desire for full Black citizenship, however, they were wrong. The Mechanics Institute Massacre came at the precise moment that Congress was debating the ex-Rebel intransigence under the Johnson administration's version of Reconstruction and galvanized support for the more egalitarian congressional vision of Reconstruction. Monroe was removed from office and Louisiana was put back under the control of the US Army, providing Black Louisianans and their supporters with crucial protection for future organizing. In a very real sense, the sacrifice of those at the Mechanics Institute became the cornerstone of Black politics, not just in Louisiana, but nationwide, and illustrated the potential of an America that embraced its founding principles.

Though they were marked by common interests, postemancipation African American politics were far from monolithic. Rather, the development of this new, interracial body politic expanded the opportunities for anyone in the system to address perceived injustice. In Lake Providence, for example, Black worker Jessy Graham testified in favor of his employer, W. R. C. Lyons to have fellow-laborer Robert Morris kicked off the plantation. Graham testified in July 1866 that Morris was "a Quarrelsome boy" and that "the place would be better off without him" as he occasionally missed work. Graham might have been coerced into testifying, he may have hoped to curry favor with his employer, or perhaps he was truly frustrated with Morris's behavior.[16] Likewise, Nero Mack was removed from J. U. Ball's plantation in West Feliciana Parish in part because of a dispute with George May over which of them had the right to use a bridle. May was roughly fifty years old, more than twenty years Mack's senior. Both men worked under difficult conditions, which doubtless contributed to the mounting tensions between them when they nearly came to blows on May 7, 1867. Though we cannot fully know their reasons for siding against their coworkers, May and Graham certainly did not view African American interests as singular.[17] Rather, they show how former slaves used a newly available political and legal structure to address personal grievances. It was mobilization on a very personal scale, where, by their petitions, Black Louisianans demanded to be considered and have their concerns addressed as members of general society.

BLACK POLITICS AND LABOR

Though formerly enslaved men and women were complicated people with many, sometimes competing, desires, they did view their interests as divergent from those of their former enslavers. Indeed, as slavery and its echoes in the Black Codes illustrated, they had good reason to be suspicious. In St. Mary Parish, for example, merchant Thomas Sanders apparently colluded with local officials to impound the wages of John Davis on purchases he allegedly made in 1860. Davis's employer implored the local Bureau agent that the debt Sanders claimed of Davis was "made before the war, when the aforesaid John was a slave," which would have prevented him from signing a promissory note. This argument was to no avail. Instead, local officials garnished his wages for 1867. Though not usually as outlandish, schemes like this were not uncommon during 1866 and 1867 and speak to the contested nature of the postemancipation plantation as former enslavers looked for creative ways to avoid paying their workers.[18] In Baton Rouge, planter G. A. Umberhagen tried to charge two of his Black workers, Samuel Reese and Henry Lewis, $250 for a mule that had died under their supervision. The Bureau agent who reviewed the case explained in a letter to his superior that Reese and Lewis had refused to work with the mule months earlier because "Umberhagan had threatened to charge them with the value of the mule if it died." The men were concerned that he was trying to entrap them—to create a situation where the mule would die and then charge them for its death. Because of their earlier complaint, the agent suspected that Umberhagan was trying to defraud them and ruled in favor of Reese and Lewis. The men were more fortunate than Davis as they managed to avoid the scheme to confiscate their wages, but many more were not so lucky.[19] Plantations further became the setting of postemancipation mobilization as Black Louisianans united to protect their own against planters who frequently resorted to legal trickery to avoid paying wages. In northern Louisiana, in Carroll Parish, freedpeople intervened to prevent their employer, Beckorn, McMillan & Co., from removing Clark Gibson from their plantation. According to the complaint against them, McMillan's Black workers "detained said Gibson in a Riotous Manner and against all law" rather than allow Gibson to lose his home and wages. During the subsequent proceedings, the freedpeople charged with kidnapping Gibson repeatedly testified that they were suspicious of McMillan's motives and thought the potential expulsion of Gibson unjust. One of them, Moses Williams, explained, "I was one that went out and stopped Arnold and Gibson from coming to Town" to face censure from the Bureau agent at the request of his employers. "I thought it was not right for a man to be sent off," Williams continued, "unless they got authority to do so from the Pro[vost] Marshall." Williams also reported that they had "not been paid as Mr. McMillan agreed in his contract." If they were suspicious of their employers, he concluded, it was with good reason.[20]

Nero Mack, after being expelled from Ball's plantation because of the previously mentioned bridle dispute, led a worker revolt on Beauchamp Plantation, where he had signed on for the remainder of the year. Planter J. W. Medbery's workers had become suspicious of their employer by October 1867 and apparently worried he would try to avoid paying them for their work that year. In response to their growing frustrations, Medbery contacted West Feliciana Bureau agent A. Finch to mediate the dispute and oversee their payment. Finch visited the workers, but the meeting quickly got out of hand as Medbery's laborers accused the Bureau agent of conspiring with the planter to steal their wages. During the ensuing chaos, Finch tried to arrest Mack for making "insolent remarks." According to the testimony of Medbery and his son, Mack "laid violent hands" on Finch during the arrest before breaking away from the agent's grasp, "having left his coat in a damaged condition in the hands of Capt. Finch." Mack then "dared capt Finch to approach him saying he would whip him if he did." About thirty of Mack's fellow workers, who apparently shared his skepticism of Bureau-administered justice, defied Finch, and supported Mack. Mack then announced that "if he should be made to leave the Place Capt Finch better look to his own Safty."[21]

Mack had been turned off without pay from Ball's plantation months earlier with the help of the former Bureau agent, E. T. Lewis, which almost certainly informed his response during this second dispute. In fact, Mack had brought his previous disagreement with May and Ball to the Bureau agent in hopes that he might help them reach a resolution, which explains why it appeared he had no such hope when Finch arrived at Medbery's plantation. Instead, Mack and his comrades turned to one another for support in confronting attempts to reduce or deny their wages and rights. This informal support system spilled over into Black Louisianans' politics and helped inaugurate what remains among the most egalitarian documents in US history. The Louisiana Constitution of 1868 overturned Black Codes meant to trap men, women, and children in pseudo-slavery and embraced African American equality. It was a stunning rejection of the antebellum power structure in favor of a new legal landscape identified more by its possibility than established features. It was a landscape of political potential on which former slaves such as Mack and his supporters were eager to make their mark.[22]

KINSHIP AND THE TERRAIN OF POSTEMANCIPATION POLITICS

Black networks of kith and kin sustained African Americans through slavery and provided grassroots support for political activism in the postemancipation years. African Americans used these communities—created under slavery to help enslaved people survive—to alter the social and political landscape of the plantation region. John Gair came to power by engaging precisely this type of network. Through familial alliances forged during slavery, Gair came to dominate the political landscape in East Feliciana alongside his brothers-in-law Tony Clark and Robert Ray. Gair was elected to the Louisiana House of Representatives in 1868 after campaigning vigorously to rewrite the state constitution in 1867 to guarantee Black rights. In the words of the local Freedmen's Bureau agent, James DeGrey, "the freedmen, one and all, who had an opportunity to vote, cast the same ticket viz- 'for a convention' and for J. P. Newsham, white, of West Feliciana, and John H. Gair and Richard Lewis (col) of this parish for Delegates thereto." In a very real sense, Gair used the relationships created on the physical landscape of plantation slavery to fundamentally alter the state's political landscape by helping to write a state constitution that guaranteed racial equality. The outcome would have been astonishing for the thousands of formerly enslaved men who cast their votes, unanimously according to DeGrey, for Gair and equality in September 1867 as it represented the culmination of years of agitating for equality.[23]

The kinship that helped bring Gair to power became clear in 1872 when he helped his brother-in-law Clark get elected as parish recorder and brother-in-law Ray as sheriff. Clark had taught at the school for African Americans in Clinton since at least 1870, where he learned to read and write proficiently, while Ray worked as a policeman in New Orleans. Both men brought important relationships to their alliance with Gair. Clark doubtless formed relationships with dozens of local families as a teacher and was an important asset as a literate formerly enslaved man. Ray enlisted in the Union Army with the 82nd US Colored Infantry in 1863 when he was just eighteen. He had risen to the rank of sergeant by 1866 and knew not only local African Americans but also white Union officers and members of the state government. Thus, Clark and Ray were crucial allies for Gair as he mobilized supporters for his reelection bid in 1872.[24]

In Pointe Coupée, Émile Honoré served two terms in the Louisiana House of Representatives and drew, in part, on powerful family connections. The Afro-Creole Honorés had been planters before the Rebellion—what we today commonly call the Civil War—and were ideally situated to become prominent political figures after the war.[25] Honoré was an accomplished poet who wrote passionately in defense of Black suffrage in the African American *New Orleans Tribune.* In "Le Droit de Suffrage des Noirs," he argued that voting rights should be expanded to "black, and white, and red, and so forth." According to Honoré, even the most ardent white supremacist understood racial hierarchy to be untenable "Because he knows that all men . . . Are all the same, and we are: the sons of Adam." On July 30, 1866, less than two months after he penned this ode to universal suffrage, voting rights advocates were attacked at the Mechanics Institute in New Orleans, setting off a chain of events that would, in the bloodiest of ironies, allow Honoré and other men of color to vote and hold public office.[26]

Emile Honoré's support came from his older brother, Joseph, who had been the color bearer for the Pointe Coupée Light Brigade, a Confederate militia company mustered in the early months of the war. At the first opportunity, the twenty-four-year-old Joseph was among the first soldiers of color to join the Union Army in November 1862, and he served with the 75th US Colored Infantry through the end of the war. After the war, he became an outspoken advocate for Black rights, writing a letter to Major General Philip Sheridan in 1867 complaining that Maney, an African American woman, was held in slavery despite emancipation. Joseph boldly declared that Sheridan should "have the girl set at liberty at once and save us the trouble of sending a complaint to Washington City." Joseph served in the Republican state convention in May 1868 to help shape the party platform and elect Republicans in the November elections. His influence had also likely helped Émile get elected to the Louisiana House of Representatives in April. As with Ray, Joseph's military service introduced him to important allies and helped launch his political career while providing important support for family like Émile.[27]

Leveraging contacts to further political careers was by no means specific to the newly enfranchised African American community. Elite white planters relied heavily on family connections to better their social or political standing. What set African American politics apart was less the use of this tactic and more the reliance on it as a primary source of shaping their postemancipation environment through mobilization. Because slavery and the highly policed racial hierarchy of the 1850s suppressed even free people of color, African Americans had little opportunity to build institutions like political parties, benevolent societies, and churches. Kith and kin networks acted as a stand-in for these social and political frameworks, facilitating change by providing a kind of infrastructure. Thus, relationships dominated Black politics, not as a unique artifact of African American culture, but as the answer to a specific sociopolitical need. As these networks proved effective, white Louisianans became so suspicious of African American political activity in general that when formerly enslaved men began to form parties and political clubs, white elites claimed—and perhaps even believed—that they were plotting to ignite a race war. Gair, Honoré, and others may have been looking to define their postemancipation environment, but their efforts were not going to go uncontested.[28]

Former slaveowners were so threatened by the political landscape taking shape that they wrote to local Bureau agents to try to disband African American political clubs. Lt. William Webster reported one such bevy of complaints in Baton Rouge to his commanding officer in New Orleans. According to Webster, white locals were "making complaints that the freedmen come to their (the freedmens) mass meetings armed with shot guns, pistols." Worse still, Black politicians supposedly instructed their supporters to "come to the meetings armed under penalty of fine and imprisonment." Similar complaints were common throughout Louisiana's plantation parishes. Though it is unclear whether these allegations represented a tactic to delegitimize African American political activity or a white supremacist belief of Black inferiority, the truth was probably somewhere in between. A *New Orleans Tribune* correspondent writing under the pseudonym "A." from Baton Rouge dismissed similar rumors as "entirely false." He wrote that while planters claimed that there were "organized companies of infantry and cavalry among the colored people in Louisiana," nothing could have been further from the truth. Instead, what "A." observed was an engaged African American electorate. White elites were right to view Black democracy as revolutionary, however. It was.[29]

Though white locals complained frequently about such meetings, African Americans did not, which would have been curious if they had been forced to attend at gunpoint, as was alleged. Webster confided that though the allegations were worrisome, he was unable to locate any meetings in which armed attendees oppressed Black workers and encouraged them to carry out an armed insurrection. His missive did include important information about Black political activity, though. According to Webster, "the freedmen are all taking great interest in political matters but are working disadvantageously at present being divided into three or four different parties." These "parties" were in fact factions of the Republican Party, to which nearly all formerly enslaved people were intensely loyal because it had helped to end slavery. Though Webster did not elaborate on their roots, the factions were almost certainly based on regional networks. Each of these Black political groups had their own leaders, a loose organization which Webster worried would allow white planter-Democrats to "best them in the coming election." It did not. Like white planters, the Bureau agent saw African American political activity through the lens of race. He questioned whether formerly enslaved men could think for themselves and organize effectively without white supervision. Though he advocated for Black rights, he still imagined that Black voters would be controlled by white political leaders.

Yet as Gair, Ray, Clark, and thousands of other Black Louisianans would show, Webster was dead wrong.[30]

PLANTATION POLITICS

The political platform that grew from the kinship networks of the lower Mississippi River valley placed the physical plantation landscape front and center as former slaves looked for self-sufficiency outside of the contract worker system. Property ownership meant independence—true freedom. African Americans' changes to the political landscape under Gair and Honoré threatened to upend its physical landscape as well, dividing plantations into small plots that might guarantee Black equality. This thirst for land was a longing both Democrats and Republicans knew well. A speech by formerly enslaved minister Richmond Lewis in July 1868 captured the concerns of freedpeople and the ways these informed their politics. According to Lewis, some formerly enslaved men in St. Francisville considered supporting Democrats because of their "promise to give you twelve acres of land if you will join their party." Lewis warned that African Americans, "whose backs still bear the marks of the bull whip," should never "join the [political] ranks of their former oppressors." He reminded listeners that "ours is the party of freedom and of progress" while Democrats had supported slavery and secession. "Rather than join hands with such a party as that," Lewis declared, "I would live in the swamps, and run the risk of perishing from hunger and exposure." He alluded to marronage here, suggesting that to vote for former enslavers was to risk a return to enslavement and more dangerous forms of resistance. Instead, Lewis implored listeners to support the Republican Party and "enjoy a degree of happiness and prosperity never before known even by the richest landowner in the South."[31]

The offer of land was not only used to entice Black voters but could also be used as a threat to force Black Louisianans into subservience. Because of slavery, white planters owned the overwhelming majority of the state's arable land. They used this exclusive access to property to threaten African Americans—refusing to hire those who would not do their bidding. In East Feliciana Parish, planters tried to prevent Black voting before the election but also passed a resolution days later to impoverish African American voters who cast Republican ballots in future elections. They declared "that we will not employ for the future any freedmen who shall hereafter vote the Radical ticket, nor shall we rent lands, advance supplies, or assist in any manner such persons." Planters reasoned that if Republicans gained supports primarily through African American plantation worker networks, the most effective way to undermine them was to remove Black Republicans from their plantations.[32]

This focus on land speaks to the fundamental nature of Black politics in the postemancipation era as former slaves sought to create a political landscape from scratch. Perhaps this determination is what drew Nero Mack, who had previously been so outspoken about wage garnishments on the Medbery plantation, to support Gair in his 1872 reelection campaign. The campaign was a contentious and highly racialized affair, with white residents nearly universally opposed to Gair. These tensions came to a head on September 21, 1872, at Salem Church when a Gair campaign event erupted in violence. Gair had spoken for roughly a half-hour, but when his wealthier white opponent, Horace Champlin, began speaking, Gair's supporters drowned him out, with Nero Mack leading their raucous chorus. According to the East Feliciana *Patriot-Democrat,* Champlin's supporters demanded that the constable arrest Mack, who was "one of the most obstreperous in his demonstrations." The paper reported that "Mack resisted, and a crowd of [white] west-enders came forward to assist the officer." In the ensuing brawl, "Mack was wounded and a colored man, Henry Berryhill, was shot" and later died. Though Gair's supporters were apparently the sole victims of the violence, white locals blamed the African Americans present, and Gair in particular, for having provoked the attacks on them by being too loud.[33]

Former slaveowners recognized the grassroots nature of African American political organizations and tried to use its structure to undermine Black solidarity in Louisiana. Black men who joined Republican clubs faced the possibility of job loss, which on the postemancipation plantation also meant being expelled from housing. In Pointe Coupée, planter James Cotton fired one of his workers, Solomon Harden, for attending a Republican rally in the nearby town of New Roads in September 1868. Harden reported the matter to the local Bureau agent, H. F. Wallace, who asked Cotton to "let the boy back and try to make a better boy of him." Wallace's response indicated one of the many problems Black Louisianans faced in relying on Bureau agents for support—they could be unsympathetic allies. Wallace's comment that should Cotton make Harden a "better boy" while at the same time requesting Harden be brought back to work was at best a noncommittal response by a government agent to whom Harden had turned for help. At worst, Wallace's instruction should make the reader wonder what action Cotton took—as instructed by Wallace—to make Harden a "better boy." Given the circumstances, it is not difficult to understand why African Americans primarily sought support among their comrades on the plantation rather than rely on the support of the Freedmen's Bureau or why preacher-politicians like Richmond Lewis warned against yielding to the promise of property.[34]

A GEOGRAPHY OF VIOLENCE

Wallace's instructions to Cotton regarding Harden were partially left open to interpretation, but in St. Bernard Parish, downriver from New Orleans, white planters and politicians left no ambiguity in their intentions as they espoused overt terror to quell worker interest in Republicanism. On October 25, 1868, members of multiple Democratic clubs arrived in the parish from New Orleans and ignited a riot, during which they killed somewhere between thirty and sixty people of color. They hid many of the bodies in sugarcane fields. A. G. Thornton, a local physician who had been elected parish judge on the Republican ticket earlier that year, testified that none "of the thirty-five (35) negroes who were murdered during the riot, witness could not learn of one who had a pistol or gun on his person." He had "no hesitation in saying that it would have been the height of folly for Republicans to have attempted to vote on the 2d of November, 1868, in St. Bernard parish." Many local officials, including the sheriff, aligned themselves with the white rioters. Bringing charges against them would be nearly impossible, and no one would face justice for the murders.[35] The violence that devastated St. Bernard Parish swept the state in 1868 and continued well into the 1870s. Tony Clark was assaulted the day after his reelection as East Feliciana parish recorder in 1874 but remained in office and continued to conduct parish business. John Gair, after being shot in the head during an assassination attempt in October 1874, on the eve of the November elections, "issue[d] a card to the public, announcing his determination to remain as the Republican nominee of the district." These were bold men who knew firsthand the dangers they faced on behalf of equality but also likely understood them to pale in comparison with conceding to white supremacy.[36]

As this pattern of violence accelerated dramatically in 1873, Reconstruction in Louisiana quickly spiraled out of control. White supremacists, frustrated with their inability to muster an electoral majority, shifted their tactics from trying to sway local elections to trying to make it impossible for African Americans to hold office in rural parts of the state. On April 13, 1873, white supremacists aligned with the Fusion Party, under which more conservative Republicans temporarily merged with Democrats, massacred between sixty and one hundred African Americans in Colfax, Louisiana, a small town on the Red River near the center of the state. Black leaders, anticipating a coup, had sought shelter in the Colfax courthouse with their families and political allies. White supremacists, who had been carefully planning to exterminate the African American officeholders for some time, drew upon a vast network of Confederate veterans under the umbrella of the paramilitary Knights of the White Camellia. They even fielded a canon borrowed from the steamboat *John T. Moore.* Although the African American defenders of the courthouse had anticipated the attack and thrown up a hasty earthwork fortification around the building, they were outgunned and outnumbered. White supremacist attackers shot them indiscriminately, wiping out with one stroke the plantation-based networks that had made Grant Parish a solid Republican area in 1870 and 1872. There was simply no organization left to support Black politicians and, once it became clear that the perpetrators would not be brought to justice, there was little incentive for Black plantation laborers to risk their lives for someone else's democracy.[37]

The events in Colfax set the tone of unwinding the reforms of Reconstruction. Increasingly, white supremacists organized formal vigilante groups and expelled African American politicians from their offices. This is what happened to John Gair, Bob Ray, and Tony Clark in East Feliciana. The trouble began on June 26, 1875, when the East Feliciana *Patriot-Democrat* declared that the parish had "resolved to redeem herself from negro and carpet-bag rule." This was almost certainly meant as a general call to organize a local White League to plot the overthrow of the Republican Party in the parish. The reference was not lost on the *New Orleans Republican,* which warned that white supremacist Democrats planned to kill or expel all the Black officeholders from the parish.[38]

On July 14th, likely in response to the mounting racial tension in the parish, the *Bulletin* ran an article entitled "What the Negro is Doing." The author complained that Tony Clark and other Black officials heard testimony of African Americans who had been attacked or threatened. The *Bulletin,* which was essentially the propaganda arm of the White League, found this situation an unacceptable and escalating breach of social hierarchy, protesting that recently a "negro used some insolent language to Dr. Saunders." The paper declared that "the white people of this section have stood the rascality of the negro about long enough." They would no longer tolerate local courts and officials like Clark hearing testimony about racist threats and violence. By the end of July, Clark, Ray, and Gair had been run out of the parish by armed vigilantes.[39]

Clark later recalled that "I left in fear of my life being taken" as white locals "assembled under arms, as they had said they intended to kill the last negro office holder." He wrote to a white local attorney, D. C. Hardee, with whom he had been on friendly terms, to see if it was safe for him return. Hardee's reply, reprinted in the *New Orleans Republican,* spoke volumes about the vigilantes' motives. He wrote: "If you ask me to put you in office and to make you rule over me, then you insult me and offend my dignity. In your letter to me you say that you wish to be friendly with the white people. Don't you know that this is impossible! Don't you know that the white people will hate you as long as you hold office over them?" Hardee's letter, especially within the context of the ongoing white supremacist organizing in the parish throughout the summer of 1875, put the matter quite clearly. Clark was fundamentally, irrevocably objectionable to White Leaguers as a Black officeholder. There was no deal that he could make or alliance he could forge that would change their racial calculus.[40]

The men lobbied Governor Kellogg to help them return to their jobs, but years of neglecting the white vigilante problem facilitated its growth and undercut the legitimacy of the state government. The *Bulletin* gloated that the state seemed incapable of intervening and suggested that Gair and his colleagues willingly abandoned their posts. The *Bulletin* quoted Abe Meyer, a prominent Jewish merchant in Clinton, that the parish "was quiet and orderly." The problem, according to Meyer, was that white locals "wanted a man that commanded respect" in public office. The local Black politicians, he argued, did not. The governor impotently declared that he "hop[ed] that matters could be correctly arranged." In fact, because the White League had destroyed the state militia in its September 1874 coup, there is little he could have done anyway. By 1875, white supremacists understood that they could operate with little fear of repercussion and used this newfound freedom to wipe out, in their entirety, the grassroots networks that brought Black politicians to power.[41]

Toppling the government of East Feliciana was insufficient for white planters, who at once sought to punish Black officeholders and undermine interracial democracy. Shortly after they ousted Gair, they orchestrated his assassination.

Like his comrades, Gair left the parish in July 1875 and had been unable to return due to the threats on his life. In October, he was living in Baton Rouge with little prospect of returning to office. Based on contemporary newspaper accounts, it appears that the white elites whom Gair had governed hoped to use their newfound control of the sheriff's office and the courts to kidnap and kill him. They arrested his sister-in-law, Babe Matthews, on suspicion of attempting to poison local white supremacist physician Dr. J. W. Saunders. Saunders never showed any sign of illness. He claimed, however, that he suspected Matthews was trying to poison him, thus "uncovering" the supposed plot. Matthews allegedly confessed that Gair had conspired with her in the rumored poisoning—of which there was no contemporary evidence—and the local court issued a warrant for Gair's arrest. We cannot know whether she actually confessed or not because Matthews would never have the opportunity to contradict their story. By the end of the night of October 13, masked white supremacists, in apparent league with local officials, lynched her from the oak tree on the front lawn of the courthouse (fig. 2). The *Weekly Louisianan* theorized that white supremacists had murdered Matthews to cover up the fraudulent basis of their assassination of Gair. Though the likely conspirators left no record in which they described their plot and confessed to the crime, the circumstantial evidence supports the *Louisianan*'s theory. Matthews was almost certainly killed because of her relationship with Gair.[42]

John Gair's story ended the same night as that of his sister-in-law. He was arrested in Baton Rouge by Deputy Sheriff Woodard under the authority of the warrant based on Matthews's alleged testimony. As the *Republican* put it, "Mr. Gair was arrested as an accessory before the fact to an alleged attempt to poison a man who now lives and moves as free as the freest."[43] He was shot to death on the way back to Clinton to stand trial for the trumped-up poisoning charge. He was still in the custody of the deputy sheriff, who claimed Gair was murdered by between sixty and seventy masked vigilantes. As with Matthews's poisoning "confession," we have only Woodard's word that he acted in good faith. These were, however, the very same people that purged the parish of Black officeholders on the premise that, in the words of the local conservative press, "the black man has proved his incapability to hold office."[44] We may take them at their word, but we do so at our own peril. Indeed, the accounts of the white elites of East Feliciana are credible only if we view their actions in isolation and ignore both the interrelationship and context of their program

Figure 2. *The East Feliciana Parish Court House,* by Andrew David Lytle, 1899. This is the courthouse where white vigilantes lynched Babe Matthews. Andrew D. Lytle Collection, Mss. 893, 1254, Louisiana and Lower Mississippi Valley Collection, LSU Libraries, Baton Rouge, LA.

of destruction in the summer and fall of 1875. They organized around the total destruction of Black democracy in the parish. This was precisely what they said in the press and exactly what they accomplished.[45]

Testifying years after the official end of Reconstruction, George Andrew Jackson Swazie, state senator from neighboring West Feliciana Parish, identified two key components of the coup that ousted Gair and so many other democratically elected politicians of color. The first was the rabid white supremacy of plantation elites and the second was their alliance with white northerners. Swazie observed that "the moment any of these United States soldiers came up there, he was taken to the house of white men like you, and his hair was plaited, and whatever the [white] people wanted to do he turned his back on it." Because of their friendliness with former enslavers, Swazie theorized, "the negro stood no chance with them." This understanding between white northerners and planters, though hardly universal, laid the groundwork for the wave of white vigilantism that "commenced when John G[ai]r was killed, and never ceased until the State was in the hands of the Democratic party." "It was just a continual thing all along," Swazie recalled. "The people were scared to death, and voted just as the white people told them." Seeing scores of Black politicians and organizers killed had fundamentally altered the revolutionary political landscape of the postwar plantation. This was, to be clear, by design. White supremacists, through a counterrevolution of brazen and unprosecuted vigilantism, rejected the political and civil rights of Black Louisianans.[46]

The wave of violence that impacted East Feliciana swept the state in 1874 and 1875, and though it did not bring an immediate political end to Reconstruction, it made lasting democratic change impossible in the state. Particularly difficult was the inability of the state government in New Orleans to guarantee the safety of their constituents and even officeholders on Louisiana's plantations. Yet this outcome was hardly inevitable. Black Louisianans had mobilized throughout the state in the aftermath of the Civil War and seized widespread power between 1868 and 1874. With it, they vigorously pursued an alternate vision of the implications of emancipation. They demanded land as a consequence of liberty, wages as a consequence of work, and public office as an expression of democracy. Their efforts were hamstrung by a lack of institutional power, itself a product of slavery. The legal and judicial systems remained largely in white hands, the result of generations of access to education and capital. And this disparity had consequences—crimes against African Americans were consistently underpunished. The result of this asymmetrical pattern of violence was that white power was applied to African Americans despite the technical legal protections they enjoyed. The landscape of emancipation and equality had been transformed into one of torture and subjugation.[47]

The antebellum plantation landscape had been defined by violence. Slaveowners and overseers used their control of enslaved people's bodies—threatening beatings, rape, starvation, sale, and even death—to force slaves to till their fields, harvest their crops, cook their meals, and empty their bedpans. They only relinquished this control at the end of a bayonet. White northerners, even seemingly dedicated ones like Lt. Webster, had proved inconsistent allies. They embraced emancipation in part because African Americans in Confederate territory had refused to remain enslaved. As Reconstruction dragged on, however, their tepid commitment to enforce its reforms waned. By the time John Gair and Babe Matthews had been murdered, Congress and President Grant had refused to commit more troops to stem a rising tide of white conservative violence. Under such conditions, the radical Black politics of the postwar plantation could not survive. At the mercy of white supremacists with a state-sanctioned monopoly on violence, Black politicians began to give up the cause. White conservatives took refuge, not in the law or democracy, but in the violence through which they had dominated the plantation landscape prior to secession. Theirs was an apt assessment of the source of their power that replaced new landscapes of equality and opportunity with all-too-familiar systems of racial oppression.[48]

NOTES

1. "Reminiscence of Radical Republicanism," *St. Landry Clarion,* March 24, 1900, p. 2. A search of the Library of Congress newspaper database indicates that no copy of the *East Feliciana Columbian* has survived, so I have relied on the reprinted article. The author's memory faltered on one point: Gair had served two terms in the state legislature but had failed in his 1874 bid for state senate.

This essay builds upon an impressive and growing body of research on Louisiana's antebellum plantations and the men, women, and children who tilled their soil and harvested their crops. See Walter Johnson, *Soul by Soul: Life Inside the Antebellum Slave Market* (Cambridge, MA: Harvard University Press, 1999); John Rodrigue, *Reconstruction in the Cane Fields: From Slavery to Free Labor in Louisiana's Sugar Parishes 1862–1880* (Baton Rouge: Louisiana State University Press, 2001); Richard Follett, *The Sugar Masters: Planters and Slaves in Louisiana's Cane World, 1820–1860* (Baton Rouge: Louisiana State University Press, 2005); Rebecca Scott, *Degrees of Freedom: Louisiana and Cuba after Slavery* (Cambridge, MA: Harvard University Press, 2005); Justin Nystrom, *New Orleans after the Civil War: Race, Politics, and a New Birth of Freedom* (Baltimore, MD: Johns Hopkins University Press, 2010); Adam Rothman, *Beyond Freedom's Reach: A Kidnapping in the Twilight of Slavery* (Cambridge, MA: Harvard University Press, 2015).

2. "Politics" in this essay refers both to the contemporary usage of voting and officeholding, and also to the larger context of the general body politic: the activity and interactions of those under a governing structure, in this case the plantation.

3. The following census data illustrate the inversion of power initiated by Gair, Clark, and the formerly enslaved politicians of the postemancipation landscape. These earliest known references to these Black revolutionaries named only their enslavers, illuminating a power dynamic that Black politicians like Clark and Gair would totally upend after emancipation. B. F. Clark, 1860 Census, Clinton, East Feliciana Parish, LA, dwelling 117, household 117; B. F. Clark, 1860 Slave Schedules, East Feliciana Parish, LA, p. 27; T. M. J. Clark, 1870 Census, Clinton, East Feliciana Parish, LA, dwelling 94, household 94; Toney M. Clark, 1910 Census, District 186, Ward 11, Orleans Parish, LA, 2821 Dryades St., dwelling 464, household 542. V. Elaine Thompson, *Clinton, Louisiana: Society, Politics, and Race Relations in a Nineteenth-Century Southern Small Town* (Lafayette: University of Louisiana at Lafayette Press, 2014), 49 n. 19.

4. For the workings of slavery and its importance in the antebellum South, see Johnson, *Soul by Soul;* Ira Berlin, *Generations of Captivity: A History of African-American Slaves* (Cambridge, MA: Harvard University Press, 2003); Walter Johnson, *River of Dark Dreams: Slavery and Empire*

in the Cotton Kingdom (Cambridge, MA: Harvard University Press, 2013); Edward Baptist, *The Half Has Never Been Told: Slavery and the Making of American Capitalism* (New York: Basic Books, 2014); Daina Ramey Berry, *The Price for Their Pound of Flesh: The Value of the Enslaved, from Womb to Grave, in the Building of a Nation* (Boston: Beacon, 2017). For the development of slavery in Louisiana, see Gwendolyn Midlo Hall, *Africans in Colonial Louisiana: The Development of Afro-Creole Culture in the Eighteenth Century* (Baton Rouge: Louisiana State University Press, 1992); Rashauna Johnson, *Slavery's Metropolis: Unfree Labor in New Orleans during the Age of Revolutions* (New York: Cambridge University Press, 2016).

5. Eric Foner, *The Fiery Trial: Abraham Lincoln and American Slavery* (New York: Norton, 2010), 223–27, 231–40, 244; Phillip W. Magness and Sebastian N. Page, *Colonization after Emancipation: Lincoln and the Movement for Black Resettlement* (Columbia, MO: University of Missouri Press, 2011), 118–28.

In Oakes's words, Lincoln was "elected on a promise to put slavery on a course of ultimate extinction," a goal that Oakes claims animated Lincoln from his first days in office despite his pronouncements to the contrary. Though he skirts "the question of *who* freed the slaves" as an oversimplification in the preface to *Freedom National,* the issue totally reframes white northerners' role in abolition and their notion of its limits. The question of *who* freed the slaves, though indeed simplistic, is nonetheless essential. Oakes and others who celebrate Lincoln and his supporters as advocates of emancipation *do* make an additional, implicit claim about why the state chose emancipation that privileges formal over informal politics and archival documents produced by white actors over the actions of their Black contemporaries. In short, they give too much weight to white-dominated politics and not enough to the enslaved people who forced white northerners to make emancipation a wartime aim. For more on Black contributions to emancipation and the reason they matter, see Berlin's *Slaves No More.*

James Oakes, *Freedom National: The Destruction of Slavery in the United States, 1861–1865* (New York: Norton, 2013), xiii, xvii (quote), xxi–xxiii, 1–5, 26, 258–69, 277–81; Oakes, *The Scorpion's Sting: Antislavery and the Coming of the Civil War* (New York: Norton, 2014), 17–18 (quote); Ira Berlin et al., *Slaves No More: Three Essays on Emancipation and the Civil War* (New York: Cambridge University Press, 1992), 36–37.

6. "Maroon," from the American Spanish word *cimarron,* originally referred to a person or animal that was wild or unruly. It came to mean a slave who either repeatedly fled the plantation or who lived for an extended period of time as a runaway, specifically in the wilderness and often with others in independent communities. The act of establishing settlements of maroons became known as marronage. Neil Roberts, *Freedom as Marronage* (Chicago: University of Chicago Press, 2015), 3–6. For more, see Sylviane A. Diouf, *Slavery's Exiles: The Story of the American Maroons* (New York: New York University Press, 2014); Daniel Rasmussen, *American Uprising: The Untold Story of America's Largest Slave Revolt* (New York: Harper Collins, 2011).

7. Testimony of Corporal Octave Johnson before the American Freedmen's Inquiry Commission, February [?] 1864, filed with O-328 1863, Letters Received, ser. 12, RG 94, in *Freedom: A Documentary History of Emancipation, 1861–1867, Series 3: Volume I, Land and Labor, 1865,* ed. Ira Berlin et al. (New York: Cambridge University Press, 1985), 217. See also David Blight, *A Slave*

No More: Two Men Who Escaped to Freedom, Including Their Own Narratives of Emancipation (New York: Mariner Books, 2007).

8. Luke Camey, John Johnson and Nine (9) other f.m.c. representing the laborers on the Black Water Plantation, Case 14, February 12, 1866, Letters Sent, Volume 4, January 1866–March 1867, February–March 1868, Roll 64, Records of the Field Offices for the State of Louisiana, Bureau of Refugees, Freedmen, and Abandoned Lands, 1863–1872, Record Group 105, National Archives, Washington DC (abbreviated hereafter as LBRFAL). See also Jed Smith to A. H. Nickerson, February 27, 1866; M. A. Reno to A. H. Nickerson, March 15, 1866, Unregistered Letters Received, December 1865–December 1868, Roll 64, LBRFAL. For more, see Stephanie McCurry, *Confederate Reckoning: Power and Politics in the Civil War South* (Cambridge, MA: Harvard University Press, 2010); David Roediger, *Seizing Freedom: Slave Emancipation and Liberty for All* (New York: Verso, 2014).

9. W. E. B. Du Bois, *Black Reconstruction in America, 1860–1880* (1935; repr., New York: Meridian, 1964), 55.

10. New Orleans fell to the Union in 1862, making the Emancipation Proclamation of 1863 a moot point in the lower Mississippi River valley, as large numbers of slaves had already fled the plantations for Union camps, in essence declaring themselves free and becoming what the Union referred to as "Contraband."

11. Major General Gordon Granger, General Order No. 3, in "From Texas: Important Orders by General Granger," *New York Times,* July 7, 1865, p. 1.

12. Beginning in 1865 with South Carolina and Mississippi, Black Codes were laws passed to limit the mobility and agency of the newly freed African American population. This is not to be confused with the Code Noir of 1685.

13. Black Codes in Louisiana took the form of expanded vagrancy laws. See Dubois, *Black Reconstruction,* 177.

14. Bat Henryham v. William Barrow and Charles Barrow and Others, Miscellaneous Court Records and Complaints, September 1865–November 1868, Roll 66, LBRFAL.

15. James Hogue, *Uncivil War: Five New Orleans Street Battles and the Rise and Fall of Radical Reconstruction* (Baton Rouge: Louisiana State University Press, 2006), 40–45.

16. W. R. C. Lyons v. Robert Morris and Alfred Bartee, July 31, 1866, Lake Providence, Records Relating to Court Cases, February 1866–March 1867, Roll 82, LBRFAL.

17. Nero Mack, Case 4, Bayou Sara, LA, May 8, 1867, Register of Complaints, May 1867–August 1868, Roll 66; J. U. Ball and laborers on Hades Plantation for the year 1867, January 7, 1867, Labor Contracts, West Feliciana and Winn Parishes, Roll 51, LBRFAL.

18. *Thomas S. Sanders v. John Davis,* December 17, 1867, Pattersonville, LA, Court Records, July 1864–November 1867 Roll 77, LBRFAL; Thomas S. Sanders, 1860 Census, Western District, St. Mary Parish, LA, dwelling 697, household 697.

19. William Webster to L. O. Parker, July 31, 1867, Baton Rouge, Letters Sent, Volume 2, July 1867–May 1868, Roll 61, LBRFAL.

20. *Beckorn, McMillan & Co. v. Clark Gibson,* September 2, 1866, Lake Providence, Records Relating to Court Cases, February 1866–March 1867, Roll 82, LBRFAL.

21. Testimony of John H. Medbery, Oct. 20, 1867; Testimony of J. W. Medbery, Oct. 20, 1867, Unregistered Letters Received, December 1865–December 1868, Target 1, Roll 65, LBRFAL.

22. *Constitution Adopted by the State Constitutional Convention of the State of Louisiana, 7 March 1868* (New Orleans, LA, 1868).

23. Lt. James DeGrey to Lt. L. O. Parker, Sept. 30, 1867, Clinton, Trimonthly Reports of Operations Sent, vol. 1, January–December 1867, Roll 69, LBRFAL.

24. T. M. J. Clark, 1870 Census, Clinton, East Feliciana Parish, LA, dwelling 94, household 94; "The Howe Committee," Testimony of T. [M. J.] Clark, *New Orleans Republican,* January 6, 1877, p. 1. Thompson, *Clinton, Louisiana,* 158; Robert Ray, 1870 Census, Ward 5, New Orleans, Orleans Parish, Louisiana, dwelling 763, household 1060; Robert Ray, Company D, 82nd USCT, Compiled Military Service Records of Volunteer Union Soldiers Who Served the United States Colored Troops: 56th–138th USCT Infantry, 1864–66, Roll 82, Record Group 94, National Archives and Records Administration, Washington, DC.

25. The war was commonly referred to as the Rebellion, especially in the decades after it ended. When the most important documents of the war were published between 1880 and 1900, for example, they titled the collection *The War of the Rebellion.* A more popular example is "Rebel yell," a term we still use that comes from this earlier way of referring to the war. Many historians prefer the term Rebellion because it was used by contemporaries and because it most accurately describes secession. After the war, prominent supporters of slavery and secession began a propaganda campaign to describe the war as an act of northern aggression. By wanting slavery to end, the argument went, Republican politicians wanted to harm white southerners. This postwar, proslavery propaganda campaign is where we get a shift to terms like the "Civil War," the "War Between the States," the "War of Northern Aggression," etc., as ways of painting slavery and secession in a more favorable light. For more on the terms and why they are important, see David Blight, *Race and Reunion: The Civil War in American Memory* (Cambridge, MA: Harvard University Press, 2001).

26. "Le Droit de Suffrage des Noirs," *New Orleans Tribune,* June 10, 1866, p. 1. Original 1: "blancs, noirs et rouges, et cetera." Original 2: "Car il sait bien que tous les hommes . . . Sont tous les même, et que nous sommes; Les fils d'Adam." Charles Vincent, *Black Legislators in Louisiana during Reconstruction* (Baton Rouge: Louisiana State University Press, 1975), 74, 234.

27. Joseph Honoré to Maj. Genl. P. H. Sheridan, June 29, 1867, Registered Letters Received, April–December 1867, Roll 96 (quote); Maj. H. F. Wallace to General J. A. Mower, August 3, 1867, Letters Sent, Volume 1, March 1866–June 1868, Roll 96, LBRFAL. Perhaps unbeknownst to H. F. Wallace, the local Bureau agent who reported that Honoré was a Rebel sympathizer, the Pointe Coupée Light Brigade apparently disbanded immediately after the Union liberation of New Orleans. "From Pointe Coupée Parish," *New Orleans Republican,* April 22, 1868, p. 1; "State Representatives," *New Orleans Republican,* May 1, 1868, p. 1; "Republican State Convention," *New Orleans Republican,* May 2, 1868, p. 1.

28. Amanda Reece Mushal, "Social Networks and the Development of a Commercial Middle Class in Antebellum South Carolina," in *The Southern Middle Class in the Long Nineteenth Century: Founder of Louisiana State University,* ed. Jonathan Wells and Jennifer Green (Baton Rouge: Louisiana State University Press, 2011), 62–83.

29. Lt. William Webster to L. O. Parker, August 31, 1867, Baton Rouge, LA, Letters Sent, Volume 2, July 1867–May 1868, Roll 61, LBRFAL; A., "Letter from Baton Rouge," *New Orleans Tribune,* November 12, 1867, p. 4. For more, see Steven Hahn, *A Nation Under Our Feet: Black Political Struggles in the Rural South from Slavery to the Great Migration* (Cambridge, MA: Harvard University Press, 2003).

30. Lt. William Webster to L. O. Parker, August 31, 1867, Baton Rouge, LA, Letters Sent, Volume 2, July 1867–May 1868, Roll 61, LBRFAL.

31. "From West Feliciana: Great Republican Meeting Near St. Francisville," *New Orleans Republican,* July 14, 1868, p. 1.

32. *Supplemental Report of Joint Committee of the General Assembly of Louisiana on the Conduct of the Late Elections, and the Condition of Peace and Good Order in the State* (New Orleans: A. L. Lee, 1869), 81.

33. "We take the following from the *Patriot-Democrat,*" *Semi-Weekly Republican,* October 8, 1872, p. 1. See also "The Affray at Salem Church," *Semi-Weekly Republican,* October 15, 1872, p. 1. For more on Champlin, see "A New Parish Proposed," *New Orleans Republican,* January 12, 1872, p. 6; Horace S. Champlin, 1850 Census, Pampas Township, Dekalb County, Illinois, dwelling 3, household 4; H. S. Champlin, 1870 Census, Ward 1, East Feliciana Parish, Louisiana, dwelling 731, household 659.

34. H. F. Wallace to Lt. L. O. Parker, Sept. 10, 1867, New Roads, Trimonthly and Special Reports, vol. 1, April 1866–May 1868, Target 1, Roll 97, LBRFAL.

35. *Supplemental Report,* 67–70, 68 (quote), 70 (quote). For more, see Chris Dier, *The 1868 St. Bernard Parish Massacre: Blood in the Cane Fields* (Charleston: The History Press, 2017).

36. *Weekly Louisianan,* October 24, 1874, p. 2; Thompson, *Clinton, Louisiana,* 167–68.

37. LeeAnna Keith, *The Colfax Massacre: The Untold Story of Black Power, White Terror, and the Death of Reconstruction* (New York: Oxford University Press, 2008), 88–110; Charles Lane, *The Day Freedom Died: The Colfax Massacre, the Supreme Court, and the Failure of Reconstruction* (New York: Holt & Co., 2008); Hogue, *Uncivil War,* 116–28.

38. *Patriot-Democrat,* June 26, 1875, reprinted "Feliciana to be Redeemed," *New Orleans Republican,* July 10, 1875, p. 2.

39. "What the Negro is Doing," *New Orleans Bulletin,* July 14, 1875, p. 1. The White League was one of many white supremacist paramilitary organizations formed by ex-Confederates in the wake of emancipation to combat equality. The Ku Klux Klan is the best remembered of these groups.

40. "The Case Fairly Stated," *New Orleans Republican,* September 24, 1875, p. 1.

41. "The East Feliciana Matter," *New Orleans Bulletin,* August 13, 1875, p. 1.

42. "White League Diabolism," *Weekly Louisianan,* October 30, 1875, p. 2; "Blood on the Border," *New Orleans Republican,* October 15, 1875, p. 1; *Report of the Select Committee on the Recent Election in Louisiana, 44th Congress, 2nd Session, House Misc. Document 34, pts. 1–3* (Washington, DC: Government Printing Office, 1877).

Thompson examines the alleged poisoning incident but overlooks contemporary newspapers in her account. The Congressional testimony upon which she relies exclusively is incredibly important, but it gives an account of events at the distance of one and one-half years, well after white supremacists had virtually annihilated the Black revolutionary movement in East Feliciana. The devastating white supremacist onslaught during the election of 1876, which inspired the Congressional inquiry in the first place, would have clearly skewed its findings. Balancing this testimony with the contemporary newspaper record supports, I believe, a different conclusion—that the assassination of John Gair and the lynching of his sister-in-law Babe Matthews were a response to their political views rather than the alleged poisoning plot. Indeed, their murders were part of a wave of white conservative vigilantism that swept the state in the aftermath of Colfax. For more, see Samuel Hyde, *Pistols and Politics: The Dilemma of Democracy in Louisiana's Florida Parishes, 1810–1899* (Baton Rouge: Louisiana State University Press, 1996), 186–87; Thompson, *Clinton, Louisiana,* 135–45. For context, Lane, *The Day Freedom Died,* 186–228; Hogue, *Uncivil War,* 116–43; Gilles Vandal, *Rethinking Southern Violence: Homicides in Post–Civil War Louisiana, 1866–1884* (Columbus, OH: Ohio State University Press, 2000).

43. "Blood on the Border," *New Orleans Republican,* October 15, 1875, p. 1.

44. Excerpt from the Clinton *Patriot-Democrat* reprinted in "A Prelude to the Murder of John Gair," *New Orleans Republican,* October 16, 1875, p. 1.

45. "The White Line Disorders" and "A Prelude to the Murder of John Gair," October 16, 1875, *New Orleans Republican,* October 16, 1875, p. 1; "The East Feliciana Crime," *New Orleans Republican,* October 23, 1875, p. 1.

46. Testimony of George Andrew Jackson Swazie, November 26, 1879, Spofford v. Kellogg, *Reports of the Committees of the Senate of the United States for the First and Second Sessions of the Forty-Sixth Congress, 1879–80* (Washington, DC: Government Printing Office, 1880), 768.

47. Vandal, *Rethinking Southern Violence,* 162–63.

48. Eric Foner, *Reconstruction: America's Unfinished Revolution, 1863–1877* (New York: Harper and Rowe, 1988), 565–75.

AFTER PERSAC

Imagining the Plantation Landscape from the Civil War to the Great Depression

JOCHEN WIERICH

For painters and photographers of the Civil War and Reconstruction eras, portraying the southern plantation landscape was a challenge. The land and buildings that once represented the power of white landowners and the dehumanization of enslaved people had been ravaged and lay in ruins. Crop production on the plantations had diminished or stopped altogether, plantation houses fell into disrepair, homes were converted into hospitals. All of these historic myths and realities later made it into Margaret Mitchell's literary epic *Gone with the Wind* (1936) and the resulting Hollywood movie (1939). This essay offers an overview of the plantation image as it was reconstituted in the visual arts between the Civil War and 1940. The plantation views painted by Marie Adrien Persac right before the Civil War represent an artist's idealized image, an architectural dream that set a visual standard for subsequent artists to revise and reimagine. Persac's mapmaking and paintings form a kind of visual mastery that was almost unattainable by the artists who followed him.

Persac's *Norman's Chart of the Lower Mississippi River* (fig. 1) compresses the plantation landscape of the lower Mississippi River valley into a vertical engraving that alters the flatness of river and land boundaries with deeper perspectival vignettes of places. Initially, one might wonder why Persac did not include a view of Natchez in the top part, given the map's title and subject, instead of Baton Rouge. Most likely, he did not have the opportunity to visit Natchez or spend any extended time there to create a drawing. Or perhaps he

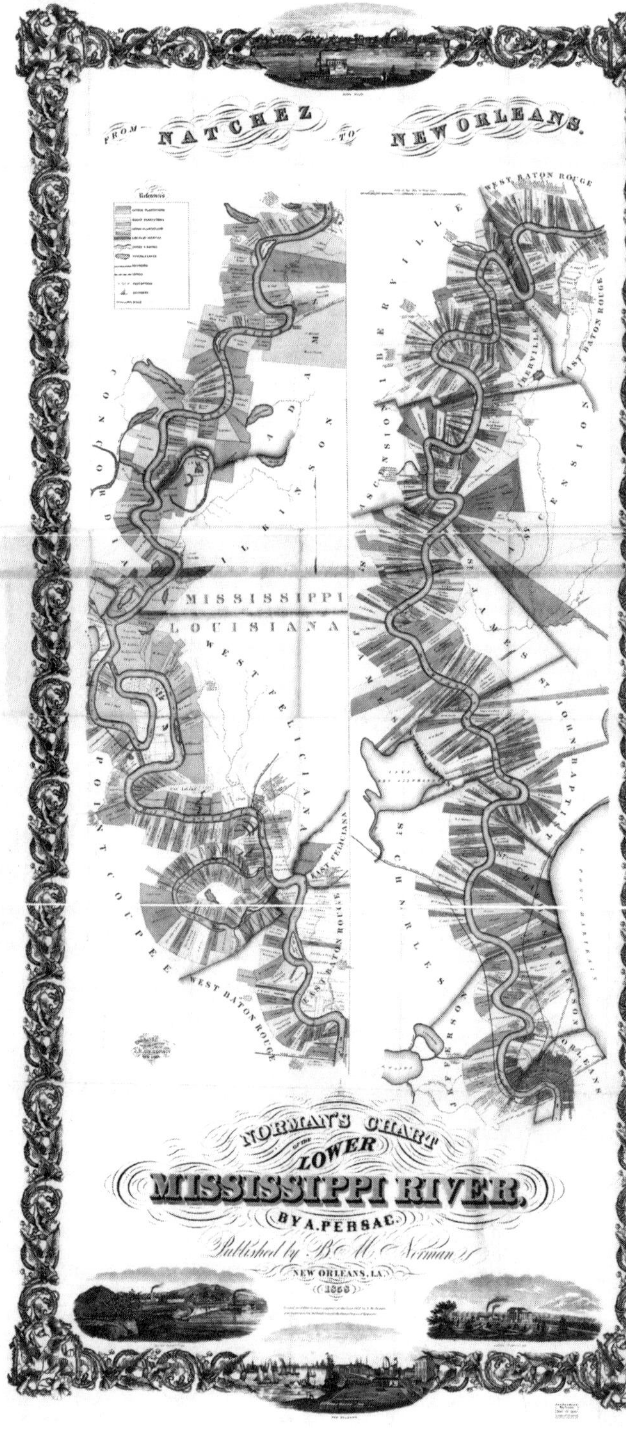
FROM NATCHEZ TO NEW ORLEANS.
MISSISSIPPI
LOUISIANA
CONCORDIA
WEST FELICIANA
POINT COUPEE
EAST FELICIANA
EAST BATON ROUGE
WEST BATON ROUGE
IBERVILLE
ASCENSION
ST. JAMES
ST. JOHN BAPTIST
ST. CHARLES
JEFFERSON
ORLEANS
NORMAN'S CHART OF THE LOWER MISSISSIPPI RIVER,
BY A. PERSAC.
Published by B. M. Norman
NEW ORLEANS, LA.

decided he needed to have a vignette that would appeal to potential buyers in his hometown, Baton Rouge. Still, the absence of a Natchez vignette in the map is perplexing; certainly, Persac's New Orleans publisher, Benjamin Moore Norman, would have considered Natchez a principal market for selling the print.

Despite this omission, the map is a powerful display of landownership, color coded and separated by sugar and cotton plantations. Within the oeuvre of Persac's plantation views that he produced between 1857 and 1861, the map is a pictorial and topographic survey, allowing the viewer to bring to mind individual plantations by looking at the abstract shapes. More than the individual views on the map's border, *Norman's Chart* validates the socioeconomic status collectively shared by the planter class. It also reveals an optimism that prevailed among planters at the end of the 1850s. The cotton economy was booming, the prices for slaves were at an all-time high, and planters had disposable income to build ever-larger mansions and buy consumer goods from America and abroad. This was certainly the case in Natchez and Adams County where the number of elite families having the "luxury of great wealth" was estimated at about sixty.[1]

Had Persac worked in Natchez—there is no hard evidence he did—I suspect he would have applied the same formula for plantation views that he had developed in his gouache drawings of the Louisiana cultural landscape. Simply put, his views were panoramas that covered the architectural and agricultural elements of plantations with a high degree of detail rendered with the hand of a precise draftsman, animated by some painterly touches in the reflections of water or, occasionally, clouds. In their literal and photographic method, they encapsulate two interdependent views: one is the fact that these plantation landscapes represent the control and power that planters exerted over their dominion; second, the works reinforce the idea that the plantation landscape is a natural part of the lower Mississippi River valley cultivated by a natural order of master and enslaved. The drawings as well as the map suggest a window into the cultural landscape of the plantation with the cold, analytic eye of the architect and engineer that Persac was. The plantation views echo topographical views of European palaces and estates produced by Dutch, British, and French artists in the seventeenth and eighteenth centuries often published as engravings in

Figure 1. *Norman's Chart of the Lower Mississippi River,* by Marie Adrien Persac, Benjamin Moore Norman, and J. H. Colton & Co. (New Orleans: B. M. Norman, 1858). Available at https://www.loc.gov/item/78692178/.

bound volumes. While a direct influence is difficult to prove, a number of European prints might have served as inspiration for Persac, including the aerial views of English country estates by Dutchmen Johannes Kip (1652/53–1722) and Leonard Knyff (1650–1722) that appeared as *Britannia Illustrata* (1707), a single volume of eighty views. Or he might have been familiar with the prints of French châteaux by the Perelles family. Father Gabriel Perelle (1595–1677) and his sons Nicolas (born 1631) and Adam (1640–1695) produced aerial views of the great estates in France from Versailles to Chantilly. Their views of mansions and gardens were published by Nicolas Langlois (1640–1703) as *Veues des Belles Maisons de France* in 1703. These European estate pictures could be adopted to the plantation economy in the New World that reigned not only in the American South but also in Latin America and the Caribbean islands. The aerial view that Persac adopted for the layout of his topographic map drew on European precedents but also anticipated a mode of aerial viewing that emerged in nineteenth-century photography.[2]

While Persac's map and plantation paintings can serve as documents in the study of the cultural landscape, they are not transparent windows. They are visual constructs that incorporate historic conventions and foreshadow pictorial innovation. What is omitted in these images is just as important as what is included. It is also important to note how Persac's practice overlaps with the technology of photography and how that dialogue continues in the period after the Civil War.[3] In 1861, Persac created a view of the sumptuous interior of a Mississippi River steamboat, most likely the *Imperial* that ran between St. Louis and New Orleans (fig. 2).

Persac's gouache and collage composition is an architectural tour de force of the main cabin or saloon and places the viewer between the front office and bar looking into a long, tunnel-like dining area. These kinds of ornately designed spaces were the main feature of the steamship interior, incorporating Gothic revival architecture with rococo revival furniture. Persac worked in the photography business starting in the 1850s, and it is possible he used a photographic device to aid him in composing this remarkably detailed architectural rendering. According to one source, the portrait of the man and woman entering the space from the left resembles a contemporary photograph of Persac and his wife Odile taken after their marriage.[4] Though dating from later in the nineteenth century, the Gantry and Norman collection at Louisiana State University's Special Collections has several examples of a photographer, most likely Henry

Figure 2. *Interior of the Main Cabin of the Steamboat Princess,* 1861, by Marie Adrien Persac, gouache and collage on paper, Gift of Mrs. Mamie Persac Lusk; conservation with funds provided by Robert T. and Linda H. Bowsher. LSUMOA 75.8. Photo by David Humphreys. Several figures are standing inside the sumptuous entrance hall of a steamship main cabin. Behind them stretches a long view of the dining area with Black attendants in white service uniforms.

Norman, documenting the saloons. One photograph, dating from about 1890, entitled *Interior View of an Anchor Line Steamboat's Salon Set for a Meal, #1,* places the viewer at the center of the long dining hall (fig. 3).[5]

The perspective of Persac's image is deeper and reveals more manipulation of space beyond the limitation of camera angle. He simply went beyond what the camera could capture and included multiple details distributed with equal legibility across the entire picture plane: bottles behind the barman, top hats on the side tables, cuspidors on the floor, compotes, tureens, and bowls on the table, and the list goes on. Like his plantation views, this picture of a steamboat borders on fantasy, allowing for anyone familiar with his map to imagine the steamboat passage on the river as luxurious and privileged.

The inclusion of a Black waiter in the steamship photograph by Henry

Figure 3. *Interior View of an Anchor Line Steamboat's Salon Set for a Meal #1*, c. 1890, Norman Studio. This photograph shows the interior of a steamboat's dining area. Black waiters are standing along tables set for a meal. Louisiana State University Special Collections, Thomas H. and Joan W. Gandy Photograph Collection.

Norman, while marginal, stands in contrast to Persac's painting where Black figures are faint specks in the distant background. As John Michael Vlach has pointed out, except for a very few images, the Persac plantation paintings omit the enslaved population who worked the estates he portrayed.[6] This omission can very well be attributed to the expectations of clients who may not have wanted any reference to the forced labor system that enabled their wealth. The enslaved workers were considered irrelevant and of little consequence, a paradox since there was so much capital invested in them. The signs of labor and bondage simply did not suit the overall effect that Persac's images projected to please his clients. Their world was one of aristocratic leisure, carefully acted out by Persac's cutout figures along the picture plane of the plantations and steamship interiors.

The Civil War, emancipation, and the transformation of the plantation economy into a sharecropping system inevitably made the idealized world that

Persac portrayed an unreal and even quaint fantasy. A cursory survey of photographs taken during and shortly after the Civil War by Mathew Brady, Timothy O'Sullivan, Henry Moore, and others reveals views of emancipated African Americans that help the viewer imagine the enslaved people that Persac's world suppressed.[7] Although set in South Carolina, the O'Sullivan photographs from the J. J. Smith plantation near Beaufort (1862), allow us to picture the mass of enslaved people who worked the rice, sugar, and cotton plantations in the South (fig. 4).[8]

In one of them, the photographer looks straight at a group of African Americans; they are slaves or, more likely, former slaves who stand in front of houses or cabins as if they are newly emancipated. Another photo from the Smith plantation, now in the Getty Collection, compresses the long panorama view à la Persac and cuts out the mansion or "big house," but it includes elements one would expect from a Persac composition: the slender trees and canopies, white buildings, presumably slave cabins, and some white fence posts. However, the presence of close to one hundred African Americans posing in the heat of the

Figure 4. *Smith's Plantation, Beaufort, SC,* 1862, by Timothy H. O'Sullivan, printed later. A large group of African American men, women, and children standing in front of two cabins. Library of Congress Prints and Photographs Division, Washington, DC.

summer for a northern photographer who views the scene from an elevated position, as if on the balcony of the big house, creates a new problem of legibility. These photographs present to the viewer a multigenerational group of African Americans whose lives were defined by the plantation, but they do not provide any clue where the people are going, how they will make a livelihood, or what happened to the white people who kept them in bondage.

Photographs of African Americans in the center of the plantation landscape clearly shift the perspective from Persac's idealized aristocratic space toward the social reality of the postslavery South. By doing so, these photographs fill an important gap while posing challenging questions in interpreting the post–Civil War era of plantation images. An obvious question is how did the plantation change as a signifier as artists and photographers were reimagining the American South during Reconstruction and beyond? In my reading of the renderings of plantations from roughly between 1860 and 1940, I will focus on the lower Mississippi River valley and the two places that epitomized the continuation of the cotton economy, Natchez and Vicksburg.

The economic collapse of the plantation economy during and after the Civil War dramatically changed the southern landscape, physically and socially—masters became plantation managers or absentee landowners; slaves became freedmen, laborers, farmers, and professionals. James Surget, Alexander K. Farrar, and Haller Nutt are three representative planters from the Natchez area who lost their wealth and were fortunate to have kept their land and its structures. James Surget, for example, lost his mansion Clifton after a Union office ordered it to be demolished to make room for a fortification. Haller Nutt was unable to complete his dream house, the octagonal mansion Longwood designed by Philadelphia architect Samuel Sloan. In 1861, after news arrived that Fort Sumter had been attacked, the northern workers at Longwood walked off the job, leaving their work tools behind and Longwood forever unfinished. Near Vicksburg, on Davis Bend, the plantation previously owned by Joseph Davis (Jefferson Davis's brother) became the site of a social experiment as management of the plantation was transferred to former slave Benjamin Montgomery. Even during the antebellum years, Joseph Davis had operated his plantation Hurricane guided by the principals of utopian ideals. Joseph first leased the land to the former slaves and eventually allowed them to buy it. But with the end of Reconstruction, burdened by debt and a legal battle with the heirs of Joseph Davis, the Montgomery family lost the property.[9]

As the post–Civil War planter elite was rebuilding their economic base by regaining control of labor, very few artists were inspired to reframe the plantation image after Persac. The plantation view, including the land, main buildings, dependencies, workers, livestock, and equipment, had simply lost its status as a signifier of wealth and social order; there was no motivation for plantation owners to commission a view of a piece of property so diminished in value. With little patronage from the new class of landowners, whether from old southern wealth or new northern capital, the plantation landscape disappeared as a genre in art. For two of the visual artists who described the post–Civil War southern landscape as travelers, James Wells Champney (1843–1903) and Alfred Waud (1828–1891), the plantation was a marginal subject, a relic from the past that one ignored. However, a third artist in my discussion below, William Aiken Walker (1838–1921), reinvented the plantation view in an era of tourism and increased mobility.

Travel writer Edward King, who traveled the southern states in 1873 and 1874 accompanied by the artist and illustrator James Wells Champney, explained the planter's economic reality. Before the war, planters invested profits in more land and more slaves. After the war, they could only operate on "borrowed capital" and rely "on a merchant or middle-man to furnish food and clothing for his laborers." King continues: "Life is somewhat barren and unattractive to the man who, after a laborious season spent in cultivating one staple, finds that, after all, he has only made a living out of it. He has done nothing to make his surroundings agreeable and comfortable: his buildings are unsightly and rickety, and there are very few stores in his cellar, if indeed he has any cellar at all." In other words, paternalism prevailed in the plantation South; the planter was still a "provider," but his power was greatly diminished, emblematized by the "unsightly" outward appearance of his buildings.[10]

The travel accounts that made up *Great South* were originally commissioned and published in serial form by *Scribner's Monthly*. One might expect a popular magazine to provide some documentation of the post–Civil War plantation for its general readership, but of the hundreds of illustrations that accompanied King's reportage and subsequent book, not one depicted an architectural plantation view. The illustrations for his essays on Mississippi and Louisiana were city views of Natchez, Vicksburg, Baton Rouge, and New Orleans. Other images were of cotton steamers, African Americans as plantation workers, and cotton wagon trains. While King's text included reportage elements that focused on socioeconomic struggles and racial inequities, the illustrations by Champney were more heavily picturesque tourist views. According to King, many of the suburban planter's residencies were destroyed, but he took great delight in the survival of luxurious gardens, such as the ones belonging to Andrew Brown at Magnolia Vale at Natchez-under-the-Hill. Brown's garden dated to the 1830s when the *Natchez Weekly Courier* described it as "a gorgeous scene of magnificence of beauty, with the residence of Mr. Brown embosomed like some fairy wrought scene in the Arabian nights."[11] Visitors to post–Civil War Natchez must have understood the flourishing gardens at Magnolia Vale as a sign of southern endurance and recovery. Edward King expressed his delight with these words: "I remember no palace garden in Europe which impressed me so powerfully with the sense of richness and exquisite profusion of costly and delicate blooms."[12] King deemed Brown's garden a special visual attraction in a place that had lost so much, evidenced in that he dedicated two of Champney's illustrations to this thriving holdover of Natchez's past glory. After the demise of the plantation mansion as a symbol of southern prosperity, the gardens of Natchez were the closest thing to splendor in the eyes of these northern observers.

While he was very active as a genre, portrait, and landscape painter, Champney had a long career as a travel or tourist artist who frequently went abroad to create visual souvenirs of the places he visited. Besides traveling to the South, Champney spent time in France, England, Germany, Holland, Italy, and traveled to Africa and South America. As art historian Judy Bullington has explained, while Champney's illustrations of the southern states were, on the surface, casual travel sketches and observations, the artist was negotiating a complex set of artistic identities from anthropologist to arbiter of truth.[13] More than one-third of his almost five hundred sketches from the South were of African-American life. In a section on sharecropping, entitled "The Share System," appears the Champney sketch *Scene on a Cotton Plantation,* featuring Black women and men picking cotton. One woman stands and rests and the basket in front of her is full, a sign of her labor and productivity. While she is reminiscent of the Black female figures standing in cotton fields painted by Winslow Homer in the 1870s, Champney's figure lacks the psychological depth and narrative possibilities. In this and in other assignments for popular magazines, Champney recorded social types, a practice he shared with modes of viewing in photography. For his middle-class viewers, he presented a carefully edited panorama of the South struggling with the difficult issues of Civil War defeat and the problems of Reconstruction and its uncertain future. This is where image and text presented an editorial mechanism to frame a scene and render it innocuous. In his 1875 travelogue, King wrote the following description surrounding an image of African Americans picking cotton: "Nothing can be more beautiful than the appearance of a cotton-field, extending over many hundreds of acres, when the snowy globes of wool are ready for picking, and the swart laborers, with sacks suspended from their shoulders, wander between the rows of plants, culling the fleeces" (fig. 5).[14]

Figure 5. *Scene on a Cotton Plantation,* 1875, by John Benjamin Champney. Illustration for Edward King, *The Great South* (1875).

Another example of traveling artists who largely ignored the old plantation view are Alfred Waud and William Waud (1832–1878), artist brothers from England who worked on assignment for different American illustrated magazines. William Waud worked as a special artist for Frank Leslie's *Illustrated Newspaper* during the Civil War. Alfred Waud covered the Civil War for *New York Illustrated News* and *Harper's Weekly.* It was Alfred Waud who traveled to the post–Civil War South on at least three occasions, first in 1866 when he was still employed by *Harper's Weekly,* in 1871 on assignment for *Every Saturday,* and in 1872 as a reporter for D. Appleton Publishing Company.[15] During these extended trips in the South, Alfred Waud produced hundreds of sketches based on observations in New Orleans as well as along the Mississippi River valley. In 1871, he traveled with writer Ralph Keeler on a steamboat north on the Mississippi River, but they did not complete their chronicle all the way to the river's source in Minnesota as planned. Waud's sketches from these trips present an anthropological record of river travels, recording African Americans on the streets of New Orleans, riverboat captains, and roustabouts. His views of Natchez and Vicksburg are panoramic, often placing the viewer on a distant hill or bluff overseeing the city. So generally picturesque and pastoral are his landscapes that the viewer gets the impression the war left no mark on the South, and the cities along the river are preserved in their pre–Civil War condition. During his visits to Natchez, Waud did not produce any views of the plantations and suburban mansions, but, like Champney, he sketched inside Andrew Brown's garden (fig. 6).

Figure 6. *Glimpse of Mr. Brown's Garden in Natchez,* 1866, by Alfred Waud. Pencil and Chinese white. Along a promenade lined by trees and leading up to a mansion walk several fine-dressed women. The Historic New Orleans Collection, Acc. No. 1977.137.7.14 i,ii.

His viewpoint is on the main axis, a broad promenade that led up to the Brown mansion lined by trees, flowerbeds, and additional paths. Waud included at least five or six visitors who were strolling through the garden; well-dressed ladies with umbrellas project a sense of gentility and leisure that gave Brown's garden an air of European garden culture. Such images reinforced the notion that Natchez and perhaps the lower Mississippi River valley remained intact after the Civil War and a picturesque place to visit. Indeed, such a positive account signaled to northern readers that Natchez could be a future tourist destination.[16]

It seems befitting that when federal troops left the South in 1877, marking the end of Reconstruction, and southern whites established "Home Rule" by regaining control of public offices, a southern painter would reframe the image of the plantation. A cursory view of William Aiken Walker's long career as a southern genre and landscape painter reveals an obsession with the plantation as an economic system that could be rendered visually pleasing for tourists and other consumers of plantation images. As Cynthia Seibels, a historian of Walker's work and biographer argues, the artist was eager to align his images with a "national consensus on life in the South"; and his vehicle was stereotypical portraits of African Americans as symbols of the plantation South.[17] As Seibels suggests, the caricatured figures of Blacks that appeared in Walker's paintings throughout the 1880s and 1890s coincided with the period of Lost Cause regional nationalism and the erection of Confederate monuments in town squares, efforts coordinated and financed largely by the United Daughters of the Confederacy, an organization of the wives, sisters, mothers, and widows of Confederate veterans. In light of the current national debate around these monuments, Walker's work is problematic and laden with discriminatory meaning, yet these concerns have not diminished demand for his work at auction sales where his paintings bring high returns.[18] But it also provides an important link in understanding the reconstitution of the plantation as a domain that exists not only as a physical space organized around a master-slave hierarchy but also as a "racial imaginary."[19]

Poet Claudia Rankine has used the term racial imaginary in speaking to contemporary issues in literary criticism. Here it applies to Walker's visual constructs of Blackness and their ability to speak to white audiences, both North and South, captivated by a postwar "mystique of black subjects."[20] In other words, Walker's images provided a visual space for viewers to enter the plantation and reimagine it as a landscape that was largely and almost exclusively populated by Black workers. By displacing the plantation house as the natural center into the far distance or by eliminating it altogether, Walker entirely revised the plantation view on which Persac had concentrated. Walker reconstituted the plantation view through a binary relationship of absence and presence, the absentee white plantation owner and the omnipresent Black laborer.

It seems naïve to see Walker's paintings as faithful renditions of what he saw in the field. August P. Trovaioli and Roulhac B. Toledano, the authors of an early monograph claimed that the artist approached his subject as a disinterested observer: "Walker was probably portraying a culture simply as he saw it, with no conscious intention to editorialize or philosophize about the political, cultural, or social conditions which gave rise to what he saw."[21] The authors of this study also made him out to be a preservationist who captured a people before the "forces of the New South had penetrated their lives."[22] Accordingly, Walker's role is akin to artists and photographers such as George Catlin, Edward S. Curtis, and Frank Rinehart who preserved the likenesses of Native Americans presumably threatened by extinction or modernization. But the notion that Walker's achievement was to record an authentic Black image is fraught with historical blindness. Along with other artists and writers, Walker created what Henry Louis Gates Jr. has called the "public fiction of the Negro" as "capable of expressing only two emotions, humor and pity."[23] In the benevolent and nonthreatening images of Walker's plantation Blacks, one can find a legacy of stereotyping that evolved into the endearing "retainer" figure of Mammy and Sambo and appropriated for Black movie characters and product mascots (Uncle Ben and Aunt Jemima). The idea that Walker was a preservationist of the plantation Black was later revised by Seibels who, in her biography of Walker, described him as a product of postwar nostalgia for the old plantation South, who was "presenting scenes of his world—the white world of the Old South—made right again."[24] Similarly, John Michael Vlach has argued that Walker's plantation views were "visual odes to the New South," which he linked with "the quasi-sacred agrarian ideals of the previous generation."[25]

Walker was the quintessential travel artist of the late nineteenth century. Born in Charleston, South Carolina, in 1838, he traveled extensively throughout eastern Florida; Augusta and Savannah, Georgia; the Delta and Gulf Coast of Mississippi; and New Orleans, Louisiana. He frequently traveled to the mountains of North Carolina and spent long periods in Arden, not far from Asheville. He died at the Charleston home of his nephew in 1921. Regarding the plantation landscape, Walker's oeuvre can be divided into three main subjects: the small full-length portraits, the small cabin scenes, and the larger plantation scenes. Starting in the mid-1870s, Walker made New Orleans his winter home and found a ready market for his work through dealers and auctioneers.[26] Walker was very systematic and business-minded as he worked through these types. He painted the smaller portraits on a larger board and then sold them as individual pieces on the streets of New Orleans or to tourists at resort hotels. According to Trovaioli and Toledano, Walker found his clients at the new southern resorts that catered to mostly northern tourists, including the Bon Air in Augusta, the Duval in Jacksonville, the DeSoto in Savannah, and the Battery Park in Asheville. Though these historians have claimed he was a compassionate observer, Walkers portraits were created for the tourist's gaze, popular fiction constructed for white audiences through spectatorship, nostalgia, and anthropological curiosity. To satisfy the tourist appetite for ethnic types, Walker, during one trip to South Carolina, took portrait photographs of African Americans and wrote the names of their African tribal origin on the margin of the print: Fanti, Hausa, Mandingo, and Gulla.[27]

Walker's occasional interest in ethnographic study should not distract from the fact he consistently relied on his pictorial formats to appeal to the prevailing taste for one-dimensional portraits of southern Blacks. Being predictable in style and historically ambiguous made him one of the most successful painters of the plantation landscape of the late nineteenth century in America. It is true that he constructed images of the plantation South that appealed to his own romance with an Old South of racial and social hierarchy that he nurtured growing up in Charleston, South Carolina. But to explain Walker's contribution fully to a postwar plantation iconography in American art, it is necessary to examine closely his pictorial strategies. His portraits of country Blacks are "darkey" caricatures in the tradition of Black stereotyping in American genre painting that distorted the image of African Americans as visual cartoons.[28] Walker invariably painted African American men in tattered clothes and with holes in their shoes located in an environment that suggests the countryside of cotton plantations. They are surrounded by cotton fields, baskets, and bales. Walker focused on elderly Black men who would have been young or middle-aged adults at the time of emancipation. With their white beards, cartoonish grins, corn pipes in their mouth, or leaning on an old walking stick, these characters become the emblem of a plantation South that transitioned from slavery toward a kind of country pauperism under the sharecropping system. Occasionally these men stare to the side, mute symbols of impoverished dignity. As other scholars have observed, Walker produced these images assembly-line style during a time when Confederate monuments were erected throughout the South. While Confederate heroes stood tall in the town squares of southern towns, Walker sold his portraits of humble and stoic African Americans to tourists and souvenir hunters from all over the country.

A second type of small painting that Walker produced based on southern travels between Louisiana and South Carolina was the log cabin. He painted a range of cabin views that were of cabins made from different building materials varying with the region. In these cabin paintings, Walker included enough detail to present a slice of African American domestic life, but the view is always from the outside. The view focuses on the simple architectural abode, the fences, small Black figures on the porch or nearby field, laundry, an outside stove, yard animals, and so on. As visual souvenirs, these images serve the purpose of depicting the humble life of the African American family. Again, Walker gives enough visual indications that the cabin is a vignette that suggests a larger plantation economy. While the African American cabin evokes the memory of slave plantations, these are freedmen's cabins. Constructed closely by the edge of the cotton fields these single-pen log cabins replaced the antebellum slave cabin quarters near the big house.[29] These cabin paintings by Walker isolate the plantation experience of rural Blacks into a small frame of reference. In their vignette-like composition, they stabilize the difficult economic reality of subsistence farming as a way to survive for the southern family during Reconstruction and beyond.

The widest possible view of the cotton landscape that Walker depicted were a few panoramic paintings of plantations based on travels to the Mississippi Delta above Vicksburg, where he had befriended planter families. One of his acquaintances was Samuel Wragg Ferguson, who was a Charleston native and had a distinguished career in the Confederate army. Through marriage to Catherine Lee, he became the owner of Ditchley, a cotton plantation near Greenville, Mississippi. Walker was in the area of Greenville in the early 1880s, though exact dates are hard to determine, since he painted a portrait of the general's daughter in 1882. Dating from the following year is a small portrait of a banana peddler from Greenville. As early as 1876, the artist was in Vicksburg, painting a sumptuous wedding portrait of local gentry (*Portrait of Kate Wilson Smith*).[30] He befriended the Mitchell family in Vicksburg and in 1880 painted a portrait of their daughter Charlotte Mitchell.[31] In Vicksburg, Walker stayed at the home of John Orr Bradfield, who owned a plantation across the river from Vicksburg and again painted the portrait of a child. Another portrait of a Confederate war veteran from Vicksburg was that of Austin A. Trescott posing in Confederate uniform and holding his Mississippi regimental flag.[32]

It is noteworthy that Walker painted the plantation as a complete economic unit where the mansion becomes an element within a production system with little architectural distinction besides a certain size. The presence of the plantation house in Walker's panoramas suggests order, supervision, and economic integration. This compositional strategy obfuscates the socioeconomic trend toward segregation and absentee ownership on the plantation. Walker never paid much attention to the planter's townhouse or suburban villa. As noted before, even before the war, the planter's home was often separate from the plantation where overseers and slaves lived. In antebellum Natchez, there already existed a spatial divide between the opulent town mansions and the agricultural production managed by an overseer on plantations that often were across the Mississippi River in Louisiana. This physical and psychological separation continued during Reconstruction. What Walker painted were plantation views that ostensibly functioned without white supervision but left it up to the viewer to imagine a planter's or property owner's presence. The planter's role was marginal as cotton made it through the hands of Black workers into baskets and onto carts, to be processed in a gin, packed into bales, and shipped to distant markets. Walker honed his artistic process to be efficient and mechanical. He owned a camera and created a collection of photographic prints that he could use as *aide memoir* for his compositions. The Walker scholars Trovaioli and Toledano established the artist's regular use of the camera as a tool of observation, calling it "the one continuous influence in Walker's work."[33] For his paintings, he began brushing a broad area of sky and sienna ground, added a layer of cotton bolls, and inserted people and buildings on the surface.

Cynthia Seibels has discussed six larger plantation paintings that range from 20 inches in height to 40 inches width. Two were painted for patrons who were cotton brokers with offices in South Carolina or Boston. Called *Big B Cotton Plantation* (1881), *The Sunny South* (1881), or *Plantation Economy in the Old South* (circa 1881), these paintings follow very similar compositional formats with rows of cotton laid out in the direction of receding lines toward a vanishing point with a broader road or path off to the side that leads toward a fence, a river, or a gin house. Along the horizon line is a middle ground of buildings, smokestacks, tree lines, or a steamboat landing. Walker had a stock of plantation imagery that he reworked for each composition. In at least four of these paintings, the artist included the plantation's big house, all variations of a three-story brick house with a double balcony surrounded by dependencies such as kitchen, smokehouse, ice house, and stable. While they are exact in their detail, these plantation paintings are quite indeterminate in their specific location and time. *Plantation Economy in the Old South* is more specific in placing it in a time before the Civil War and in asserting its association with slavery by including a row of slave cabins. The slave quarters culminate in a building on the far left that has a small tower suggesting a church or school. While one would expect that to be a fabrication, if indeed Walker intended the viewer to read it that way, the entire row suggests a peaceful village. The big house is a modest two-story dwelling with multiple chimneys but no architectural adornment. Could this be Walker's way of romanticizing the past?

As these larger plantation scenes reveal, Walker deliberately blended the Old South and New South plantation landscapes by providing a sense of continuum across time and place. Never does the viewer know the exact location of a plantation or even whether it is historical past or present. In other paintings by Walker, the log cabin is referred to as "Quarters," a term that was military in origin and referred to an area of dedicated housing for soldiers. In the context of Walker's painting, the title was an anachronism referring to the cabins where enslaved people lived. In other works, elderly Blacks are associated with vernacular, a pre–Civil War dialect that also became a staple of post–Civil War plantation literature. Thomas Nelson Page's "Gran'mammy Tales," published in northern periodicals in the 1870s, and the more famous Joel Chandler Harris's *Uncle Remus: His Songs and His Sayings* (1880), to name a few examples, were written by white authors in Black dialect.[34]

Nowhere is the temporal slippage more pronounced than in the transformation of the painting *A Cotton Plantation on the Mississippi* (1883) into a lithographic print made by the New York firm of Currier and Ives (fig. 7). The painting, possibly based on Walker's visits to the area around Greenville or Vicksburg, employs his compositional formula of broad areas of sky, fields, and earth, punctuated with people, cotton bolls, and architectural detail. Unlike his other plantation views, this painting's cotton field extends across the entire picture plane, giving no indication of a central axis road that leads into space. There is no indication that a plantation home or big house is associated with this plantation, and the houses in the distance are quite substantial and larger than typical "quarters." Steam rises from the cotton gin house, the most prominent structure in the scene, complemented by the darker smoke of the steamship. The steamer is undoubtedly a riverboat and not a packet boat exclusively dedicated to transporting cotton bales. The painting is one of three that Currier and Ives chose for reproduction as color lithographs.[35] If the painting seems to suggest a plantation of the New South, where workers work unsupervised, either as sharecroppers, tenants, or wage laborers, the print complicates such a reading.

Figure 7. *A Cotton Plantation on the Mississippi,* 1883, by William Aiken Walker. This horizontal view of a large plantation includes a wagon loaded with cotton bales, African Americans picking cotton in the field across the middle distance, and a plantation house and a steamboat in the far distance. Gilcrease Museum, Tulsa, Oklahoma.

The publisher added a white couple in the foreground standing between a group of cotton pickers on the right and the group of workers distributed around a mule-drawn wagon with bales (fig. 8). The identity of the white couple is ambiguous; their dress cannot be identified with certainty as antebellum or New South. The bustle of the lady's white dress suggests an older style, but it was not out of fashion in the 1880s. Regardless of whether the artist or the publisher decided to add the couple to the print, their inclusion in the print added another level of pastiche to the scene. Walker's plantation scenes were perhaps accepted as authentic representations of plantation economy, but they were fantasies that concocted the illusion that the Old and New Souths formed one harmonious continuum.

Figure 8. *A Cotton Plantation on the Mississippi,* Currier & Ives lithograph. This print is a copy after the original painting by William Aiken Walker Aiken. This print deviates from Walker's painting by including a white couple in the foreground. Library of Congress Prints and Photographs Division, Washington, DC.

Being able to draw on photographs as visual aids, Walker was able to include the specific numbers inscribed on cotton bales, or the specific construction of a cotton gin. This photographic working technique is combined with a compositional structure that lines up almost every component parallel to the picture plane, making each piece a kind of plantation survey reminiscent of Persac's paintings. In other ways, Walker's plantation images depart from his predecessor in significant ways. Walker's paintings are more populated and more animated than Persac's, and they focus on work, not leisure. But they provide a murky and perhaps intentionally unclear view of the post-Reconstruction relationship between planters, workers, and the land. The plantations that we see are large and run by up to thirty African Americans, always men and women, and a child or two accompanying a parent. As historians of the post–Civil War cotton plantations have pointed out, the plantation economy went through many adjustments in the first few years following the war, and different modes of labor contracts prevailed into the 1880s, including wage labor, sharecropping, and tenant farming. It is difficult to say from Walker's images whether the African Americans are tenants who own certain implements or a mule; sharecroppers who own no tools and only have their labor to supply; or wage laborers who work the cotton fields in "squads," a term that replaced the pre–Civil War term "gangs." The typical size of a squad was six to eight workers but could be up to twenty-six, and they were made of extended families working as a unit. It is also not entirely clear who supervises the workers. As indicated earlier, many planters became absentee owners who left the management of the plantation to the overseer. During Reconstruction, however, African Americans sought greater independence from a supervision system that owners adapted from slavery. Planters addressed this issue by recruiting an African American to be the foreman. In some of Walker's scenes one can see a single figure of an African American man, riding a horse or mule, but his role in the plantation hierarchy is unclear.[36] All these elements combined to imbue Walker's plantation landscapes with a prevailing sense of racial order that was also the foundation of a New South under white rule.

In the end, Walker was more invested in the pictorial effect and marketability of his paintings than in visualizing the complex drama of race relations in the post-Reconstruction South. His pictures were innocuous and romanticized enough to have a wide appeal. Had the artist further developed his network with publishers and periodicals in New York, such as with *Harper's Weekly* or *Frank Leslie's Illustrated Newspaper,* most likely his work would have had a much wider distribution in print form. That his work could easily be adopted for commercial use is evidenced by the curious career of his painting *A Cotton Plantation in Mississippi.* The Currier and Ives color lithograph had included a significant change, the addition of a white couple. Sometime after the Currier and Ives print was produced, the image with the added figures and slightly cropped on both sides appeared as a chromolithograph published by Kitson Machine Company in Charleston as an advertisement with the title *A Cotton Plantation near Charleston, S.C.* While this commercial print displaced the original scene in Walker's painting, moving its location from Mississippi to South Carolina, the artist had all along constructed a series of plantation views that had many interchangeable parts. In all their compositional balance, technical efficiency, and sense of order, Walker's paintings and their reproductions barely concealed the instability of the plantation as it transformed itself into a post-Reconstruction economy ruled by whites.[37]

Except for Walker, no artist after Persac pursued a sustained preoccupation with plantation views of the lower Mississippi River valley. The Reconstruction illustrator artists Waud and Champney presented an interlude of forgetting, directing their artistic attention toward other southern iconic places. Walker created plantation images that were photographic yet impossibly real; they were historic and topographic recreations, but, in my reading, ultimately they were non-places. It was predominantly the work of late nineteenth- and early twentieth-century photographers to reclaim the plantation as a historic and lived landscape.

As art historian Alexis Boylan has demonstrated in her essay on the plantation painting after the era of Reconstruction, the subject was anachronistic and out of step with a modern artistic search for new subjects. Boylan identifies the prevailing plantation representations as the "abandoned plantation scene" and the "plantation as symbolized by African American workers."[38] Such image types can easily be isolated within the larger visual record that photographers compiled. But beyond sharing with painting certain subjects and compositional strategies, plantation photography followed another trajectory toward restoration and reimagining. Though working separately on different assignments, the photographers discussed in the remainder of this essay assembled a visual archive that helped incorporate the plantation into modern forms of image consumption, from heritage tourism to cinema.

In the late nineteenth century, the American photographer William H. Jackson (1843–1942) visited the South and produced a small body of plantation photographs. Jackson had already established himself as a pioneer in photographing the American West, and his breathtaking views of Western mountains and canyons were already well known nationally and internationally. He was an inveterate traveler who may have made a detour through the South or came specifically to see a part of the country that had once been the old Southwest. Several Jackson and Company photographs from Mississippi and Louisiana are now in the Library of Congress, dated broadly between 1885 and 1898, including some from the Dahomey plantation in Mississippi. In this series of images, Jackson focused on a group of children standing by a storage or loading facility. Behind them are numerous sacks and piled up cotton bales with numbers and inscriptions, including the word "Dahomey." These images of anonymous children and a few unidentified adults are random observations made by a passing photographer, but they have a greater intimacy than either Walker's plantation views or his portraits of African Americans. In one of the photographs, the taller girl in the group turns her face and engages the viewer (fig. 9). This photographic glance creates an exchange and tension that none of the Walker paintings possess.

Figure 9. Untitled photograph. Scene at a cotton plantation, c. 1880–97, by William H. Jackson, dry plate negative. Three Black children stand in front of a platform that holds cotton bales; in the distance two Black workers look in the direction of the camera. Library of Congress Prints and Photographs Division, Washington, DC.

Also in the Library of Congress collection is a Jackson photograph of a house and garden entitled *Planter's Home on the Mississippi,* which can be identified as San Francisco Plantation in St. John Parish, Louisiana (fig. 10).[39] The camera is positioned at street level looking beyond two girls passing a white fence. Beyond the fence is a sumptuous garden with a fountain and a distant view of the mansion. The girls' heads are fully covered in white hats of the kind that female workers wore in the field picking cotton.[40]

Figure 10. *Planter's Home on the Mississippi,* c. 1880–97, by William H. Jackson, dry plate negative. Two female figures, presumably African Americans, walk along a white fence. Behind the fence is a lush garden and a large plantation house. Library of Congress Prints and Photographs Division, Washington, DC.

Such occasional plantation photographs by visiting artists added to an inventory of plantation views established by local photographers in Natchez and Vicksburg. From the studio of the Natchez photographer Henry Norman, discussed earlier, came a series of images of Natchez mansions that could all be considered suburban villas and townhomes. While there are some earlier and later dated photographs in the collection housed at Louisiana State University's Special Collections, the majority of them date from around 1930. In the collection are postcard-style images of all the plantation homes that have since become part of the heritage tourism industry whether as historic museums, event spaces, or bed and breakfast inns. What these photographic records did was to provide a new identity for the planter's home toward becoming a historic landmark. The urge to record and classify antebellum plantation homes also motivated photographers who worked for the Historic American Building Survey (HABS). Founded in 1933 in partnership with the National Park Service and the Library of Congress, HABS began as a relief program for unemployed architects and artists to create a repository of drawings and photographs of early American architecture. The drawings of building types were reminiscent of Persac's architectural drawings, but the mission now was historic preservation and not idealization of the antebellum past.[41]

The 1930s was a decade of simultaneous photographic projects to inventory the architectural heritage of the South. In 1933, Frances Benjamin Johnston (1864–1952) received private funds from the Carnegie Corporation to survey the architecture of the South and deposit the photographs in the Library of Congress. Over the next few years she traveled by car thousands of miles across the South, producing a total of 7, 100 photographs. In 1937–39, she had Carnegie funds to travel to Louisiana and Mississippi, and during this assignment she photographed all the major antebellum mansions in Natchez. In the late 1930s, Clarence John Laughlin (1905–1985) began his survey of Louisiana plantations, yet with a different sensibility. In the preface to his book *Ghosts Along the Mississippi,* which included photographs from 1938 and 1939 and, for the majority, from 1946 and 1947, Laughlin stated his goal as a synthesis of "historico-architectural and 'poetic' vision." Indeed, throughout his book, there is a prevailing mood of elegy, reinforced by both text and image. The Louisiana plantations in his photographs are framed and veiled by Spanish moss; they appear phantom-like and abandoned.[42]

It is almost impossible then to interpret the images that emerge from the first few decades of the twentieth century without imagining a photographic lens as partner in the making those images. The camera assists the viewer in determining what are important historic sites in the South, how a historic structure is associated with the plantation as a cultural landmark, but also where it is a landscape for poetic meditation. In all of these instances of historic surveying, there are few if any signs that the photographers were interested in recording a working plantation. This distinction between plantation culture and plantation work is one that emerged more clearly if one examines the records left by photographers who arrived in the South during the New Deal era, including Walker Evans (1903–1975), Dorothea Lange (1895–1965), and Marion Post Wolcott (1910–1990). All of them worked for the Resettlement Administration, organized in 1935, which was renamed as Farm Security Administration in 1937. Walker Evans stands apart from the other New Deal photographers in that he was already drawn to southern architecture before his assignment to travel to the South for the Farm Security Administration. Evans had earlier traveled to Louisiana and Mississippi to document Greek Revival architecture and Victorian buildings in New Orleans and Natchez. In 1934, Gifford Cochran, a wealthy New Yorker whose mother was a German princess, commissioned Evans to travel South for a photographic architectural survey in preparation for a planned book on Greek Revival architecture.[43] In February 1935, Evans began a trip to the South that included, in addition to New Orleans and Natchez, photo shooting in Savannah and Macon, Georgia. In Savannah, Evans photographed slave cabins on the Hermitage Plantation. While visiting Belle Grove plantation in Louisiana, Evans photographed the façade of the abandoned plantation and took one interior view of what one scholar has referred to as "a haunting photograph about absence."[44] Evans's camera eye surrounded the Belle Grove plantation and shot it from different angles, a framing technique that suggests a state of instability and flux. A similar plantation view, but of Belle Helene (Ashland) on River Road, Louisiana, appeared in *American Photographs* (1938), the book that accompanied Evans's exhibition at the Museum of Modern Art. Photography scholar Alan Trachtenberg has argued that Evans's Belle Helene image partially obscured the frontal view of the house with a fallen tree, thereby mocking the romance of the old plantation South represented by the publication of *Gone with the Wind* in 1936.[45]

Evans's visual exploration of the plantation is more than an architectural survey of old building types and vernacular culture. Through this architectural photography project, Evans developed his own visual language and modern aesthetic. His views of southern architecture were largely ahistorical in that they focused on purely formal aspects of capturing a building type on black-and-white film. Evans admired the clarity and objectivity of Civil War photography. His views of ruined plantations are reminiscent of the photographs that Timothy Barnard and others took of destroyed buildings in the South during and after the Civil War. In one example, Evans shot an abandoned plantation near Vicksburg with his large viewfinder camera, intentionally making the center of the image blurrier than the edges; tall grass reaches into the center, enveloping the house from the ground (fig. 11).

This was not a creative accident, and one should assume that Evans willfully added a sense of natural decay and emptiness to the architectural view. Who lived in the plantation house and who worked there is irrelevant to Evans's exploration of a ruined building. Evans split the image of the plantation from its past, leaving it void and at the same time available for the modern observer to occupy its emptiness. Evans's photographs of ruined plantations not only counterbalanced the literary romance of *Gone with the Wind,* they also allowed for an imaginary rebirth, a stage setting for the Technicolor splendor of *Gone with the Wind,* the movie, directed by David O. Selznick.[46] One should not be surprised that Selznick took creative license by choosing Twelve Oaks, the mansion in Covington, Georgia, as the stand-in for the home of the Wilkes family. While Margret Mitchell had described a more modestly sized house in her book and expressed dismay at the discrepancy, both book and movie

Figure 11. *Abandoned Plantation House, Vicksburg, Mississippi,* 1936, by Walker Evans, nitrate negative. Library of Congress Prints and Photographs Division, Washington, DC.

were reinventing what Evans's photographs marked as lost. Evans's exhibition *American Photographs* at the Museum of Modern Art (1938) included sixty-three images that were from recent trips to the South, ranging in subject from a *House in New Orleans* to a *Butcher sign in Vicksburg.* Referring to Evans's photographs from Louisiana, Mississippi, and other places, Lincoln Kirstein wrote in the catalog for the MoMA show: "His work, print after print of it, seems to call to be shown before the decay it portrays flattens all sagging roof-trees and rusts all the twisted automobile chassis. Here are the records of the age before an imminent collapse. His pictures exist to testify to the symptoms of waste and selfishness that caused the ruin and to salvage whatever was splendid for the future reference of the survivors."[47]

In late 1939, when the movie *Gone with the Wind* premiered in Atlanta, it celebrated a different type of cultural and historic salvage. On Friday, December 15, the entrance to the Lowe's Grand Theatre was decorated as Tara with fake columns and a pediment. In the words of film historian Steve Wilson, it was an epic that clashed between "historical accuracy and breathtaking spectacle."[48] Thus, two very distinct cultural spheres, a modern art museum exhibit and a Hollywood production, contributed to the survival of the plantation image as a powerful signifier of twentieth-century antebellum nostalgia.

The 1930s were an important period in the displacement and reorganization of the plantation in American visual culture from black-and-white photos to Technicolor costume drama. The 1930s and 1940s were also decades of major changes in the cotton fields, where corporations were displacing tenants, migrant workers were hired for seasonal work, and mechanization became more prevalent. Two photographers working for the Farm Security Administration documented this shifting landscape in Mississippi through extensive visual archives. Dorothea Lange showed a wide range of plantation experiences, including a sharecropper's cabin, elderly African Americans referred to as "Old Time Negro Living on Cotton Patch," young African American women who worked as cotton hoers, the children of an evicted sharecropper, cooperatives that worked with tractors, and Mexican migrant workers on their way back to California, to name a few. Another photograph by Lange showed the owner's house on the Aldridge Plantation. It is a two-story house with a small portico with a carport on one side and a screened-in porch on the other (fig. 12). It is a standardized suburban home type built in the twentieth century.

Figure 12. *The Aldridge Plantation Big House, Leland, Mississippi,* 1937, by Dorothea Lange, nitrate negative. Library of Congress Prints and Photographs Division, Washington, DC.

Like Lange, Marion Post Wolcott created a sequence of Mississippi photographs that she took around different plantations and towns in the Mississippi Delta, allowing the viewer to "read" a narrative of changing plantation economy. In her archive one finds Mexican seasonal workers, plantation managers, plantation offices, harvesting machines, cotton gins, and interior views of cabins inhabited by Black families. In the collection of negatives in the Library of Congress, there is one photo by Wolcott that she took of the ruins of Windsor mansion, south of Vicksburg near Port Gibson, in 1940. Windsor was originally built in 1859–61 on a large plantation, and after it burned to the ground in 1890, twenty-three of its twenty-nine Corinthian columns were still standing. Wolcott photographed this landmark (fig. 13) about a year before Clarence John Laughlin took his photo of the site entitled *The Enigma* (*Windsor Plantation, near Port Gibson, Mississippi*) (1941) and two years before Eudora Welty took her famous photograph of the same subject, *Ruins of Windsor* (1942).

Figure 13. *Port Gibson, Mississippi, Ruins of Windsor,* 1940, by Marion Post Wolcott, safety films negative. Columns stand abandoned in a landscape of trees and tall grasses. Library of Congress Prints and Photographs Division, Washington, DC.

At first sight, Wolcott's and Welty's images look very similar. Both are taken from about the same distance, though Wolcott is standing closer to the ruins than Welty, and the camera's eye takes the viewer along a path and some wooden fence posts toward the ruins of the structure. Yet in Wolcott's photograph the columns are extensively covered and almost swallowed by tall grass, trees, and vines. Welty probably recorded Windsor during the winter season, and the growth of trees and grasses is less enveloping (possibly cleared by humans). But by placing herself where she was, she gave the ruins a different presence. One could call the Welty photograph a souvenir, a visual image that holds time and allows for revisiting. Wolcott's photograph, in contrast, was an image of inevitable change, of the plantation past on the verge of disappearing and replaced by the suburban cookie-cutter buildings she photographed elsewhere in Mississippi. It was an image of the plantation without a hint of nostalgia.

Pictorial approaches to understanding and interpreting the southern plantation landscape evolved between about 1860 and 1940. Broadly described, painters and photographers gravitated toward representations of plantations as models of productivity and order, as historically important landscapes, or as places of abandonment and haunted memory. The cultural responses to the plantation as a place identified with slavery continue to evolve, as evidenced by the exhibition *Landscape of Slavery: The Plantation in American Art* (2008), organized by Angela Mack and Stephen Hoffius for the Gibbes Museum of Art in Charleston, South Carolina. The exhibition, which is referenced in several places in this essay, included many examples of artistic imaging and imagining in art created after 1940. After the end of slavery, the plantation maintained an undeniable physical reality in the American South, and some of the image producers discussed in this essay depicted the plantation as an economic system that kept African Americans in a state of bondage. Others skirted the post–Civil War plantation altogether, as they developed a new visual narrative describing the southern landscape and its cultural identity as a place to visit and explore. It was only in the twentieth century that the cultural and economic forces of heritage tourism, architectural preservation, and modern photography combined to "revive" the plantation image. In summary, it appears that the plantation landscape after the Civil War became a burdensome subject, casting shadows on the past while continuing to shape southern life in the present, a place of historic memory difficult to erase.

NOTES

The author wishes to thank Laura Kilcer VanHuss, Lake Douglas, Alexis Boylan, Angela Mack, and Mimi Miller for their support and comments at various stages of preparing this essay.

1. David G. Sansing, Sim C. Callon, and Carolyn Vance Smith, *Natchez: An Illustrated History* (Natchez: Plantation Publishing Company, 1992), 85.

2. For further study of Persac and topographic painting traditions, see Barbara SoRelle Bacot, "Marie Adrien Persac—Artist of an American Landscape," in H. Parrott Bacot et al., *Marie Adrien Persac: Louisiana Artist* (Baton Rouge: Louisiana State University Press, 2000), 12–13. Throughout my discussion of Persac I rely on this excellent book.

3. Persac went into the photography business on two occasions, first in Baton Rouge around 1856 and later, from about 1865 to 1867, in New Orleans. See Bacot et al., *Marie Adrien Persac*, 4–5.

4. For a detailed discussion of this image, see Bacot, *Marie Adrien Persac*, 68–69.

5. The Thomas H. and Joan W. Gandy Photograph Collection in the Louisiana State University Library Special Collections contains views of steamboat interiors that can be attributed to Henry Norman. Henry Norman was hired by Natchez photographer Henry Gurney in 1870. By 1876 Norman had bought out Gurney's studio and opened his own business. The glass negatives are available at www.louisianadigitallibrary.org.

6. John Michael Vlach, *The Planter's Prospect: Privilege and Slavery in Plantation Paintings* (Chapel Hill: University of North Carolina Press, 2002), 105.

7. For a good survey of photographs, see Deborah Willis and Barbara Krauthamer, *Envisioning Emancipation: Black Americans and the End of Slavery* (Philadelphia: Temple University Press, 2013).

8. "Slaves on J. J. Smith plantation, near Beaufort, S.C." is illustrated in Willis and Krauthamer, *Envisioning Emancipation,* 79. The original carte de visite photo is at the J. Paul Getty Museum in Los Angeles.

9. See Janet Sharp Hermann, *The Pursuit of a Dream* (New York: Oxford University Press, 1981).

10. Edward King, *Great South* (Hartford, CT: American Publishing Company, 1875), 272.

11. *Natchez Weekly Courier,* August 16, 1839, 1.

12. King, *Great South,* 293.

13. Throughout my discussion of Champney, I am indebted to Judy Bullington's extensive research files. For a specific reference to Champney's practice as travel artist, see Judy Bullington, "'Champ'—The Artist as a Model Traveler," in "The Artist-as-Traveler and Expanding Horizons of American Cosmopolitanism in the Gilded Age" (PhD diss., Indiana University, 1992), 174–241.

14. King, *Great South,* 307.

15. Frederic E. Ray, *Alfred Waud, Civil War Artist* (New York: Viking Press, 1974).

16. According to Natchez historian Mimi Miller, it was after 1882 when Natchez was fully connected by railroad and the grand hotels such as the Natchez (1890) and the Eola (1927) were built that the city began to attract a tourism industry in the modern sense. Plantations did not become a major part of the tourist business in Natchez until the beginning of heritage tourism in the 1930s when Natchez garden clubs began to open historic homes and offer public tours. Mimi Miller, email correspondence with the author, August 18, 2018.

17. Cynthia Seibels, *The Sunny South: The Life and Art of William Aiken Walker* (Spartanburg, SC: Saraland Press, 1995), 83.

18. This statement is based on a survey of auction house records from the past four years (au: include years here), including results from Christie's, Sotheby's, Neal Auction Company, and Brunk Auction. At a Christie's auction in November 2017, one of Walker's plantation paintings entitled *Big B Cotton Plantation* (1881) sold for $648,500 (Askart.com, consulted on August 19, 2018). The tradition of topographical plantation views is currently being revived by watercolor artist Jim Blanchard. In 2018, when the Ogden Museum of Southern Art exhibited Blanchard's watercolors of Louisiana plantations, it described the works as follows: "In the tradition of the great 19th century architect and painter, Marie Adrien Persac, the paintings of Jim Blanchard combine history, aesthetic and skill to create a visual document that is both accurate and idealized. Through these works, grand homes rise from the ashes of the past, crumbling facades are restored and faded images glow with the color of life." See https://ogdenmuseum.org/exhibition/a-precise-vision/.

19. See Claudia Rankine and Beth Loffreta, *The Racial Imaginary: Writers on Race in the Life of the Mind* (Albany, NY: Fence Books, 2016).

20. Guy C. McElroy, ed., *Facing History: The Black Image in American Art 1790–1940* (Washington, DC: Corcoran Gallery of Art, 1990), 94.

21. August P. Trovaioli and Roulhac B. Toledano, *William Aiken Walker: Southern Genre Painting* (Baton Rouge: Louisiana State University Press, 1972), 4.

22. Trovaioli and Toledano, *William Aiken Walker,* 107.

23. Henry Louis Gates Jr., "The Face and Voice of Blackness," in *Facing History,* ed. McElroy, xxix.

24. Seibels, *The Sunny South,* 100.

25. John Michael Vlach, "Perpetuating the Past: Plantation Landscape Paintings Then and Now," in *Landscape of Slavery: The Plantation in American Art,* ed. Angela D. Mack and Stephen G. Hoffius (Columbia: University of South Carolina Press, 2008), 21, 22.

26. See Seibels, *The Sunny South,* 84–90.

27. See Trovaioli and Toledano, *William Aiken Walker,* 12, 107.

28. McElroy, ed., *Facing History,* xiii–xix.

29. See Charles S. Aiken, *The Cotton Plantation South since the Civil War* (Baltimore: Johns Hopkins University Press, 1998), 51.

30. This portrait is illustrated in Seibels, *The Sunny South,* 77.

31. Ibid., 74.

32. See Trovaioli and Toledano, *William Aiken Walker,* 66; Seibels, *The Sunny South,* 75–76.

33. Trovaioli and Toledano, *William Aiken Walker,* 106. The book contains several illustrations of photos of African Americans from Walker's collection (see pp. 107–9).

34. For a literary history of the plantation literature, see Lucinda H. Mackethan, "Plantation Fiction, 1865–1900," in Louis D. Rubin Jr., ed., *The History of Southern Literature* (Baton Rouge: Louisiana State University Press, 1985), 209–18.

35. The other two Walker images that Currier and Ives printed were *A Free Lunch* (1872) and the *Levee-New Orleans* (1884). See Seibels, *The Sunny South,* 238–39. It is difficult to determine how many hand-colored lithographs Currier and Ives would have produced of each image. Since they did not produce a print unless they could sell 100 copies, an estimate of several hundred seems reasonable. See Robert K. Newman, "Brief History of N. Currier and Currier & Ives" (2010), http://www.oldprintshop.com.

36. For two informative accounts of the southern plantation economy after the Civil War, see James Roark, *Masters without Slaves: Southern Planters in the Civil War and Reconstruction* (New York: W. W. Norton, 1977), and Michael Wayne, *The Reshaping of Plantation Society: The Natchez District, 1860–1880* (Baton Rouge: Louisiana State University Press, 1981).

37. The Kitson Machine Company print is illustrated in Trovaioli and Toledano, *William Aiken Walker,* 84. See also Seibels, *The Sunny South,* 239–39.

38. Alexis Boylan, "From Gilded Age to Gone with the Wind," in *Landscape of Slavery,* ed. Mack and Hoffius, 120.

39. I am thankful to Lake Douglas for his help in identifying San Francisco plantation.

40. Other views from Mississippi in the Library of Congress attributed to Jackson are of Natchez, Vicksburg, and Richmond cotton plantations. The image *Mississippi River at Natchez, Mississippi* from the collection of the George Eastman House was recently included in the exhibition *East of the Mississippi: Nineteenth-Century American Landscape Photography.* See Diane Waggoner, Russell Lord, and Jennifer Raab, *East of the Mississippi: Nineteenth-Century American Landscape Photography* (Washington, DC: National Gallery of Art), 2017.

41. The entire HABS digital archive is available at *Built in America: Historic American Buildings Survey/Historic American Engineering Record, 1933–Present,* http://memory.loc.gov/ammem/collections/habs_haer/.

42. Clarence John Laughlin, "Prologue," *Ghosts along the Mississippi: An Essay in the Poetic Interpretation of Louisiana's Plantation Architecture* (New York: Bonanza Books, 1948), n.p. For biographical information on Frances Benjamin Johnston and a survey of her plantation images, I consulted the Library of Congress Prints and Drawing Section at https://www.loc.gov/rr/print/coll/fbjchron.html.

43. See Jeff L. Rosenheim, "'The Cruel Radiance of What Is': Walker Evans and the South," in *Walker Evans,* ed. Maria Morris Hambourg et al. (New York: Metropolitan Museum of Art, 2000), 59–66, 99n28.

44. Ibid., 65.

45. Alan Trachtenberg, *Reading American Photographs: Image as History, Mathew Brady to Walker Evans* (Toronto: Hill and Wang, 1989), 265.

46. For a study of the film production of *Gone with the Wind,* see Steve Wilson, *The Making of "Gone with the Wind"* (Austin: University of Texas Press, 2014).

47. Lincoln Kirstein, "Photographs of America: Walker Evans," in *Walker Evans American Photographs* (New York: Museum of Modern Art, 1938), 193.

48. Wilson, *The Making of "Gone with the Wind,"* Introduction, n.p.

THE RISE AND FALL OF UNCLE SAM PLANTATION

CHRISTOPHER MORRIS

The story of the demise of Uncle Sam Plantation, as it is told in books and newspaper articles, is one of humans against nature. "Time and River Win Again," declared a *New Orleans Times-Picayune* headline on the eve of the plantation home's demolition.[1] Built before the Civil War, Uncle Sam, in east St. James Parish, once offered a prime example of the human conquest of nature. In 1890, however, nature turned the tables on the plantation when a flood destroyed the entire crop of sugarcane, machinery, and infrastructure, and left the plantation enterprise on the verge of bankruptcy. Through succeeding decades, the river never relented. It continued to chisel away at the levee's foundations and, fearing catastrophic failure, engineers drew up a plan proposing to set a new levee farther back from the river. With much regret, and following some political machinations, the Pontchartrain Levee District Board, established in 1895 by the state legislature and charged with maintaining and improving 115 miles of the east bank levee from Baton Rouge to St. Charles, accepted the plan and authorized the dismantling of the Uncle Sam Plantation structures, which comprised the most pristine example of an antebellum sugar plantation along the Mississippi River.[2]

It is easy to understand the appeal of this story at the time it was first told. It was 1940, and the Great Depression had brought new energy to the human struggle against nature in the high plains of the Dust Bowl and in the valleys of the Tennessee and Cumberland Rivers. The Great Mississippi River Flood of 1927 was still fresh in the minds of many in Louisiana. New flood-control devices designed in response to the Great Flood were being installed from Missouri to the delta marshes below New Orleans. New levees, including the one that brought about the end of Uncle Sam, represented progress and a new push against nature. Under President Franklin D. Roosevelt, the centralized modern nation-state promised to end economic misery, tame nature, and, before the year was out, serve as the arsenal of democracy.[3]

What the levee board that approved the demolition plan had not anticipated was the strong romantic attachment of many in Louisiana and around the country to a decaying southern landscape. The film *Gone with the Wind,* released only a few months before Uncle Sam came down and still playing in theaters around the country, was only the most recent of many examples of the nation's new romance with the South and its "Lost Cause."[4] In the words of one Louisiana reporter, "written in the masonry" of Uncle Sam was "the rise and fall of the South as it was before the war."[5] Photographers hired by the Farm Security Administration to document rural poverty were especially drawn to Louisiana's landscape of abandoned mansions. The destruction of the Uncle Sam Plantation structures and the construction of a myth of lost southern glory were joined. At the same time, a powerful romance with the human struggle against nature explained why Uncle Sam had to come down. It and other relics of the Old South had to give way to a twentieth-century America of centralized planning and modern engineering backed by all the resources of the modern state so that abandoned landscapes, whether in the dusty plains of Oklahoma or the floodplains of Louisiana, could be reclaimed and made productive once again.

The story of Uncle Sam that dwells on loss and sacrifice in the name of progress has little to say about the plantation's creation or about environmental transformations and their human and ecological costs at that location and by extension in the riverside plantation district generally. "Erected by owner Samuel P. A. Fagot," the plaque near the former home site states. How did Samuel Fagot erect Uncle Sam? What did the plantation's establishment entail? How did he, and hundreds of others not given the slightest nod on the plaque, wrest a plantation from the floodplain? Studies of the sugar plantations of Louisiana—while their authors can hardly fail to discuss the unique qualities of the plantation landscape, its swamps in particular—nevertheless tend to treat landscape as a stage on which history unfolds. In addition, they typically focus on particular periods, such as the antebellum era, the Reconstruction era, and so forth. This essay views the land and water as active participants in the human-environmental history of one prominent sugar plantation, from its founding early in the nineteenth century to its height of productivity and control of nature at about the time it appeared on Persac's map, to its demise and disappearance in the mid-twentieth century.[6] If we are to appreciate what was lost when Uncle Sam came down, we might consider what was gained and lost when Uncle Sam went up.

Photographs taken by the Historic American Buildings Survey (HABS) of the plantation's last days offer clues to a largely obscured history. For example, none of them show the levee; however, in several cases it is clear from the angle of view that the photographer had set the camera on it (fig. 1). Some photographs show cisterns, constructed to catch and hold rainwater (fig. 2). Water management was central to the construction and operation of all plantations as well as to the demise of Uncle Sam. Photographs from the 1930s show overgrown lawns, grasses, and vines entangled in leaning fences of weathered wood and iron. They also tell of a landscape deforested, drained, and planted. Uncle Sam's cane fields were extensive, and ornamental gardens and lawns filled the

Figure 1. *Main House, West Elevation (Front)—Uncle Sam Plantation, Convent, St. James Parish, LA,* 1936, by Richard Koch. View of Uncle Sam Plantation home from atop the levee. Library of Congress, Prints & Photographs Division, HABS LA,47-CONV.V, 1-1.

Figure 2. *Uncle Sam Plantation, Convent, St. James Parish, LA,* 1940, by Richard Koch. Uncle Sam in the process of being dismantled. At the left corner of the mansion are the remains of a cistern. Library of Congress, Prints & Photographs Division, HABS LA,47-CONV.V, 1-7.

yard between the big house and the levee.[7] In the images of this period, livestock graze, seemingly untended, as if part of the natural landscape. In the mid-nineteenth century, Uncle Sam's managers raised, pastured, and slaughtered herds of cattle and sheep, in part to feed field laborers who lived in the cabins captured quite by accident in some of the twentieth-century photos. Of course, livestock, along with the income from sugar, also sustained the sumptuous lifestyle of Uncle Sam's owners.[8]

As Jochen Wierich explains in his essay, empty buildings overgrown with grasses, vines, and trees, captured in photographs of the South's plantation landscape, presented images of decay and ruin reminiscent of the war-ravaged landscape photographs of the Civil War era. In the photographs of Uncle Sam—and Uncle Sam has to be one of the most photographed of the "lost" southern plantations—nature appears rampant amidst the abandoned structures that once housed the people who transformed floodplain marshes, forests, and canebrakes into what one writer described as "a superficial area," a managed landscape, most of it cultivated, with an "up-to-date sugar factory," a barrel factory, buildings, fences, "seven miles of narrow gauge tracks, locomotives and cars, seventy odd first class mules, and a full complement of agricultural implements."[9] The complex still operated almost up to the moment of demolition. Indeed, the seemingly romantic landscape of abandon and ruin was, in fact, not abandoned at all. When the wrecking crew arrived, field laborers still occupied cabins that had housed slaves. They worked for the plantation's owners, who, although absent for twenty-eight years, profited from sugar raised in the fertile soil of the Louisiana floodplain, just as Samuel Fagot had done more than a century earlier. The romance of Uncle Sam Plantation was a twentieth-century construction and a legacy of the plantation's destruction. But when Fagot and his partner first established Uncle Sam, there was no romance about it. This plantation was all business.

In the early 1820s, Samuel P. A. Fagot left France for New Orleans. He was a native of La Rochelle, a city with ties to Louisiana dating back to explorations by René-Robert Cavelier, Sieur de La Salle. He may have had personal connections to New Orleans, although what likely drew him there, besides opportunity, was that he could conduct business in his native language. French remained the city's common language a generation after the acquisition of Louisiana by the United States. Fagot was a storekeeper, and being able to converse easily with customers and suppliers would have been essential for his success. Meanwhile, sixty miles north on the Mississippi River, a few hundred landowners were putting three thousand enslaved laborers to work at transforming wetlands into sugarcane fields. Whether Samuel Fagot, as he was settling into business in the city, always aspired to a life of mastery by the Mississippi riverside is not known. Opportunity to take up planting came with marriage and the business partnership he established with his wealthy father-in-law.[10]

Upriver from New Orleans lay a broad, flat, and forested floodplain. Long before the first manmade levees, which date to the early 1700s, natural levees lined the Mississippi River, formed over thousands of years from sediment deposited during annual floods. In some places they rose five or more feet above the floodplain and were, for most of the year, sufficiently dry to support a variety of bottomland hardwoods, including live and water oaks, elm, ash, and cottonwoods. Beyond the natural levees, what geologists call the levee toe sloped gradually downward and away for two or three miles before reaching what are called backswamps. Along the toe, between levee and backswamp, bottomland hardwoods gave way to a wetland forest dominated by water tupelo (*Nyssa aquatica*), bald cypress (*Taxodium distichum*), and the smaller wax myrtle (*Myrica cerifera*) trees. The soil changed, too, from the reasonably dry but coarse dirt of the levee to the fairly well-drained but clayey dirt of the levee toe to a mucky mixture of clay and organic matter near the backswamp.[11]

Native peoples had lived in the area for centuries. There are in St. James Parish ceremonial mounds that appear to date to the Meso-Indian Period (6000–2000 BCE), placing them among the oldest in North America. One such mound, nearly thirty feet high, stands in a field about one-half mile from a corner of the original Uncle Sam Plantation.[12] Europeans—and in particular, French-speaking refugees from Acadia, in Nova Scotia, Canada—began to settle this stretch of the Mississippi River in the latter half of the eighteenth century. For the most part, they lived as herders and subsistence farmers, keeping cattle along the river and in low-lying meadows and raising food in small plots for themselves and for local exchange. They also hunted and fished, living off the natural resources of the wetlands much as the native peoples they displaced. A few grew agricultural commodities for export, primarily indigo and, in some locations, tobacco.[13]

Louisiana's first sugarcane plantations were located near New Orleans and dated back to the colonial era. The transformation of St. James Parish, established in 1807, into sugarcane fields came later. The annexation of Louisiana to the United States (1803) brought people and investors, while the conclusion of the War of 1812 brought access to oversees sugar markets. In addition, both the Haitian Revolution (1791–1804), which disrupted sugar production in what had been the French colony of Saint-Domingue, and the turmoil in Europe brought by the Napoleonic Wars (1803–15), created opportunities for North American sugar producers.

The transformation of floodplain into plantation took time, perseverance, and tremendous capital resources, which the first owners of what became Uncle Sam lacked. As a result, the construction of the plantation proceeded in fits and starts.

The man who first built what became Uncle Sam Plantation was a soldier in the War of 1812. Joseph Constant—sometimes in Louisiana records the name appears as Constance—was a New Yorker, the son of a Presbyterian minister, a former New York City sheriff, and a military man. In June of 1812, when

President James Madison signed a declaration of war against Great Britain, the thirty-two-year-old Colonel Constant commanded the Third US Infantry in the territories of New Orleans, Mississippi, and West Florida. The next month he secured US authority over Pass Christian, on the Mississippi Gulf Coast, and then returned to New Orleans where he remained through the first year of war. In August of 1813, Constant resigned his army commission in protest of being overlooked for promotion and joined the Louisiana militia. When the British moved on New Orleans in December of 1814, Constant was aide-de-camp for Brigadier General Stephan A. Hopkins, commander, Second Brigade, First Division, Louisiana General Militia, and stationed at Galvez Town on the Amite River in Ascension Parish, twenty miles north of the location of what would become Uncle Sam Plantation.[14]

Constant was an ambitious man. At one time he hoped to be appointed the first US governor of Florida but was disappointed despite having received the endorsement of his friend New York governor Daniel Tompkins.[15] Upon leaving the army and joining the state militia, Constant traded his New York connections, which had let him down, for Louisiana connections that included Hopkins, who served several terms in the Louisiana legislature, and Major General Jacques Philippe Villeré, who in 1816 become the second governor of Louisiana. Constant finished the war as a militia colonel with ties to Louisiana's elite, which would be of use to him in civilian life.[16]

In 1815 or 1816, Joseph Constant began to build a sugar plantation in St. James, one of the parishes assigned to his brigade during the war. Like many army officers, George Washington perhaps most famously, Constant speculated in real estate. In addition to property in New York, he owned lands in Ohio that he purchased while stationed in Pittsburgh. His Louisiana property may have meant nothing more to him than a simple addition to his collection of land speculations. Then again, he did name his property, Constantia, sometimes spelled Constancia, which hints at grandiose ambitions for a new life as a Louisiana planter.

How much of the construction of his plantation Constant personally oversaw is not known. Three years later he was back in New York, dying. Something may have gone wrong for Constant in Louisiana, or he may have wished to spend his final days among family and old friends, although he clearly had friends in Louisiana. Colonel Philip Hickey was a veteran of the War of 1812 and of the Louisiana militia. George Mather owned a plantation almost next door to Constantia. Both men had participated in an attempt to overthrow the Spanish regime at Baton Rouge, which precipitated a US military intervention in which Constant was involved. The condition of Constantia at the time Constant left for New York is not known, but progress at transforming forested floodplain into sugar fields must have been well-advanced, for Hickey and Mather, whom Constant placed in charge of his Louisiana affairs, arranged for the sale of the plantation for the incredible sum of $150,000.[17] The introduction of what was commonly called ribbon cane (*Saccharum officinarum,* var. *ribbon*), a new variety of sugarcane better able to withstand the fall frosts that could ruin crops north of New Orleans, initiated something of a rush that inflated real estate values in areas formerly deemed risky for sugar.[18]

The new owner of Constantia was an Englishman named Samuel McMaster. During the war, US officials monitored English immigrants, whose loyalty they distrusted, and often removed them to locations where they could not easily aid the enemy. McMaster had been ordered to Opelousas, more than one hundred miles northwest of New Orleans, although he shortly snuck back to the city to tend to his mercantile business. He seems to have been ignored by the authorities. His wife was a New Orleans native, which may have allayed suspicions. If McMaster was a successful merchant who could afford a very expensive plantation, he proved to be an unsuccessful planter who could not hold on to his purchase. By 1826 Constantia Plantation was back in the hands of the Constant family, McMaster having defaulted on his mortgage. Joseph Constant's heirs were no more interested in a Louisiana plantation now than they had been seven years earlier and quickly began to look for a new buyer. In 1828 they found two buyers, Samuel Fagot and his father-in-law Jean Joseph Jourdan.[19]

When they took control of Constantia Plantation, the land had been significantly transformed. However encumbered the McMasters had been, they commanded the labor of nearly seventy enslaved people, most of whom Joseph Constant and his heirs sold with the plantation. By the mid-1820s, Timothy Flint, a Massachusetts missionary and man of letters, observed that Constantia was part of a continuous landscape, "a rich and highly cultivated tract," where "plantation touches plantation," each skirted by fields of cotton, sugarcane, and rice, forming "one continued village" along "a perfectly uniform strip" about two miles wide, sixty miles long, bound by river in front and forested swamp in back. In 1826 Flint saw plantation homes that were "noble," "neat," and "airy," many of them ornamented with gardens of jasmine, roses, altheas, and in some places, groves of oranges. Despite the novelty and beauty, "the country is so level, the mansions so uniform, the fields so exactly alike," that, to Flint's eye, the landscape exhibited "a tiresome sameness." It was not what Flint saw that most struck him, but what he heard. From the raised deck of a steamboat, itself elevated above the plantation landscape by a rise in the river, the "strokes of the axe and the report of guns have a singular sound in the ear, as though the noise commenced under water." What Flint heard were the sounds of trees being cleared, animals being eradicated, enslaved humans being made to work, and water being drained from the land. This was a landscape still very much in the making.[20]

Plantation development required labor and capital. How Joseph Constant found the resources necessary to establish Constantia is not clear, although his connections to some of Louisiana's leading men surely helped. Samuel McMaster never did succeed in scraping together resources sufficient to succeed at planting. The investment capital that Samuel Fagot and Jean Joseph Jourdan brought to bear at Constantia were of another magnitude.

Jean Joseph Jourdan, his wife Victoire, and their children migrated from Aubagne in the south of France to Spanish colonial New Orleans, where Jean Joseph established himself as a *boulanger,* a baker. He also began to collect real estate, including several town lots, a grant of 1,000 Spanish acres along Catahoula Creek in present-day Hancock County, Mississippi, and a small farm on Bayou Barataria, southwest of New Orleans. The latter property held special interest for Jourdan. His primary business concerns, at least initially, were in New Orleans, where he raised his children at the family's Bourbon Street home, but he enjoyed his visits to Barataria where, with several slaves, he tended a herd of cattle and raised corn, rice, and poultry. He "liked the life of the woods and slept there often," recalled Louis Bouligny, a neighbor who kept a dairy herd at Barataria, but he was always alone. "Jourdan's wife never went to Barataria" and perhaps for good reason. By the 1810s, Jourdan was smuggling slaves from the West Indies or Africa into the United States.[21]

Legal importation of slaves into the United States ended in 1808, just as development of new cotton and sugar districts in the Mississippi and Louisiana territories stimulated demand for enslaved labor. Jean Lafitte and other Gulf pirates supplied a thriving black market. They centered their operations at Barataria Bay, which provided cover for their vessels, proximity to Spanish slave traders, and easy access to the New Orleans slave markets. During the War of 1812, the US Navy broke up the pirate rings, although Andrew Jackson offered clemency to any pirates who assisted him in the fight against the British, which most did. Following the war, Lafitte and others reestablished their criminal operations at Galveston Island on the Texas coast. Once again, Barataria Bay became an important point of entry for black-market slave traders bound for New Orleans and plantations upriver.

How involved Jourdan was in this business is not known. Evidence is circumstantial. He seems to have done very well, perhaps too well for a baker. Hancock County, Mississippi, where in 1820 Jourdan had two dozen slaves working his land, is supposed to have been home to pirates and slave smugglers, including Lafitte. Whichever of Jourdan's activities—baking, farming, or slave trading—provided the bulk of his income, he invested his earnings into New Orleans real estate, accumulating sixty city lots in the new suburb of St. Marie. From Barataria on the Louisiana Gulf Coast to Hancock County, Mississippi, to suburban New Orleans, Jourdan brought three landscapes into combination to raise the capital needed to engineer a fourth landscape, a sugarcane plantation in St. James Parish.

In the spring of 1828, the beginning of planting season, Jean Joseph Jourdan and Samuel Fagot purchased Constantia Plantation in its entirety: land, livestock, implements, and seventy-seven enslaved people. To the labor force Jourdan added forty slaves and Fagot added eleven, for a total of 128 enslaved laborers. Jourdan contributed the bulk of the cash investment, for which Fagot made up by assuming responsibility for managing the enterprise, which Jourdan, at seventy-three years and in poor health, could not have done. The 1830 census indicates that the Jourdans, the Fagots, and the Fagot children—three generations—lived together at Constantia, probably in the original plantation home built by Constant or McMaster.[22]

Little is known of Constantia's enslaved workforce beyond general demographic contours. In 1830 there were fifty-three males and fifty-six females of all ages, including nineteen young children. The total number, down from what it had been two years earlier, indicates deaths, sales, and few births. Both the sex ratio and age distribution differed from those for the state's entire enslaved population, which had more males than females and a much higher ratio of children per woman. The sex and in particular the age distributions at Constantia were those of a labor force assembled by businessmen who purchased men and women, but not children, for immediate placement in sugarcane fields. Over the next decade, the age distribution barely changed. Either women were not having children, children were dying, or owners were selling children. Over time, the sex ratio changed. By 1840, men significantly outnumbered women. Occasionally, and perhaps more often than records reveal, enslaved men ran away from Fagot's plantation, five in September and October of 1844, six in May and June of 1855.[23]

When his in-laws died, Samuel Fagot inherited through his wife one quarter of the Jourdan estate, which included Jean Joseph's share of the plantation and more than $195,000 in New Orleans real estate.[24] With tremendous capital resources at his disposal, Fagot set about building Constantia into one of the most prosperous and imposing sugar plantations in Louisiana. He bought land: over the next decade Fagot added nine hundred acres to the back of the plantation, extending the property five miles from the Mississippi River to Bayou des Acadiens, which drained east St. James into Lake Maurepas, bringing the total area of Constantia to 2,500 acres.[25] He bought slaves: by 1850, the enslaved laborers numbered 156, nearly two-thirds of them men, most of them in their twenties or thirties.[26] Fagot's backswamp land acquisitions facilitated the draining and clearing of dry land. His human acquisitions provided the labor for ditching, chopping, and hauling.

While the plantation's previous owners, Constant and McMaster, began the process of clearing land and planting sugarcane, Fagot, with his tremendous cash reserves, expanded, intensified, and quickened the pace of development. Crucial to his success was the construction of a sophisticated system for controlling water. Fagot designed a drainage network with a central or "grand" canal nearly two miles long down the center of the plantation, with connecting ditches three to six feet wide, to funnel rain and river water downhill to the backswamp. Enslaved men dug the entire works by hand. During dry months, when the river was low, they lifted mud out of the ditches and piled it alongside, from where other laborers carted it to the plantation edges and there piled it to form levees. Other work crews cleared forest, first girdling trees to kill and dry them, then felling and bucking them the next year. The easiest time to remove logs was during the spring rise, when they could be floated to nearby mills, of which there were several in the parish.[27] The drainage system, fitted with a gate so that it held water year round, was essential because of "the difficulty of getting the lumber out, unless [one] should first dig a canal."[28]

Finally, teams working with mules pulled stumps from the mud. As each acre was cleared of water, trees, and debris, and secured, more or less, from inundation, more teams of laborers planted seed cane and corn. Into the 1840s, Constantia was a landscape in motion: fields were expanding, wetland forests were receding, and in between fields and forests there was an area still wet and only partially cleared, an area in transformation and in continual movement downhill from front to back lot. Water moved downhill into the canal and out into the swamp. Logs moved uphill in the canal, hauled by men and mules.

By 1850 all of the original Constantia tract, from river to backswamp, one thousand acres in all, was uniformly cleared, drained, enclosed, and planted. There was no more land to be brought into cultivation. At the back of the plantation, nearly twenty feet below the high ground along the river, the land leveled and ceased to drain. This was the bottom of the bowl. In 1850 a surveyor located a bearing tree—a tupelo, he observed, not a gum as reported in earlier field notes—that an earlier surveyor had notched to denote a boundary at a back corner of Constantia. All around the tree the land lay beneath eighteen inches of stagnant water.[29] But even here, laborers cut trees continually, not to prepare fields, but for building material and, more important, to provide fuel for the plantation sugar mill, which Fagot converted from horse to steam power. The cost of steam machinery, between $6,000 and $12,000, was too high for some, but not for Fagot.[30]

Steam-powered sugar mills could be voracious consumers of wood, burning three to four cords to produce a single hogshead of sugar. In 1844 Constantia Plantation produced 725 hogsheads at an approximate cost of two to three thousand cords of wood cut from 100 to 150 acres, the better part of a quarter section of cypress forest.[31] By the 1850s, the only trees remaining on the plantation that were not ornamental or shade trees were to be found in the cypress swamp, where the work of felling them was especially difficult. Trees standing in areas that drained, if only briefly, were the first to be taken. In areas that were permanently inundated, woodcutters worked with one foot on a pirogue and another on an axe lodged firmly in the trunk of the tree.[32] The work necessary for supplying wood for the mill, planting and cutting sugar, cleaning ditches, and maintaining levees all competed for the plantation's substantial but nevertheless limited workforce of enslaved laborers.

Elsewhere in Louisiana's sugar parishes, as timber extraction moved deeper into the swamps, some plantation owners flirted with coal as a fuel. However, by the 1850s furnaces designed to burn crushed and dried cane stalks, or bagasse, replaced coal and wood-burning furnaces on most sugar plantations. Some planters in Louisiana's sugar parishes used bagasse as a fertilizer, applying it to fields after first composting it for a year. One plantation overseer claimed bagasse doubled the size of his crop. Using bagasse as fuel saved trees and the expense of cutting them, but at the cost of soil restoration, although ashes from the boiler room could be spread onto fields.[33]

Most of the cultivated land at Constantia, about 600 acres, was planted with sugar. Another 300 acres was planted with hay and corn, which, along with molasses, provided the primary source of food energy for all plantation labor, including more than 150 slaves and fifty or more mules. The remaining one hundred acres were devoted to plots of sweet potatoes, gardens, lawns, the canal, levees, barns, the mill, cabins, and the Fagot family home.[34]

In the late 1840s or early 1850s, Samuel Fagot oversaw the construction of a new plantation big house. Paid for with sugar planted on the floodplain and built of bricks made of bottomland clay and sand, Fagot's mansion rose quite literally out of the Mississippi mud. His brickmaking operation impressed the respected agriculturalist Solon Robinson. "Owing to the very frequent showers in this country, brickmaking is a very 'catching [i.e., precarious] business,'" Robinson noted, but Fagot had a drying shed large enough to keep 30,000 bricks safe until they were ready for a kiln, in which they would bake for eight to twelve days. There must have been several kilns burning round the clock during the years that the plantation big house was under construction. The structure demolished in 1940 by the levee board had approximately 250,000 bricks in its exterior and interior walls. The first-story porch, chimneys, columns, and several outbuildings, including the *garçonnières* (traditionally, bachelor quarters, but more commonly used as guest cottages) and *pigeonniers* (dovecotes) were also made of brick. The upper verandas, all floors, joists, rafters, and roofs were made of cypress cut from the back of the plantation.[35]

In 1854, the surviving documentary record identified the plantation for the first time as Uncle Sam Plantation.[36] Unfortunately there are no descriptions of it that survive from that moment. Solon Robinson commented on several plantation homes, and was quite struck by the "very imposing-looking structure" of Sacred Heart Convent, which was just downriver from Constantia, but said nothing about Fagot's home. In 1860 J. W. Dorr left perhaps the most detailed descriptions of the pre–Civil War landscape between St. Charles Parish and Baton Rouge in a series of letters he wrote for the *New Orleans Crescent.* He noted that the residences of most of the largest plantations, including the Fagot plantation, were "really magnificent," but offered no details. Maps from the pre–Civil War era, including the Persac map, indicate property boundaries, but not plantation structures. The earliest document to depict what became known as the Uncle Sam Plantation big house and outbuildings is the Corps of Topographical Engineers Mississippi River Survey map for St. James Parish. Published in 1877, it indicates the Uncle Sam structures precisely as they appeared later in HABS drawings.[37]

When Fagot or his heirs completed construction of their home, the whole plantation scene must have been beautiful, especially in late summer, with the soft pastel-toned sugarcane and the more intense hue of the corn presenting a sea of green enclosed by a grass-covered levee upon which cattle and sheep grazed, and in the midst the mansion, painted a pale yellow so that the surrounding landscape appeared to be reflected on its walls and columns. Such a pastoral scene would have hidden the hard labor that produced and maintained it, hidden, too, the ecology that sustained it, even as the scene offered proof that human enterprise could transform untilled wetland into rich farmland. Most of all, the scene would have distracted the viewer's gaze from the fact that it was all one fabulous money-making machine. In 1859, the year following Fagot's death , the gross plantation income on sales of sugar and molasses amounted to $80,000.[38]

Samuel Fagot died on October 31, 1858, and was interred at St. Michael's Cemetery in Convent. His widow Emilie took over management of Uncle Sam.[39] The sugar harvest that year, at 894 hogsheads, was the fourth largest in a decade of large harvests. It would not be surpassed for the next thirty years. Fagot left a plantation valued at $315,000, including land, buildings, slaves, livestock, and machinery, and was the most highly valued plantation in St. James Parish.[40] He did not live to see the upheavals of war and emancipation, although Uncle Sam fared better than many plantations elsewhere in the South. Early occupation of the New Orleans region by Union forces spared the area from much destruction of life and property and even permitted, to some extent, daily life to continue as normal.[41]

Throughout the war the plantation produced marketable crops of sugar and cotton, the latter of special interest to the US Army, and paid US taxes on income from sales. In 1863 Emilie Fagot's net income from sugar sales amounted to $5,800. In 1865 she netted $6,973 on sugar and $2,755 on cotton.[42] While elsewhere in the war-torn South people suffered from food deprivation, she purchased imported cognac and had French bread shipped sixty miles upriver from New Orleans. In 1865, with the war over and the Thirteenth Amendment in force, she paid wages to plantation laborers, marking the end of slavery and the start of a new era at Uncle Sam. Not all change came as a result of war and constitutional amendment. Regular purchases of fertilizer, which began in the 1870s, indicated that rich bottomland once thought to be infinitely fertile was suffering the effects of years of cultivation and flood control, which deprived the floodplain of annual silt deposits. The fields at Uncle Sam needed to be supplemented with fertilizer to remain productive.[43]

In the first half of the nineteenth century, sugar and cotton planters transformed the natural environment along much of the lower Mississippi River. In the latter half of the century, plantation owners began to experience several effects of those transformations that they had not anticipated. Levees served two essential purposes: they protected the plantation, its fields, structures, animals, and people from inundation; and they helped plantation overseers manage water for their crops, which varied depending on the crop. In the case of sugarcane, water is essential. The soil around the roots must be moist throughout the growing season, and yet too much water can be ruinous. In the cooler winter months, moisture encourages the growth of a fungus that causes root rot.[44] Whatever the time of year, sugarcane roots cannot tolerate saturated soil. There was nothing landowners could do about weather, but their systems of water management were designed to keep soils moist yet well drained. With levees, ditches, and canals operated in the best interest of sugarcane, plantation owners ignored other dimensions of the floodplain ecology. Levees prevented the river from fertilizing the floodplain with annual deposits of silt. While they reduced the frequency of floods, they increased their destructive power. Moreover, levees trapped rainwater in low-lying areas not adequately drained by canals, while in well-drained areas cleared of trees and other natural vegetation in preparation for tilling, erosion became a problem, as floodwater and rainwater moved unimpeded over even the flattest land, carrying topsoil into canals and into the back swamp. Pooled water and erosion reduced soil biodiversity by drowning earthworms and by washing away microbes that kept nematodes and fungi in check or that fixed nitrogen. Periodic dredging of canals, with the collected mud spread on fields as a fertilizer, helped to restore the land. Sugarcane planters also manured fields with filter cake, the residue strained from cane juice. Monocropping—raising one crop year after year on the same land—depleted the soil of many minerals, nutrients, and organisms. Denitrification was a serious problem in the sugarcane fields along the Mississippi River, as it was in corn and cotton fields across the South. There is no indication that managers at Uncle Sam ever practiced crop rotation or fallowing, even though the positive effect of clover, soybeans, and other legumes on soil fertility had been understood by farmers the world over for centuries. The focus at Uncle Sam was singleminded and on the incoming-earning crop of sugarcane.[45] Beginning in the spring of 1870, Uncle Sam's owners compensated for a loss in soil fertility by applying fertilizers of nitrogen-rich cottonseed meal, bone black—a charcoal made of animal bones that was rich in phosphate and that was unrelatedly used in the sugar refining process—and combinations of lime, potash, and ammonia mixed especially for sugarcane according to recipes devised by French chemist Georges Ville. Flood control, monocropping, and artificial fertilization, not just at Uncle Sam but up and down the Mississippi River Valley, represented significant human intrusions into and alterations of the natural processes of the floodplain ecology, which raised the financial and labor costs of plantation operations, which became, in effect, a battle against nature. The plantation landscape along the Mississippi River was a disaster—environmental, financial, or both—waiting to happen, although no one saw that in the picturesque green fields and grand yellow mansion at Uncle Sam.[46]

The effects of clearing, draining, and leveeing at Uncle Sam and at neighboring plantations are illustrated in the history of Bayou des Acadiens. When Samuel Fagot acquired Constantia Plantation, surveys of landholdings in St. James Parish placed the bayou to the north, flowing east-northeast from the natural levee along the river toward Lake Maurepas. The appearance of this bayou and no others on the surveys indicated its significance as the primary channel for draining the parish of rainwater and river overflow. In the days before steamboats, and even after their appearance, the bayou also served as a canoe route to and from New Orleans via lakes Maurepas and Pontchartrain, Bayou St. John, and the Carondelet Canal.[47] In 1845, Fagot completed the land purchases that extended his holdings north two miles through cypress swamp to Bayou des Acadiens, perhaps with the intention of floating out rafts of timber. However, later maps have the bayou beginning south of Uncle Sam, where no stream appeared previously, and the original stream, renamed Blind River, is shown as much diminished in size. Twentieth-century maps return the primary stream to its original location, north of Uncle Sam, although they label it Blind River, while the stream they identify as Bayou des Acadiens runs south of Uncle Sam and appears as a short and insignificant creek that disappears abruptly into the swamp. The apparent confusion in parish maps over the location of Bayou des Acadiens also exists in textual sources. For example, writing in 1881, E. W. Hilgard, a pioneer soil scientist at the University of California, Berkeley, who surveyed much of the Mississippi Valley, where he had lived for many years, identified the primary drainage channel of east St. James as Bayou des Acadiens, located to the north of the sugar plantations that fronted the river. Several years later, George W. Cable set *Bonaventure,* his story of Acadian Louisiana, along Bayou des Acadiens, which he located in the far southeast of the parish.[48]

Between 1800 and 1950 the primary drainage system for St. James Parish shifted from north to south and back again. The primary causes were levee construction and wetland drainage, which dramatically reduced the volume of water that annually ran downhill through the parish from the Mississippi River to Lake Maurepas, which in turn reconfigured the runoff channels. It appears that flood control and drainage systems put in place by the last half of the nineteenth century prevented water from running into the original Bayou des Acadiens while at the same time forced more water into a low area in the southern end of the parish, creating a new branch that eventually became known as Bayou des Acadiens.

Catastrophic floods, which occurred when levees collapsed under the pressure of a swollen Mississippi River, also affected drainage patterns in new ways. Compared to the seasonal flooding patterns from the pre-levee era, catastrophic floods rushed over the land with greater force and carried silt to far greater distances. The massive levees of the post-1927 Mississippi River flood era, as well as the parish canal system completed in the 1950s, further reconfigured the area's drainage system, reducing the new Bayou des Acadiens and enlarging the original, although differently named, bayou.

The annual Mississippi River rise came early in 1890. On the night of Thursday, March 13, the river in front of New Orleans reached an unprecedented height. It topped the levee in several places, and engineers feared a crevasse at Ninth Street was unavoidable. Then, abruptly, river levels began to fall, two to four inches over the next twenty-four hours, and the people of New Orleans breathed a collective sigh of relief. What saved the city that year was a catastrophic levee failure that same Thursday night, sixty-five miles upriver at the Nita Plantation.[49]

The Nita crevasse opened in a portion of new levee that was structurally weakened by a wooden irrigation trough—a rice flume—notched into the top of the embankment. At first, high water simply rushed down the trough and into empty rice fields, but it quickly eroded the levee, and within two hours a hole 25 feet wide appeared. Word spread and teams of managers and laborers from Nita and neighboring plantations worked in vain to repair the break. Over the next several weeks the crevasse widened to 3,000 feet and water poured through at a rate of 400,000 cubic feet per second, digging a crater that is visible more than a century later. The Corps of Engineers estimated that half the normal volume of the Mississippi River discharged through the break, from where it ran into Bayou des Acadiens, or Blind River, as the bayou was then called, and into Lake Maurepas, and eventually into Lake Pontchartrain and the Gulf of Mexico.[50]

Water from the Nita crevasse interrupted train traffic along the Illinois Central and Mississippi Valley lines, halted work in lumber yards, and swept away gardens and truck farms. Coastal fishermen as far as Biloxi, Mississippi, observed changes in current and water color. Instead of pompano, mackerel, and redfish, they hauled in nets full of Mississippi River catfish and buffalo fish. "Vast amounts of mud" buried thousands of acres of coastal oyster beds.[51]

Under normal circumstances, floodwaters that topped natural levees deposited the heaviest particles of sediment first, with finer, lighter grains drifting toward the backswamps. The flood caused by the Nita crevasse was different. Water surged through the human-made levee with such force that it scoured a large and deep hole in the floor of the floodplain. Water already laden with sediment picked up more dirt from that hole and from the levee, and carried it all to the back of the plantation several miles away, and there dropped it, forming a ridge a foot or more in height and four miles long. This ridge impeded flow into Blind River, or Bayou des Acadiens, forcing water across Uncle Sam Plantation, where the sugarcane crop was in the ground and corn planting had probably begun. The plantation's owners hastily organized all laborers to shore up the four-foot high levee that surrounded the estate, but it failed and river water inundated Uncle Sam, destroying crops and machinery, and rendering uninhabitable all buildings but the upper stories of the big house.[52]

At the turn of the century, sugarcane planters in Louisiana struggled with many problems, ranging from global competition to fungus in the soil, but for the descendants of Samuel Fagot, his granddaughters Emilie and Felicie Malus and their husbands Jules and Camille Jacob, the flood of 1890 sent the plantation business into near bankruptcy.[53]

Henry Studniczka was a fertilizer manufacturer and merchant with storefronts in St. Louis and New Orleans. He specialized in bone phosphates designed specifically for sugarcane cultivation and made from the waste of Chicago slaughterhouses. When the levee broke at Nita, he was about to ship twenty tons of phosphate to Uncle Sam Plantation, but he held it at Memphis until he got word that the plantation was safe. "I do sincerely hope that you will be able to save your entire crop," Studniczka wrote to Jules Jacob. A week later, after he received word of the devastation at Uncle Sam, Studniczka sympathized and offered support: "We exceedingly regret to hear of your calamity. Should you be able to cultivate sufficient cane for seed we would be very thankful if you accept from us, whatever you may need for tankage to fertilize same, so that you may obtain a fine tonnage. If the above is impossible we will be glad to hear from you, if there is any way that we could assist or help to carry your loss." In the interest of maintaining a good customer and receiving payment on accounts owing, Studniczka was willing to give Jacob the fertilizer necessary to replant his crop.[54]

Sugar production at Uncle Sam plantation in 1890, the year of the Nita crevasse, fell nearly 90 percent.[55] To repair damage and to live for a year without income from sugar sales, on which the entire plantation operation depended, the Jacob family borrowed heavily. Half of the family abandoned Uncle Sam altogether: at a family meeting in 1891, Emilie and Camille Jacob sold their shares in the family business to Felicie and Jules Jacob, who proceeded to rebuild.[56] Subsequent years saw some of the largest sugar crops ever produced at Uncle Sam. The crop for 1904–5 surpassed four million pounds, attesting to the beneficial effects of mechanization and fertilization.[57] However, every spring rise also brought the threat of another devastating flood, attesting to the risks of environmental manipulation. Over the next two years, there were in St. James Parish alone five levee breaks, including one at Uncle Sam, which sandbaggers successfully closed after three days. The Belmont crevasse of 1892 rivaled the Nita crevasse in its destructive effects, but it occurred below Uncle Sam. In response, state engineers continually built new levees and enhanced existing ones, including, in 1893, adding a 2,200-foot improvement at Uncle Sam plantation.[58]

In 1907, when Felicie Malus Jacob died, the plantation was so indebted that her children renounced their inheritance to avoid subjection to the claims of creditors. In accord with the Napoleonic Code, Felicie's half interest in the Uncle Sam plantation enterprise transferred to her husband, Jules Jacob, who became sole owner of the business. Soon after, Jules retired to New Orleans, leaving the plantation in the care of his son, Jules Jr. In 1914, Uncle Sam fell into receivership. The next year, Jules Jr. and receiver Firmin Reynaud, "the well known banker, planter, and financier" from nearby Lutcher, sold the estate to Moise Hymel and Walter James Stebbins, both of St. John the Baptist Parish, and the plantation passed out of the hands of the descendants of Jean Joseph Jourdan and Samuel Fagot.[59]

Hymel and Stebbins incorporated Uncle Sam as the Uncle Sam Planting and Manufacturing Co., kept Jules Jacob Jr., on as manager, and sold stock to raise funds to pay down debt. Over the next fifteen years, debts mounted once again as stockholders quarreled over finances. Law firms were the biggest winners of what one reporter called "a football of litigation." There were other problems. For example, the grinding and boiling plant repeatedly broke down and required expensive repairs or upgrades. Natural disasters frequently struck the Uncle Sam. In 1906 a tornado ripped up trees and destroyed the primary drainage pump. Three years later a hurricane tore the roofs off of several buildings and severally damaged the sugarcane crop, costing the plantation enterprise, by one estimate, $50,000. In 1917, drought ruined half of the plantation's sugarcane crop.[60]

In 1921, with a mortgage of $80,000, payments in arrears, and the company "again in trouble," the St. James Parish sheriff seized Uncle Sam for sale at auction, but all that resulted was a transfer in shares among stockholders. Throughout most of this period, Hymel and Stebbins remained the primary directors.[61] Meanwhile, the global price for sugar steadily fell so much that the plantation needed to produce three times as much sugar as in Samuel Fagot's day to maintain the same earnings.[62] For a few seasons, Hymel and Stebbins made rice the primary crop. Rice was more flood resilient than was sugar, but retooling entailed costs, and the global price for rice was also low. For the most part, the Uncle Sam Planting and Manufacturing Company limped along behind the levee as a sugarcane planting and sugar manufacturing corporation. And the Mississippi River steadily ate away at the levee in front of the plantation.

This was a time when many sugarcane plantations were incorporating, following a nationwide trend in agriculture and in business in general. Incorporation enabled landowners to raise capital for improvements and expansions and to pay down debt. Incorporation also meant that owners had to put investors' interests ahead of their own personal interests, and because none of Uncle Sam's investors lived on the plantation, they took no financial interest in the plantation as a residence.

The big house and the grounds around it fell steadily into disrepair. Heirs of the Jacobs family emptied the big house of furnishings and art, removing most of it to a home in New Orleans. "Weeds and rank grass" colonized the lawns and gardens.[63] Jules Jacob Jr. managed Uncle Sam on behalf of Hymel and Stebbins, but he lived in one of the *garçonnières.* He was now a tenant on the plantation where he grew up, no longer responsible for maintaining its residences. In addition, with the turn of the century, new ideas of the good life replaced those that had motivated Samuel Fagot and Joseph Constant. The life of a country squire was not for a sophisticate such as Jules Jacob Jr., who, following his father's death and the sale of the plantation, seems to have spent little time at Uncle Sam.[64] Neighbors described him as a keen student of modern, scientific agriculture, but they also celebrated his visits to St. James Parish from his home in New Orleans or following his excursions abroad. In 1932, when Jules Jacob Jr. died, the house had no official resident. By 1935, when Walker Evans photographed Uncle Sam for the Resettlement Administration, subsequently renamed the Farm Security Administration, the big house had been abandoned for years (fig. 3).

The cabins behind the big house were a different matter. More than one hundred African Americans lived in these two-room structures and in others on or very near Uncle Sam Plantation.[65] They raised the cane and produced the sugar that brought the income from which the plantation's investors profited. When the Pontchartrain Levee District Board made its decision to condemn Uncle Sam, they were the people forced off the land.

Samuel Fagot invested thousands of dollars into his struggle against the river. His twentieth-century successors lacked such tremendous wealth and power, especially after the Nita crevasse set them back. Instead, they relied on public agencies to keep the land safe from flooding, namely, on levee boards, the Army Corps of Engineers, the Mississippi River Commission, and on the

Figure 3. Photograph of the abandoned mansion, taken in March 1935 by Walker Evans, when he worked to document southern rural poverty for the Farm Security Administration. The Metropolitan Museum of Art, Walker Evans Archive, 1994 (1994.258.271). © Walker Evans Archive, The Metropolitan Museum of Art.

taxpayers and elected officials who funded them. For the most part, Fagot and other landowners built their plantation landscapes as independent men of property and business. In 1940, public agencies waged the battle against the Mississippi River, in the interest of communities, parishes, states, and nation. The Pontchartrain Levee District Board sacrificed Uncle Sam, its unoccupied big house and its occupied cabins, and there was little that Uncle Sam's owners and residents could do. In the era of Jim Crow segregation, African American laborers had no political recourse, no means for challenging the board's decision. The plantation company's investors appear not to have put up a fight, although it is not clear what they could have done. The consensus among landowners in St. James favored the proposed new levee. Meanwhile, the big house sat empty. Managing partner Walter Stebbins, a levee board member, resided in St. John the Baptist Parish. Whatever sentimental feelings Stebbins may have had for Uncle Sam, and for the plantation landscapes in which he grew up, as a practical man of business, he may have agreed with the assessment of the board that a new levee was best for all.[66]

The strongest objections to the demolition of Uncle Sam came from the Historic American Buildings Survey. Architectural photographer Richard Koch convinced HABS director Charles Peterson to prevail upon his superior, National Park Service director Arno Cammerer, to halt proceedings, but when Cammerer's telegram arrived at the Corps of Engineers Office in New Orleans, the demolition of Uncle Sam was well underway.[67]

The HABS had hoped to preserve the Uncle Sam big house and adjacent structures as a "national monument or historic site" or, as a *Times-Picayune* article declared, a "glorious memorial of an era long gone." However, the agency expressed little interest in the history of the struggle against nature or in the history of the people who worked on the front lines of that struggle. Architectural photographers saw art in columns and pigeon houses but not in ditches, canals, and slave cabins. The HABS photographs of the big house, *garçonnières,* and *pigeonniers,* of mantel pieces and cornices, abstracted those objects from the context of the full plantation landscape and history, much as the nation at that time abstracted the romantic story of the Lost Cause from the full history of the Old South and the Civil War. Drawings made by HABS draftsmen presented aerial perspectives of the assemblage of structures on the plantation grounds, including in the distance the former slave cabins, but no fields. In contrast, an aerial photograph of the Uncle Sam Plantation, taken in 1939, its last full year, shows a working plantation, with plowed fields, ditches, gravel roads, and well-worn paths, as well as workers' cabins surrounded by fences and kitchen gardens (fig. 4).

Following the demolition of the Uncle Sam plantation structures, the Corps of Engineers set a new levee back from the river, right over top of the site of the former big house. Hymel and Stebbins, their company now registered as Uncle Sam Plantation, Inc., continued to hire farm laborers and to plant sugarcane in the same fields Samuel Fagot had overseen, but they also optioned the property and looked to sell. The post–World War II growth of the chemical industry in Louisiana presented new opportunities to riverside landowners. In 1961 Walter Stebbins died. In 1966 his surviving partner, Moise Hymel, sold a large portion of the former plantation to the Freeport Sulphur Company, a fertilizer producer, since subsumed by IMC Global. Mosaic, a fertilizer company formed by IMC Global and Cargill, currently owns the former plantation lands.[68]

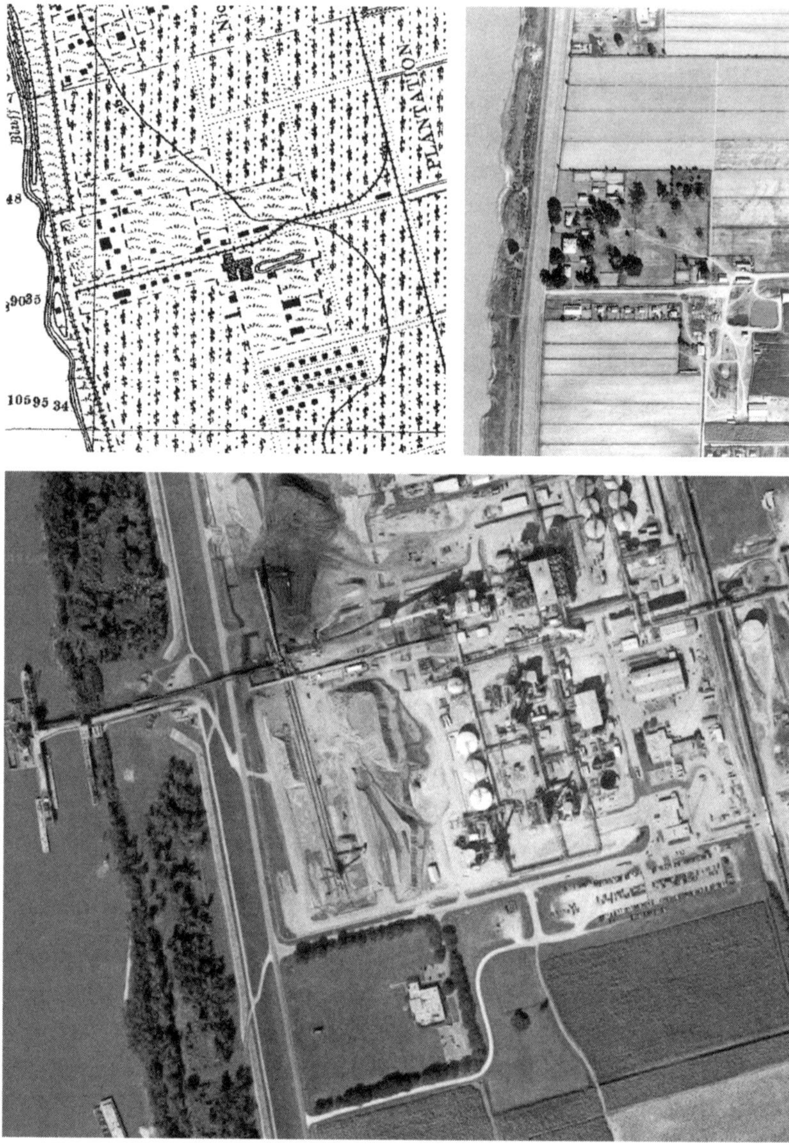

Figure 4. *Clockwise:* Survey chart of the plantation area, 1877; aerial photograph of the working plantation, 1939; satellite image of the former plantation site, now a chemical plant, 2018.

In the years after World War II, the river bank from Baton Rouge to New Orleans was industrialized, and the agricultural landscape built a century or more before was once again transformed. Since 1966, the fertilizer factory at what is still known as Uncle Sam has altered considerably the landscape of the former plantation, although much land between it and other factories nearby is still planted with sugar. Some of the property boundaries demarcating Constantia—Uncle Sam—on the Persac map are visible in aerial photographs of the chemical plant that operates there now, as are portions of Fagor's drainage canal, for which the plant has some use. Industrialized fertilizer production, like sugar production in Louisiana, depends on careful management of water.

NOTES

1. "Time and River Win Again," *New Orleans Times-Picayune,* March 10, 1940, section 2, p. 6.

2. The Pontchartrain Levee District had its headquarters at Lutcher, in St. James Parish, downriver from Uncle Sam. The Board of Commissioners represented six parishes and the Illinois Central Railroad. On the history of the Pontchartrain Levee District, see http://leveedistrict.org/history/.

3. Susan Scott Parrish, *The Flood Year 1927: A Cultural History* (Princeton: Princeton University Press, 2017). On the New Deal's reconstruction of rural America, and in particular, those places devastated by environmental disaster, see Sarah T. Phillips, *This Land, This Nation: Conservation, Rural America, and the New Deal* (New York: Cambridge University Press, 2007).

4. On the image of the South in early twentieth-century popular culture, see Karen L. Cox, *Dreaming of Dixie: How the South Was Created in American Popular Culture* (Chapel Hill: University of North Carolina Press, 2011). See also the special issue of *Southern Quarterly* devoted to *Gone with the Wind:* no. 55 (Winter/Spring 2018).

5. C. W. Price Jr., "Hungry Waters of Mississippi Threaten to Destroy Uncle Sam Plantation," *The Progress* (Hammond, LA), August 19, 1938, p. 12.

6. Richard Follett, *The Sugar Masters: Planters and Slaves in Louisiana's Cane World, 1820–1860* (Baton Rouge: Louisiana State University Press, 2005); John C. Rodrigue, *Reconstruction in the Cane Fields: From Slavery to Free Labor in Louisiana's Sugar Parishes* (Baton Rouge: Louisiana State University Press, 2001); John B. Rehder, *Delta Sugar: Louisiana's Vanishing Plantation Landscape* (Baltimore: Johns Hopkins University Press, 1999). Rehder's cultural geography focuses mostly on the late-twentieth-century demise of six plantations. His discussion of the formative history of the sugar landscape discusses the French or English or Irish, and so forth, traditions visible in plantation design. The best economic history of the entire era of sugar planting in Louisiana and elsewhere in the South remains J. Carlyle Sitterson, *Sugar Country: The Cane Sugar Industry in the South, 1753–1950* (Lexington: University of Kentucky Press, 1953). Two model plantation environmental histories are Lynn A. Nelson, *Pharsalia: An Environmental Biography of a Southern Plantation, 1780–1880* (Athens: University of Georgia Press, 2009), and Drew A.

Swanson, *Remaking Wormsloe Plantation: The Environmental History of a Lowcountry Landscape* (Athens: University of Georgia Press, 2012).

7. Agathine H. Goldstein, "Plantation Relic of Steamboat Days," *Ruston Daily Leader,* February 20, 1933, p. 4.

8. Photos, Historic American Buildings Survey (HABS), Uncle Sam Plantation, Convent, St. James Parish, LA, Library of Congress Prints and Photographs Division, Washington, DC. http://www.loc.gov/pictures/item/la0030/, hereafter cited as HABS. Eighth Census, 1860, Schedule 4, Agriculture, Louisiana, St. James Parish, Convent Post Office, p. 5.

9. Quote is from *New Orleans Item,* March 6, 1914, p. 7. In 1926 New Orleans architect Richard Koch commissioned New Jersey architectural photographer Robert W. Tebbs to undertake a photographic survey of Louisiana plantations, including Uncle Sam, that was itself part of a project funded by the Press of the American Institute of Architects. Richard Anthony Lewis situates Tebbs's photographs within a "broadly romantic view of plantation life" that culminated in *Gone with the Wind.* Richard Anthony Lewis, *Robert W. Tebbs, Photographer to Architects: Louisiana Plantations in 1926* (Baton Rouge: Louisiana State University Press, 2011), 1. In 1936 and 1940, Richard Koch, then director of the Louisiana Division of HABS, photographed Uncle Sam. In the 1930s, Dorothea Lange, Marion Post Wolcott, Ben Shahn, and Walker Evans were among the Farm Security Administration photographers to document the South's landscape of poverty and abandonment. In 1935, Evans took several photographs of Uncle Sam. Also in the 1930s, Louisiana photographer Clarence John Laughlin, a pioneer of photographic surrealism, photographed Uncle Sam as part of a series commissioned by the US Army Corps of Engineers, which Laughlin adapted for his "Elegy for the Old South" series, included in *Ghosts Along the Mississippi* (1948). On the photographers who depicted a ruined and abandoned plantation landscape, see Jochen Wierich's essay in this volume.

10. In 1825 Fagot sailed from Nantes, France, to New Orleans. He gave his country of residence as the United States, so this was likely not his first voyage to America. He also gave his occupation as merchant. Passenger Lists of Vessels Arriving at New Orleans, Louisiana, 1820–1902, NAI Number 2824927, Records of the Immigration and Naturalization Service, Record Group 85, National Archives, Washington, DC.

11. Mark F. Martinkovic, "Management Summary Phase I Cultural Resources Survey of the Longview Canal Drainage Project St. James Parish, Louisiana," Draft Report, US Department of Homeland Security, FEMA, Hazard Mitigation Grant Program, Algiers, Louisiana, May 27, 2011; Bradley E. Spicer et al., *Soil Survey of Iberville Parish* (Washington, DC: United States Department of Agriculture, 1977), 28–30.

12. Daniel Tyler Gooden, "St. James Mounds Tested," *L'Observateur*, March 10, 2001. http://www.lobservateur.com/2001/03/10/st-james-mounds-tested/. Earthen ceremonial mounds from different eras and representing different cultures have been found throughout the Mississippi Valley and around the southeastern United States. In addition, there are shell midden mounds scattered around the Mississippi River Delta and elsewhere. Dennis Jones and Malcolm Shuman, *Archaeological Atlas and Report of Prehistoric Indian Mounds in Louisiana: Volume II—Ascension, Iberville, Pointe Coupée, St. James and West Feliciana* (Baton Rouge: Louisiana Division of Ar-

chaeology, Office of Cultural Resource Development, Department of Culture, Recreation and Tourism, 1987).

13. Lillian C. Bourgeois, *Cabanocey: The History, Customs, and Folklore of St. James Parish* (Gretna, LA: Pelican Press, 1998), 1–9, 170; William C. Rense, "The Perique Tobacco Industry of St. James Parish, Louisiana: A World Monopoly," *Economic Botany* 24, no. 2 (1970): 123–30.

14. *New York, Marriage Newspaper Extracts, 1801–1880 (Barber Collection)* [database on-line] (Provo, UT: Ancestry.com); *Military minutes of the Council of Appointment of the State of New York, 1783–1821* [database on-line] (Provo, UT: Ancestry.com); Register of Enlistments in the US Army, 1798–1914 (National Archives Microfilm Publication M233, 81 rolls); Records of the Adjutant General's Office, 1780s–1917, Record Group 94; National Archives, Washington, DC (Provo, UT: Ancestry.com); *US Army, Register of Enlistments, 1798–1914* [database on-line] (Provo, UT: Ancestry.com Operations Inc., 2007); Theophilus Francis Rodenbaugh and William Lawrence Haskin, eds., *The Army of the United States: Historical Sketches of Staff and Line with Portraits of Generals-In-Chief* (New York: Maynard, Merrill & Co., 1896), 432; Logan Esarey, ed., *Governors Messages and Letters, Messages and Letters of William Henry Harrison, Vol. 1, 1800–1811* (Indianapolis: Indiana Historical Commission, 1922), 472; Joseph Constant to Andrew Jackson, December 28, 1814, Library of Congress, Manuscript Division, Andrew Jackson Papers: Series 1, General Correspondence and Related Items, 1775 to 1885.

15. Hugh Hastings, *The Public Papers of Daniel D. Tompkins, Governor of New York, 1807–1817, Military* (Albany, NY: J. B. Lyon Co., 1902), vol. II, 363–64, 366–67; vol. III, 361.

16. *Membership in the Louisiana House of Representatives 1812–2020,* David R. Poynter Legislative Research Library, Louisiana House of Representatives, June 19, 2017, at house.louisiana .gov/H_PDFdocs/HouseMembership_History_CURRENT.pdf.

17. According to MeasuringWorth.com, $150,000 in 1820 would today equal between $3 million and $4 billion.

18. *Record of Wills, 1665–1916; Index to Wills, 1662–1923 (New York County),* New York, Surrogate's Court (New York County), Ancestry.com; *New York, Wills and Probate Records, 1659–1999* [database on-line] (Provo, UT: Ancestry.com Operations, Inc., 2015); R. Christopher Goodwin et al., *Cultural Resources Survey of Five Mississippi River Revetment Items, Final Report,* US Army Corps of Engineers New Orleans District, Report No. COELMN/PD-85/03, at www.dtic.mil /dtic/tr/fulltext/u2/a158908.pdf. It is possible that Constant sold his plantation just before returning to New York. His will refers to Louisiana property without specifically identifying it and appoints Philip Hickey and George Mather to take care of it.

On ribbon cane, see Follett, *Sugar Masters,* 22, and Kenneth A. Gravois and Keith P. Bischoff, "New Sugarcane Varieties to the Rescue," *Louisiana Agriculture* (Spring 2008), at https:// www.lsuagcenter.com/~/media/system/4/a/0/9/4a0957a5c38f740abc6bed0859012 41c/spring 2008louisianaagriculture web1.pdf.

19. Kenneth Scott, *British Aliens in the United States during the War of 1812* (Baltimore, MD: Genealogical Publishing Co., 1979). McMaster owned the land during passage of the 1820 Land Act and so was recorded as the original patentee and his name appears as such on surveys of St. James Parish (Louisiana-St. Helena, Township 11S, Range 4E). The government did not issue a

certificate until 1846, by which time Samuel McMaster was deceased. Patent no. 396 is in the name of Samuel's widow, Helen Ross McMaster. Both the patent and the original survey may be found at United States Bureau of Land Management, General Land Office Records, Washington, DC, at http://www.glorecords.blm.gov/.

20. Timothy Flint, *Recollections of the last ten years: passed in occasional residences and journeyings in the valley of the Mississippi . . .* (Boston: Cummings, Hilliard, 1826), 299–301; W. (William) Bullock, *Sketch of a journey through the western states of North America . . .* (London: John Miller, 1827), xiii.

21. "United States Census, 1810," NARA microfilm publication M252 (Washington, DC: National Archives and Records Administration, n.d.), roll 10, p. 442; FHL microfilm 181,355; Jill-Karen Yakubik et al., "Archaeological Data Recovery of the Camino Site (16JE223), A Spanish Colonial Period Site Near New Orleans, Louisiana," US Army Corps of Engineers Cultural Resources Survey, Final Report (March 1996), 61, at https://apps.dtic.mil/dtic/tr/fulltext/u2/a286872.pdf.

22. Ancestry.com, *Louisiana, Wills and Probate Records, 1756–1984,* Fifth Census, 1830, Population Schedules, Louisiana, St. James Parish, at https://archive.org/stream/populations-c18300043unit#page/n551/mode/2up.

23. See https://archive.org/stream/populationsc18400135unit#page/n107/mode/2up. *Baton-Rouge Gazette,* October 12, 1844, p.1, and *Le Messager* (Bringier, Paroisee Saint-Jacques, Louisiana), June 2, 1855, p. 2, and June 30, 1855, p. 2, include notices of runaway slaves.

24. Succession of J. J. Jourdan and Victoire Celeste His Wife, Court of Probates, J Surnames, Jackson 1832-Jordan 1833, Louisiana, Orleans Parish Estate Files, City Archives, New Orleans, Louisiana. Process Verbal of the Sale of the Property Belonging the Estate of Jean Joseph Jourdan and Victoire Celest His Wife, Inventories of Estates, J Surnames, Jeanflos, 1825-Jordan, 1833, Louisiana, Orleans Parish Estate Files, City Archives, New Orleans, Louisiana. Jourdan's estate of $195,000 would in 2018 be worth between $5 million and $3.7 billion, according to MeasuringWorth.com.

25. Original Survey, and Accession Numbers LA0150.242, LA0150.243, LA0170.185, LA0170.186, Survey Plats, Louisiana, St. James, Township 11 S, Range 4 E, United States Bureau of Land Management, General Land Office Records. Washington, DC, at http://www.glorecords.blm.gov/. Land surveys and maps from the early nineteenth century, including *Norman's Chart,* identified the stream as Bayou des Acadiens, which later maps identified as Blind River. Later maps identify a different stream, to the south of Uncle Sam near Convent, as Bayou Acadien. This second stream is not on early maps.

26. Seventh Census, 1850, Slave Schedules, Louisiana, St. James Parish, at https://archive.org/stream/populationscheduo246unix#page/n211/mode/2up.

27. Andrew Moore, *Brown and Cypress Lumbering in the Old Southwest* (Baton Rouge: Louisiana State University Press, 1967), 64.

28. Solon Robinson, "Agricultural Tour of the South and West.—No. 7," *American Agriculturalist* 8 (1849): 219.

29. The surveyor may have made a distinction between a water tupelo and a black gum, both of the genus *Nyssa,* both commonly and confusingly referred to today as tupelo or tupelo gum.

30. Uncle Sam Plantation Papers, 1805–1914, Mss. 408, 602, 1252, Louisiana and Lower Mississippi Valley Collections, Special Collections, Hill Memorial Library, Louisiana State University,

Baton Rouge, hereafter cited as US Plantation Papers. On ditching, see: Series I, UU:217, box 1, folders 32, 37, box 3, folder 81; Plantation Diary for 1873, March 11, 12, 14, 17, 27, June 18, and October 8, and the March 12, 1850. A survey of the plantation, undertaken by A. W. Warren, mentions "Fagot's Canal" and may be found in UU:228, box 15, Legal Material, folder 421, in the US Plantation Papers. In 1850 the Louisiana sugar census noted that the Samuel Fagot plantation used a steam mill. Pierre Antoine Champomier, *Statement of Sugar Crop Made in Louisiana, 1850–51* (New Orleans: Cook, Young & Co., 1851), 16.

31. Follett, *Sugar Masters,* 35. Calculations are rough estimates based on the following: the standard weight equivalent of a hardwood cord is two tons; in Louisiana, on average, there are forty-one tons of trees, dead and alive, per acre. See Sonja N. Oswalt and James W. Bentley, "Louisiana's Forests, 2005, SRS-192" (Asheville, NC: US Department of Agriculture Forest Service, Southern Research Station, 2013), 13.

32. Ervin Mancil, "An Historical Geography of Industrial Cypress Lumbering in Louisiana" (PhD diss., Louisiana State University, 1972), *LSU Historical Dissertations and Theses,* at http://digitalcommons.lsu.edu/gradschool_disstheses/2296.

33. Benjamin Silliman, *Manual on the Cultivation of the Sugar Cane and the Fabrication and the Refinement of Sugar* (Washington, DC: Francis Preston Blair, 1833), 15, 64; Solon Robinson, "Mr. Robinson's Tour.—No. 10," *American Agriculturalist* 8 (1849): 314.

34. Eighth Census of the United States, 1860, Agricultural Schedules, Louisiana, St. James Parish. Crop acreages are estimated based on crop size reported in the census, 700 hogsheads of sugar and 6,000 bushels of corn. Louisiana sugar yields averaged two to three hogsheads per acre, less for ratoon sugar. Estimates allow for seed cane held back from milling. Corn averaged eighteen to twenty-five bushels per acre. On sugar yields, see Joseph Carlyle Sitterson, *Sugar Country: The Cane Sugar Industry in the South, 1753–1950* (Lexington: University of Kentucky Press, 1953), 155; J. D. B. DeBow, *The Industrial Resources, Etc., of the Southern and Western States* (New Orleans: Office of DeBow's Review, 1853), 199; Follett, *The Sugar Masters,* 12. On corn yields, see Christopher Morris, *Becoming Southern: The Evolution of a Way of Life, Warren County and Vicksburg, Mississippi, 1770–1860* (New York: Oxford University Press, 1995), 212n28; "Letter from Panola," *Southern Cultivator* 27 (1869): 304; Price, "Hungry Waters of Mississippi."

35. Data Pages, Historic American Buildings Survey; Robinson, "Agricultural Tour of the South and West.—No. 7," 219; Frederick J. H. Merrill and Heinrich Ries, *Bulletin of the New York State Museum, Volume 3, Clay Industries of New York* (Albany: University of the State of New York, 1895), 155–73. There is some uncertainty as to when construction of the mansion that stood until 1940 was completed. An estate inventory undertaken in 1872, following Emilie Fagot's death, indicates a home with six rooms—two bedrooms, a dining room, a hall, a reception room, and a kitchen. In contrast, the Uncle Sam Plantation mansion that was demolished in 1940 had seven rooms on each floor and a detached kitchen. "Agreement of Heirs of Emilie Jourdan Fagot," Nicholas B. Trist, 23 April 1872, Act 470, New Orleans Notarial Archives. Box 2, Folder 47, US Plantation Papers. In its 1940 report on Uncle Sam, HABS cited Lyle Saxon as an authority on the date of construction. A New Orleans writer and journalist, Saxon claimed in his book *Old Louisiana* that the building dated from 1836, but provided no source for his information. The HABS report also cited a fourth-hand account from architect F. Ray Leimkuehler, who claimed

to have seen a letter written by architectural photographer Richard Koch, in which Koch claimed to have been told by Edward Trist Waldo, a great grandson of Samuel Fagot, that construction on the mansion had begun in 1837, that a fire had taken the house before construction was completed, leaving only the brick walls. Construction on the big house began anew, Waldo told Koch, but not until 1850 was it completed. Lyle Saxon, *Old Louisiana* (New York: The Century Co., 1929), 301. William P. Spratling and Natalie Scott, *Old Plantation Houses in Louisiana* (New York: William Helburn, 1927), describes Uncle Sam but offers no date of construction.

36. Pierre Antoine Champomier, *Statement of Sugar Crop Made in Louisiana, 1853–54* (New Orleans: Cook, Young & Co., 1854), 16.

37. Robinson, "Agricultural Tour of the South and West.—No. 7," 219; Walter Prichard, ed., "A Tourist's Description of Louisiana in 1860," *Louisiana Historical Quarterly* 21 (October 1938): 1120. Englishwoman and travel writer Frances Milton Trollope also mentioned the convent in her description of the region between New Orleans and Baton Rouge, but she said nothing on plantation homes. See Frances Milton Trollope, *Domestic Manners of the Americans,* vol. 1 (New York: Whittaker, Treacher and Co., 1832), 37.

38. See Saxon, *Old Louisiana,* 301, and Spratling and Scott, *Old Plantation Houses,* 13, 15. Saxon states that the mansion was painted a soft yellow. Spratling and Scott state, confusingly, that the building was originally painted white but that by 1927 much of the white paint had washed down to an earlier tan. In April of 1902, Jules Jacob white-washed the sugar house and cabins at Uncle Sam. See "St. James, Left Bank," *Louisiana Planter and Sugar Manufacturer* (April 12, 1902): 237. Receipt for sales, 1859, Series I, UU:217, box 1, folder 13, US Plantation Papers. According to Measuringworth.com, $80,000 in 1859 equaled $1.8 million to $352 million in 2018.

39. Some accounts assume Samuel Fagot's son-in-law, Lucien Malus, assumed management responsibilities, but he lived in New Orleans, where he owned a mercantile business. Plantation records indicate very clearly that Emilie managed the family business.

40. The amount of $315,000 in 1858 equaled $7.1 million to $1.5 billion in 2018, according to Measuringworth.com.

41. Pierre Antoine Champomier, *Statement of Sugar Crop Made in Louisiana, 1858–59* (New Orleans: Cook, Young & Co., 1859), 15; Eighth Census, 1860, Population Schedules, Louisiana, St. James Parish, at https://archive.org/stream/populationschedu423unit#page/n569/mode/2up.

42. The amount $6,973 in 1865 equaled between $90 thousand and $13.6 million in 2018; $2,755 in 1865 equaled between $35 thousand and $5.4 million in 2018. Both estimates are according to MeasuringWorth.com.

43. Series I, Financial Records, UU:217, Box 1, Folders 26–28, 37, US Plantation Papers.

44. H. H. Flor, "Factors Influencing the Severity of the Root Rot Troubles of Sugar Cane," *LSU Agricultural Experiment Station Reports* (May 1930): 576.

45. Not until 1888 did agroscientists learn how legumes worked to improve soil fertility through their relationship with a particular species of nitrogen-fixing bacteria. Anne Willems, "The Taxonomy of Rhizobia: An Overview," *Plant and Soil* 287 (September 2006): 3–14.

46. US Plantation Papers, Series I, Financial Records, UU:217, Box 1, Folder 37, Box 2, Folders 59, 71, Box 3, Folders 111, 118; Series II, Correspondence, UU:226, box 10, Folders 340 and 341.

47. Prichard, ed., "A Tourist's Description of Louisiana in 1860," 1124.

48. Matthew Carey, *Louisiana.* [S.1, 1814] map. Retrieved from the Library of Congress, at https://www.loc.gov/item/2002624016/; David H. Burr and John Arrowsmith, *Map of Mississippi, Louisiana & Arkansas* (London: J. Arrowsmith, 1839), retrieved from the Library of Congress at https://www.loc.gov/item/98688404/; John La Tourrette, *La Tourrette's reference map of the state of Louisiana* (New Orleans: John La Tourrette, 1848), retrieved from the Library of Congress at https://www.loc.gov/item/2006629760/; G. W. R. Bayley, and Childs & Hammond, *Map of a part of the State of Louisiana exhibiting the route of the New-Orleans, Opelousas & Great Western Rail Road* (New Orleans: Eng. by Childs & Hammond, 1853), retrieved from the Library of Congress at https://www.loc.gov/item/gm72003017/; Charles Mahon, *Map of the alluvial region of the Mississippi* [S.1, 1861], retrieved from the Library of Congress at https://www.loc.gov/item/99447038/; Mississippi River Commission, *Survey of the Mississippi River, Chart 71* (1877), retrieved from the National Oceanic and Atmospheric Administration, Coast Survey at https://historicalcharts.noaa.gov/historicals/preview/image/MR71; US Geological Survey, Topographic Division, *Topographic Maps, Louisiana—Donaldsonville* (1892). For the twentieth century, see the USGS Historical Topographic Map Explorer at http://historicalmaps.arcgis.com/usgs/. E. W. Hilgard, "St. James Parish," in William H. Harris, *Louisiana. Products, Resources and Attractions, with a Sketch of the Parishes* (New Orleans: Times-Democrat, 1881), 208. George W. Cable, "Grande Pointe," *Century Magazine* 33 (March 1887): 659–84; George W. Cable, *Bonaventure: A Prose Pastoral of Acadian Louisiana* (New York: Charles Scribner's Sons, 1888), 86.

49. *New Orleans Times-Picayune,* March 15, 1890, p. 1.

50. "The Mississippi River," *Louisiana Planter and Sugar Manufacturer* 9 (October 15, 1892): 288.

51. Eugene A. Smith, Lawrence C. Johnson, and Daniel W. Langdon Jr., *Geological Survey of Alabama, Report on the Geology of the Coastal Plain of Alabama* (Montgomery, AL: Brown Printing Co., 1894), 30–32; Lawrence C. Johnson, "The Nita Crevasse," *Bulletin of the Geological Society of America, Volume II* (Rochester, NY: Geological Society of America, 1891), 20–25.

52. *New Orleans Times-Picayune,* March 19, 1890, p. 1; F. W. Brode of Memphis to Jules J. Jacob, March 17, 1890, US Plantation Papers, Series II, Correspondence, UU:226, box 10, Folder 340.

53. Flor, "Root Rot Troubles of Sugar Cane."

54. Henry Studniczka to Jules J. Jacob, March 18 and March 24, 1890, US Plantation Papers, Series II, Correspondence, UU:226, box 10, Folder 340.

55. Alcée Bouchereau, *Statement of the Sugar and Rice Crops Made in Louisiana in 1889–90* (New Orleans: L. Graham and Sons, 1890), 42; Bouchereau, *Statement of the Sugar and Rice Crops Made in Louisiana in 1890–92* (New Orleans: Alcée Bouchereau, 1892), 86.

56. US Plantation Papers, Series II, Correspondence, UU:226, box 10, Folders 341.

57. Alcée Bouchereau, *Statement of the Sugar and Rice Crops Made in Louisiana in 1904–05* (New Orleans: Alcée Bouchereau, 1908), 42.

58. "Three More Levee Breaks," *Bolivar Bulletin* (Bolivar, TN), June 23, 1893; *Report of the Board of State Engineers of the State of Louisiana* (Baton Rouge: News Publishing Co., 1894), 74, 151, 157.

59. *New Orleans Item* (March 6, 1914), p. 7.

60. Jacob v. Uncle Sam Planting and Mfg. Co. et al., 81 So. 604 (1919); Jacob et al. v Falgoust et al., 90 So. 426 (1922); *Louisiana Planter and Sugar Manufacturer* 37 (October 13, 1906): 231;

38 (January 24, 1907): 55; 43 (October 2, 1909): 215; 66 (February 5, 1921): 91; 66 (April 2, 1921): 219; "Louisiana Cane Sustains Damage," *Hattiesburg News* (Hattiesburg, MS) (September 22, 1909), p. 8; "Sugar Grinding Season Opens with Prospects of Reduced Output," *Times-Picayune* (October 31, 1917), p. 28.

61. Reynaud v. Uncle Sam Planting Manufacturing Co., 94 So. 405 (La. 1922).

62. "Sugar Plants Closed by Free Trade," *Hartford Republican* (Hartford, KY) (January 29, 1915), p. 7; David S. Jacks, "From Boom to Bust: A Typology of Real Commodity Prices in the Long Run," *NBER Working Paper 18874* (2013), at http://www.nber.org/papers/w18874.

63. Many items, formerly of Uncle Sam Plantation, were in the Garden District home of Benjamin T. Waldo, whose wife was a great-granddaughter of Samuel Fagot. *Times-Picayune,* August 17, 1930, section 4, p. 11 (p. 49); Annette Duchein, "Superb Plantation Homes Fall Before 'Ole Man River,'" *New Orleans Times-Picayune,* June 1, 1930, p. 20.

64. "St. James, Left Bank," *Louisiana Planter and Sugar Manufacturer* 47 (October 14, 1911): 262.

65. Jules J. Jacob Jr. and his uncle, Camille Jacob, are both on the 1920 census, but they are separated by 155 people, of whom 119 were African Americans. Jules lived at Uncle Sam. If the census taker found Camille living there or nearby, then he must have found the other people living in the same proximity. Fourteenth Census, 1920, Population Schedules, Louisiana, St. James Parish. Duchein, "Superb Plantation Homes Fall Before 'Ole Man River.'" In 1830, Duchein reported that there were forty "negro cabins" at Uncle Sam. Writing in 1938, C. W. Price stated that "until recently . . . forty slave cabins" stood at Uncle Sam. Price, "Hungry Waters of Mississippi." In 1940, HABS drawings indicated twenty or so. Aerial View, Uncle Sam Plantation, Convent, St. James Parish, LA, Library of Congress Prints and Photographs Division, Washington, DC, at http://www.loc.gov/pictures/item/la0030.sheet.00002a/resource/.

66. "Walter James Stebbins Life Written by His Two Daughters," unpublished. The authors posted this record on Ancestry.com.

67. Goodwin et al., *Cultural Resources Survey,* 98.

68. Index to Conveyances, St. James Parish, http://www.stjamesparishclerkofcourt.com. Joseph A. Lucia, "Convent to Get Freeport Plant," *New Orleans Times-Picayune,* October 12, 1966, p. 1. Mark Schleifstein, "Mosaic Fertilizer Pledges $2 Billion to Settle Hazardous Waste Complaints," NOLA.com, October 2, 2015, at https://www.nola.com/news/environment/article_696f8455-b497-5ac6-9dcd-c94c17ced6e3.html.

EPILOGUE

An enthusiastic plantation guide stood in front of a group of tourists, the Persac map hanging behind him. With a dramatic sweep of his arm, he announced that in the map, visitors were getting to see the "millionaires' row" of the 1800s. He pointed out with great pride where the artist had outlined "our plantation" (the plantation being toured) and "our neighbors." In the hands of the guide, what visitors had just experienced—a tour filled with nostalgia and short on fact—was in fact a beautiful window into a lost, successful gentry. And the Persac map was the proof.[1]

The described tour, which took place in 2010, was by no means an anomaly. While Persac's map was not always as overtly referenced, throughout the twentieth century and into the twenty-first century the world it illustrated was mirrored in the content and messages shared at plantation sites from Natchez to New Orleans. Rapt audiences, having no reason to question what was being presented, absorbed formulaic presentations as "windows into the past" and tangible myths. They were there for the "antebellum experience"; eccentric hoopskirts or wild misrepresentations of history were merely "Southern Belle charm" and "quaint stories." Material jeopardizing the prevailing message of nostalgia was either pushed aside or reimagined and carefully repackaged in a form that was appropriately marketable and harmless (to the mythmaker). Why run the risk of damaging the vision of the antebellum lifestyle by talking about enslaved men and women when instead the guide could share ghost stories of "old mammie" and her voodoo or of the faithful nursery maid? Such a path was certainly much safer, and the more outrageous the story, the better the visitor response. It was an ideal arrangement for those crafting the narrative.

The planter-dominated landscape remained untainted, with slavery tucked safely in the appropriately frightful corners.[2] Even as recently as 2007, a plantation tourism participant declared to an interviewer, "[Tourists] come for the hoopskirts, the grandeur and the elegance. That's a part of the story, and maybe a better part to tell."[3]

It was a statement curiously prophetic, though surely not as the owner intended—162 years after Persac printed his map, and more than seventy years after the first Natchez Pilgrimage, there were rumbles of a cultural awakening. In 2012 "Slavery at Thomas Jefferson's Monticello: Paradox of Liberty" was unveiled at the Smithsonian's National Museum of American History. For the first time, a national museum framed its exhibit of the man who penned the Declaration of Independence with his identity as slaveowning planter. The following year—and seventy-four years after *Gone with the Wind* took the honor—*12 Years a Slave* won the Academy Award for Best Picture and Solomon Northup's interaction with the plantation landscape began to supplant Scarlett O'Hara's Tara as the plantation reference in popular culture. Public interest in plantations in general and in slavery specifically continued to grow. Less than ten years after the plantation owner's hoopskirt assertion—an assertion that had held true for decades—visitors were indeed visiting plantations but it was Northup's experience, not Scarlett's story, that had their attention. Nostalgia was being replaced with an interest in historical accuracy, in scholarship, and in its interpretation. Adding to this increasing public interest in plantation history, visitors' experiences were contextualized by their awareness of racial tension in Ferguson (2014), Baltimore (2015), and Baton Rouge (2017). As a result, the plantation landscape was quickly being brought into the lens of popular culture as "ground zero" for current social issues. Plantation sites were now being compared with Auschwitz and less often to the imaginative Tara.[4]

The Old South was changing. In 2015, Whitney Plantation opened in Wallace, Louisiana, as the first to use a former plantation as its medium to interpret American slavery. In 2017 James Madison's Montpelier opened its permanent exhibit "A Mere Distinction of Colour." In 2018, the *New York Times* announced, "Monticello is done avoiding Thomas Jefferson's relationship with Sally Hemings" and revealed that Hemings's former quarters at Monticello had been identified and would be opened to the public.[5] In 2018, the Owens-Thomas House in Savannah, Georgia, changed its name to include "and Slave Quarters." The scholarship put forth by historians John Wesley Blassingame,

Michael Vlach, and others now found an audience outside academia in the form of public discussion and heritage tourism.

That is not to say that this rush of scholarship-based interpretation has been universally adopted by plantations in the South or unchallenged by the public. Some sites appear to have recommitted to narratives that further the idealized landscape of Persac's map, avoiding unpleasant realities altogether.[6] Others who have changed their interpretation have been met with resistant or angry visitors who once looked to such sites to confirm their own belief in plantation mythology, cultural supremacy, and Lost Cause ideology.[7] Visitor response has in and of itself become a subject of study, with cultural geographers Stephen P. Hanna, David Butler, and others leading research efforts in the area of plantation representation and tourism mapping. And academic research became public discourse in 2019 after congressional candidate Saira Rao tweeted a plantation visitor's negative online review of McLeod Plantation in Charleston, South Carolina.[8] Rao's tweet unleashed a firestorm of social media activity, followed by press, as the public realized what Butler and others knew for a number of years: studying how visitors react to these contested landscapes offers an immediate perspective on the complexity of America's relationship with its own history.

Adding to the current plantation debate is the question of plantation weddings. In the tradition of early automobile groups looking for beauty and a view, brides have long considered plantations ideal venues, their definition of plantation informed (often almost entirely) by the site's aesthetic narrative. A plantation in the wedding venue context is an impressive example of architecture with bucolic surroundings—nothing more. On the part of the bride-to-be, the reality that institutionalized, multigenerational enslavement made what they admire—those columns, those gardens (even if they are modern inventions)—possible, is often simply not part of the wedding-venue equation.

Yet the reality is that it is impossible to accurately consider the plantation landscape without slavery, and in 2019, following petitions by the civil rights advocacy group Color of Change, online wedding promoters Theknot.com and Pinterest.com announced that they would no longer be promoting weddings at plantation venues or associating romanticized hashtags such as #elegant, #romantic, or #glamorous, with plantation wedding listings. Zola.com followed soon after, announcing it had removed all plantation venues from its wedding planning website.[9]

It is the hope of the contributors and editor of this volume that, moving forward, works such as this one become increasingly common, so that as we discuss plantations—as tourism sites, memorials, sites of architectural significance, sites of bondage, cultural landscapes, and wedding venues—we have at our grasp material that can inform our understanding of these places not just with accuracy but with sharp attention to complexity. We seek to offer a vocabulary and context that moves the plantation away from oversimplification to a place of meaningful discussion that considers the plantation as a space of identifiable markers and their relationship—a *landscape.* By considering these sites in their true, comprehensive form, discussion of their use can be moved from touchpoints and reactionary language to a place of meaningful conversation.

The significance of the plantation landscape is far from being merely a history footnote or solely a tourism question. If debates on interpretation, significance, and weddings are not enough to spur us to know more about plantations, in 2019 a House Judiciary Subcommittee held a hearing debating the need for a commission to "study and develop reparations proposals for African-Americans." At no point has there been a greater need for accessible scholarship on what Persac outlined 162 years ago: a geographic place, a sociopolitical assemblage, an agroeconomic system, and a legal construct—the plantation landscape of the American South.

NOTES

1. Author's experience of tourist event, 2010.

2. Tiya Miles's *Tales from the Haunted South: Dark Tourism and Memories of Slavery from the Civil War Era* (Chapel Hill: University of North Carolina Press, 2015) expounds on this industry and its impact.

3. J. Adams, *Wounds of Returning: Race, Memory and Property on the Post-Slavery Plantation* (Chapel Hill: University of North Carolina Press, 2007), 67.

4. Jared Keller, "Inside America's Auschwitz," SmithsonianMag.com, April 4, 2016.

5. Farah Stockman, "Monticello Is Done Avoiding Jefferson's Relationship with Sally Hemings," *New York Times,* June 16, 2018, https://www.nytimes.com/2018/06/16/us/sally-hemings-exhibit-monticello.html.

6. Houmas House, a plantation in Darrow, Louisiana, that was once owned by one of the largest slaveholders in Louisiana, has been using the phrasing "Houmas House Estate" (as opposed to "Plantation") in much of their material. Visitors are encouraged to see Whitney Plantation if they are interested in learning about slavery, as it is not discussed at Houmas House, per tour guide.

7. Gillian Brockwell, "Some White People Don't Want to Hear about Slavery at Plantations Built by Slaves," *Washington Post,* August 8, 2019.

8. Saira Rao, Twitter post, August 7, 2019, 3:03 p.m., at https://twitter.com/sairasameerarao/status/1159193443467481090?lang=en.

9. Clarissa-Jan Lim, "Pinterest and The Knot Will Stop Promoting Wedding Content that Romanticizes Former Slave Plantations," *Buzzfeed News,* December 4, 2019, at https://www.buzzfeednews.com/article/clarissajanlim/plantation-weddings-pinterest-knot.

CONTRIBUTORS

Laura Ewen Blokker is a lecturer at the Tulane School of Architecture, where she teaches courses in the history of American architecture and preservation. She has been working in the field of historic preservation since 1998. Her work includes investigation of physical characteristics and material properties as well as history and contextual significance. She holds a master's of preservation studies from the Tulane University School of Architecture and a BA in creative writing with an individually designed minor in architecture from Trinity College in Hartford, Connecticut.

Charles D. Chamberlain III is president of Historia LLC, a history consulting and museum services business. After receiving his PhD in US history from Tulane University in 1999, he worked for ten years as the museum historian at the Louisiana State Museum, curating the Louisiana Sports Hall of Fame, and at Northwest Louisiana History Museum in Natchitoches from 2009 to 2012. Chamberlain currently teaches history at the University of New Orleans.

William Horne is an Arthur J. Ennis Postdoctoral Fellow at Villanova University. His research interests include systems of power revolving around concepts of race, labor, incarceration, and capitalism with particular emphasis on their expression in the state. His current project, "'Peculiarly Disposed to Insanity': Racing Madness in Louisiana," examines the imprint of racial science on Louisiana's schools, hospitals, and insane asylums. He holds a PhD in history from George Washington University and is a cofounder and associate editor of the *Activist History Review.*

Christopher Morris is professor of history at the University of Texas, Arlington. He is the author of two books, *Becoming Southern: The Evolution of a Way of Life, Warren County and Vicksburg, Mississippi, 1770–1860,* and *The Big Muddy: An Environmental History of the Mississippi and Its Peoples from Hernando de Soto to Hurricane Katrina.* He has received several awards, including a Pulitzer nomination and a senior fellowship at the Stanford Humanities Center.

Suzanne Turner is principal of the Baton Rouge–based firm Suzanne Turner Associates, whose projects include the National Trust sites Shadows-on-the-Teche and Drayton Hall; Oakland and Magnolia plantations in Natchitoches, Louisiana; National Park Service properties Bayou Bend and Rienzi; properties of the Houston Museum of Fine Arts; and Olana New York State Park. Turner taught at Louisiana State University's Robert Reich School of Landscape Architecture for twenty-five years. She is editor of *The Garden Diary of Martha Turnbull, Mistress of Rosedown Plantation* (Baton Rouge: Louisiana State University Press, 2012) and coauthor of *The Gardens of Louisiana: Places of Work and Wonder* (Baton Rouge: Louisiana State University Press, 1997).

Laura Kilcer VanHuss is the curator at Oak Alley Foundation, an institution dedicated to the preservation and interpretation of Oak Alley Plantation, a historic site in Vacherie, Louisiana. Her work concentrates on the act of meaning-making in historic built environments, and her research focuses on the degree to which meaning is assigned, defined, or shaped by influences such as history, design, and popular culture. She holds a BA in English from Hillsdale College and an MA in Museum Studies from Johns Hopkins University.

Jochen Wierich began his museum career at the Terra Museum of American Art, Chicago. His curatorial work includes exhibitions at the Northwest Museum of Arts & Culture and at the Cheekwood Botanical Garden and Museum of Art. Wierich has taught at Vanderbilt University, Whitman College, and Belmont University, as well as at the John F. Kennedy Institute in Berlin. His articles on American art have appeared in various journals, including *Winterthur Portfolio, American Art,* and *American Art Review.* He was the coeditor and contributing author for the anthology *Internationalizing the History of*

American Art: A Reader (2009) and is the author of *Grand Themes: Emanuel Leutze, Washington Crossing the Delaware, and American History Painting* (2012).

Christopher D. E. Willoughby is a historian of medicine and Atlantic slavery and a postdoctoral fellow at the Lapidus Center for the Historical Analysis of Transatlantic Slavery at the Schomburg Center for Research in Black Culture in New York. His research focuses on how slavery and racism have shaped some of the most influential institutions in American medicine, most notably medical schools. Currently, he is working on a book on the history of racial science and slavery in American medical schools from 1765 to 1861. Willoughby holds a PhD from Tulane University.

INDEX

Note: Page numbers in italic refer to figures.